# AIN'T I A WOMANIST, TOO?

# AIN'T I A WOMANIST, TOO?

## THIRD-WAVE WOMANIST RELIGIOUS THOUGHT

MONICA A. COLEMAN, EDITOR

Fortress Press
Minneapolis

AIN'T I A WOMANIST, TOO?

Third-Wave Womanist Religious Thought



Cover design: Justin Korhonen

*Library of Congress Cataloging-in-Publication Data is available*

Print ISBN: 978-0-8006-9876-6

eBook ISBN: 978-1-4514-2642-7

The paper used in this publication meets the minimum requirements of American National Standard for Information Sciences — Permanence of Paper for Printed Library Materials, ANSI Z329.48-1984.

Manufactured in the U.S.A.

This book was produced using PressBooks.com, and PDF rendering was done by PrinceXML.

*To the first generation of womanist religious scholars*
*who dared, centered, and named the religious experiences of black women*
*To G-d be the glory*

# CONTENTS



## Part I. Religious Pluralism



## Part II. Popular Culture

## Part III. Gender and Sexuality



## Part IV. Politics

# Acknowledgments

This volume started as a small idea in an article I began writing in 2004 in the midst of lively conversations with Karen Baker-Fletcher about black feminism and womanism. The conversations took form in my essay, "Must I Be Womanist?" in *Journal of Feminist Studies in Religion* (2006). The editorial staff of *JFSR* was amazingly supportive in offering me space, validation, and interlocutors as I worked through these ideas. For years, Melanie L. Harris was a lively conversation partner, encouraging me to give more attention to the concept of a third wave in womanist religious scholarship. Likewise, Victor Anderson also pressed me for greater specificity about this concept. Layli Maparyan has been a sister-comrade for decades now, and keeps me from staying in the religious studies bubble.

Ivan Petrella, more than anyone, encouraged me to put these ideas in a book-length volume. He asked about my own sense of vision and community, lending his name, energy, and effort to the concretization of the ideas.

To the colleagues who teach "Must I Be Womanist?" or stopped me at a conference to encourage me, I thank you for the added energy to do this kind of volume.

All the contributors of this volume put in time, travel, and most importantly, their research in becoming a part of this project. I appreciate your support, your scholarship, and your friendship. I did my best to present your unique voices and fascinating work. I hope you all feel good about your role in this book. I hope that this work draws the circle wider, rather than circumscribes, the discourse we all have joined.

This book is largely the outcome of my inaugural lecture and conference at Claremont School of Theology (CST) in February 2010. There were many people who worked to make this endeavor a reality: my deans at CST, the late Susan L. Nelson and Philip D. Clayton; CST president Jerry Campbell; then-dean of the School of Religion at Claremont Graduate University Karen Torjesen; Bishop Charles Wesley Jordan, Elaine Walker, Gamward Quan, Lynn O'Leary Archer, Duane Dyer, Gary Oba, Lisa Marcia, Donna Porras, Sansu Woodmancy, Mark Whitlock, Trina Armstrong, Jon I. Gill, Richard Newton, Theresa Yugar, Paula McGee, John Erickson, Deidre Green, Janis Brown, Vera Alice Bagneris, Jon Hooten, David Musick, Jared Reeder at

Question Mark to Period, Elonda Clay, Raedorah C. Stewart, Jason Taylor, Charles Dorsey, Garlinda Burton, and Anne C. Walker. Financial assistance came from: Southern California Edison Foundation, the Wabash Center for Teaching and Learning in Theology and Religion; Women's Studies in Religion at the School of Religion at Claremont Graduate University; the Pat Reif Memorial Lectureship; Process and Faith; Center for Process Studies; Commission on the Status and Role of Women in the California Pacific Annual Conference, United Methodist Church; Henry Jefferson; Kenny and Michelle Walden; Gary Oba; Bishop Charles Jordan; Kim-Monique Johnson; Cornish R. Rogers; Karen Clark Ristine; Nancy L. Jones; African American Clergy Women in the California Pacific Annual Conference, United Methodist Church. I had the time to organize this conference because I was on a sabbatical leave with significant support from the Career Enhancement Fellowship for Junior Faculty from the Woodrow Wilson National Fellowship Foundation.

I thank Katie G. Cannon and Anthony B. Pinn for their ongoing support of both this project, specifically, but more so their commitment to giving space to novel voices in black and womanist theologies. I appreciate their confidence in the future of the field we love, and in my voice in the conversation. I am grateful to the entire editorial team at Fortress Press with whom I worked on this book: Michael West, David Lott, Susan Johnson, Will Bergkamp, Lisa Gruenisen, Marissa Wold, and the production team at Fortress Press.

Words cannot express my gratitude to Monica R. Miller and C. Yvonne Augustine, who served as assistants (in different phases of this project). Tireless, invested, and capable, they carried the details and minutiae with excellence, skill, and grace—especially in the seasons when health challenges slowed me down. To my life's partner, Michael Datcher, whose love and camaraderie undergird me no matter the details of the project—I owe to you my sense of humanity in the midst of work.

# Foreword

**Layli Maparyan**

> *"Repeatedly, Thurman asks, 'How can I believe that life has meaning if I do not believe that my own life has meaning?' Thurman poses this question/affirmation to stress how one's autobiography is connected to spirituality. Whatever one seeks to discover about the meaning of life in general must take into consideration how such meaning is found in one's own life."*
>
> –Luther Smith[1]

> *". . . it was the first time that I could be all of who I was in the same place."*
>
> –Barbara Smith[2]

Womanism stands out as a liberatory spiritual praxis because of the depth to which it honors the personal spiritual journey. In the early twenty-first century, we find ourselves at a place where, if popular polls can be believed, at least in the United States of America, large segments of the population have rejected traditional, mainstream religious adherence in favor of various hybrids of spiritual belief and practice that embrace multiple religious threads and even various forms of secularity. Some people claim multiple religious affiliations, while others simply identify as "spiritual but not religious." Many people question the faiths into which they were born, the faiths of their parents and ancestors. Some leave for good; others leave, then come back with a different perspective and renewed passion. Still others create highly idiosyncratic hybrids by bringing additional faiths or philosophies into their core religion—or dispensing with a core altogether.[3] For many people, the new normal is, "I am the organizing principle of my own spirituality."

In the beginning, the womanist tradition in religious studies came from a place of deeply self-respecting reflexivity—a place of "respects herself, *regardless*"—against the backdrop of religious histories of gender-, race-, and sexuality-based exclusions and oppressions. The question posed seemed to be, how do I need to relate to this faith and its institution in ways that respect me and my community? Also, how can I forge new pathways (*à la* Harriet Tubman) for myself and others to escape religious oppression, marginalization, or colonization while remaining connected to Spirit? The answers that came from womanists were—and continue to be—polyform and ingenious. We see in third wave womanist religious thought the latest iteration of this liberatory thinking.

The Internet Age—which hadn't even been born when womanism first asserted itself three decades ago now—has allowed us to explore many traditions and belief systems from the comfort of our couches and kitchen tables. No longer do we wait for interpreters to tell us the meaning of distant practices. In my own Baha'i Faith, the principle is called "The independent investigation of truth"—the notion that external arbiters are no longer needed for us to find meaning, truth, or even Divinity itself. While we revere sacred traditions in their wholeness, we find our courage to question, indeed to interrogate, and even to mix and match them in ways that, from our own diverse perspectives, not only suit us personally, but also create new pathways of political and spiritual liberation for others. Womanism is very much about the personal spiritual journey—bringing it from behind the shadows, owning it, and forging new pathways through dialogue and interpersonal sharing that allow us all to be enriched by one another's personal spiritual journeys and reimagine community along new lines of affinity and sacredness.

Third wave womanist religious thought, as showcased in this landmark volume, exposes the inner workings of these hybrid spiritual journeys, their resulting belief systems, and highly varied modes of practice—particularly as they relate to people for whom the terms "womanism" and "womanist" resonate. Sometimes, but not always, these are black women or other women of color; sometimes these are people of other genders or colors. Indeed, many of these authors are people who define their own identities in ways that defy established categories. This work simultaneously embraces, confronts, and transcends intersectionality in ways that some will find maddening, others will find confusing, and still others will find exhilarating.

In early 2010, Monica A. Coleman asked me to serve as a discussant at the Third Wave Womanist Religious Thought conference she was organizing in conjunction with her inaugural lecture at Claremont School of Theology. I was invited to serve as a bridge between the religious and nonreligious domains of womanist scholarship on spirituality. This was only my second or third time circulating within a religion-focused womanist scholarly arena, and I was wide-eyed with delight, given that my own scholarship was increasingly focusing on spirituality and spiritual activism. What I found at this conference was a welcome eclecticism and "out loud" questioning with regard to how we understand both womanist religiosity and spirituality. I also found provocative explorations of both personal experience and theory/theology at the juncture where religion and spirituality meet issues of social justice and identity, including sexuality, popular culture, politics, and ecology. *Wow*, I thought, *this is what's next!*: vibrant womanist polyvocality, movement intersections, cross-pollination, lovingly rebellious uprisings from within, new members at the table, new topics of conversation, and, of course, new versions of "outrageous, audacious, courageous, [and] *willful*" behavior . . . Would we expect anything else from womanists? Paper after paper, presenter after presenter, impressed me with a breathtaking fearlessness, creativity, innovativeness, or ingenuity.

What I observed at this conference is that third wave womanist religious thought bridges religious studies, women's studies, queer studies, ethnic studies, theory, media studies, peace studies, ecology, sustainability studies, even futurism, and brings together divergent thought communities in an artful and alchemical act of synthesis. But, stated differently, what it really does is just talk about life with a candor and realness that one only finds when one lets down the guard of the academic walls—kind of like taking the classroom discussion to your living room sofa, spreading out with it, and unbuttoning the top button so that you can breathe with it and really exhale. It is about getting truthful, and messy, and deep—and then putting it all back together so that it makes sense and advances knowledge . . . and human well-being. This is what third wave womanist religious thought is like.

The brave authors whose work is now collected in this volume enable us to confront a host of questions that whisper along the edges of religious studies and religious life. How do we deal spiritually, for example, with issues, experiences, and identities that established religions reject or fail to address? How do we "Love ourselves, *regardless*," even when our religions refuse to do so, or do so only partially and contingently? How do we love each other—"the Folk"—when religions tell us not to deal with certain kinds or classes of people—yet our compulsions toward universal love and our commitments to peace and justice compel us to break bread and find peace with—even love—all kinds of people? Third wave womanist religious thought gives us space to wrestle with all of these questions and many more. And it delivers us to this realization: Spirit is often the answer, even when religion isn't. So how do we talk about that? Womanist thought, especially third wave womanist religious thought, helps create the language with which we can traverse these tricky terrains.[4]

What you hold in your hands is the fruit of the conference, the conversations, and the gestational trajectory created by third wave–identified womanists—female, male, LGBTQ, and straight, black, white, Asian, mixed, Christian, Muslim, indigenous identified, spiritual-but-not-religious, agnostic, reverent, irreverent, insiders, outsiders, one and all—who seek to forge a harmonizing and inclusive dialogue around that toward which womanism tends: a better world in which we can all live as who we are with justice, wellness, ecological vitality, and peace. The bottom line is this: womanism exists to draw us together at the same time that we transform ourselves and the world, to help us figure out how everybody can be included as we hurtle through space on a changing planet, uncertain of our future destination but knowing that, once we get there, we will only survive if we have found how to be "committed to survival and wholeness of entire people." *Really.*

Layli Maparyan
Wellesley, Massachusetts
December 2012

# Notes

1. Luther E. Smith, "Introduction," *Howard Thurman: Essential Writings* (Maryknoll, NY: Orbis, 2006), 14.

2. Barbara Smith qtd. In Duchess, "'All of Who I Am in the Same Place': The Combahee River Collective," *Womanist Theory and Research* 2, no. 1 (Fall 1999): 10. There is a video interview by Susan Goodwillie that is referenced in Duchess Harris's more recent book, Black Feminist Politics from Kennedy to Obama (Palgrave Macmillan, 2011).

3. From recent research studies by the Pew Forum on Religion and Public Life (www.pewforum.org).

4. Select quotes scattered throughout this foreword were taken or paraphrased from Alice Walker's definition of "Womanist" from *In Search of Our Mothers' Gardens: Womanist Prose* (New York: Harcourt Brace Jovanovich, 1983).

# Contributors

**Victor Anderson** is John Frederick Oberlin Theological School Professor of Ethics and Society at Vanderbilt University Divinity School and Professor of African American and Diaspora Studies and Religious Studies at Vanderbilt University. He is the author of *Beyond Ontological Blackness: An Essay on African American Religious and Cultural Criticism* (1994), *Pragmatic Theology: Negotiating the Intersections of an American Philosophy of Religion and Public Theology* (1998), and *Creative Exchange: A Constructive Theology of African American Religious Experience* (2008), and numerous academic articles.

**Elonda Clay** is a Ph.D. student in Religion and Science at Lutheran School of Theology at Chicago. She grew up vibing off of Gwendolyn Brooks, Nikki Giovanni, and Maya Angelou while wylin' out to Alice Walker's poetry and prose. Spoken word, hip hop, and neo-soul are often her contemplation companions. As a writer, she operates in what her friends call "mad scientist" mode; that is, she resuscitates the alchemy of creative intellectual transmutation. She describes her works as "Awkward Black Girl Meets African American Religious Thought"!

**Monica A. Coleman** is Associate Professor of Constructive Theology and African American Religions at Claremont School of Theology in the Claremont Lincoln University consortium and Co-Director of the Center for Process Studies. She is the author of *The Dinah Project: A Handbook for Congregational Response to Sexual Violence* (2004), *Making a Way Out of No Way: A Womanist Theology* (2008), *Not Alone: Reflections on Faith and Depression* (2012) and co-editor of *Creating Women's Theology: A Movement Engaging Process Thought* (2011), the oft-cited article, "Must I Be Womanist?" in *Journal of Feminist Studies in Religion* (2006), and various other journal publications.

**Nessette Falu** is a Ph.D. candidate in Socio-Cultural Anthropology at Rice University. She completed a graduate certificate program at Rice University's Center for the Study of Women, Gender and Sexuality, as well as two years of Religious Studies doctoral work at Rice. She was a graduate assistant for Race Scholars at Rice, a program of the Kinder Institute for Urban Research. Sited in Salvador-Bahia, Brazil, her current fieldwork and research looks at black lesbians' sexual subjectivities, Candomblé women in particular, and the social and religious ethics by which they contest the silencing of their sexual subjectivities and practices within the gynecological medical care domain. She holds an M.Div. and is a Physician Assistant. She is a recipient of a generous fieldwork grant from the Ruth Landes Memorial Research Fund.

**Stephen Finley** is Assistant Professor of Religious Studies and African American Studies at Louisiana State University. His book manuscript, *In and Out of This World: Material and Extraterrestrial Bodies in the Nation of Islam*, is under review. He is also co-editor (with Margarita Guillory and Hugh Page) of *"There Is a Mystery": Esotericism, Gnosticism, and Mysticism in African American Religious Experience*. He is authoring a book on Malcolm X and gender with Eldon Birthwright (English, LSU). He continues to research for his second monograph, tentatively titled *Sojourners in a Strange Land: The Religious Lives of African American Latter-day Saints*. Dr. Finley is on the Executive Committee of the Society for the Study of Black Religion.

**Barbara A. Holmes** is President of United Theological Seminary of the Twin Cities and Professor of Ethics and African American Religious Studies. She was formerly Vice President of Academic Affairs and Dean of Memphis Theological Seminary. Ordained in the Latter Rain Apostolic Holiness Church in Dallas, she has privilege of call in the United Church of Christ and recognition of ministerial standing in the Christian Church (Disciples of Christ). Her latest book, *Dreaming*, was published by Fortress Press (Compass, Everyday Living Series) in March 2012. Other titles include: *Liberation and the Cosmos: Conversations with the Elders*; *Joy Unspeakable: Contemplative Practices of the Black Church and Race*; and *Race and the Cosmos: An Invitation to View the World Differently*.

**EL Kornegay Jr.** earned his Ph.D. in Theology, Ethics, Culture and Human Science from the Chicago Theological Seminary, Chicago, IL. He is the author of an influential article on Black masculinity and homophobia titled "Queering Black Homophobia: Black Theology as a Sexual Discourse of Transformation" in *Theology and Sexuality* (2004) and "Baldwin on Top: Towards a Hetero-Anomalous Queer Calculus of Black Theology" in *Black Theology: An International Journal* (2012). His current research considers and rethinks the importance of literary contributions—such as those of James Baldwin—as sacred mediums informing, conveying, and necessitating black religious interpretation in relation to the formation of black masculinity, sexuality, and multiple forms of homophobia.

**Debra Majeed** is Professor of Religious Studies at Beloit College. A religious historian, Majeed has published in *CrossCurrents, the Journal of Feminist Studies in Religion, the Encyclopedia of Muslim-American History, the Encyclopedia of Women and Religion in America, the Encyclopedia of Women in Islamic Cultures, the Pakistan Journal of Women's Studies,* and *Deeper Shades of Purple: Charting Twenty Years of Womanist Approaches in Religion and Society*, among others. Her current project, "Encounters of Intimate Sisterhood? Polygyny in the World of African American Muslims," is forthcoming from University Press of Florida.

**Layli Maparyan** is Executive Director of the Wellesley Centers for Women, a women- and gender-focused research institute housed at Wellesley College. As Layli Phillips, she published *The Womanist Reader* (Routledge, 2006), which documents the first quarter-century of womanist thought from an interdisciplinary perspective. Her most recent book is *The Womanist Idea* (Routledge, 2012), in which she focuses on womanist metaphysics and spiritual activism. She has been a recipient of both a Contemplative Practice Fellowship from the Center for Contemplative Mind in Society and a Fulbright Specialist Award.

**Darnise C. Martin** earned her Ph.D. in Cultural and Historical Studies of Religion from the Graduate Theological Union. She is the author of *Beyond Christianity: African Americans in a New Thought Church* (2005), and co-editor of *Women and New and Africana Religions* (2009). Her research interests include a forthcoming article, "Not Your Grandmother's Christian Church," an examination of the connections between New Thought religions, sometimes called "The Health and Wealth Philosophy," and the contemporary evangelical-based prosperity gospels.

**Monica R. Miller** is Assistant Professor of Religious and Africana Studies at Lehigh University, where her research focuses on the intersections of religion and material/popular culture. Miller currently serves as a Senior Research Fellow with the Institute for Humanist Studies (Washington, DC) and is co-chair of Critical Approaches to the Study of Hip Hop and Religion Group (AAR). Miller is the author of *Religion and Hip Hop* (Routledge, 2012) and Principal

Investigator of Remaking Religion—a large-scale survey project exploring religion in youth culture in Portland, Oregon. Miller is currently completing a book about the awkwardness of race in Portland titled *Blacklandia: The Subtleties of Race in Portland.*

**Ronald B. Neal** holds a Ph.D. in Religion, Ethics, and Culture from Vanderbilt University. He is a Visiting Assistant Professor in the Department of Religion at Wake Forest University in Winston-Salem, North Carolina. His research and writing interests include: religion, ethics, and politics, postmodern philosophy, gender studies, third world studies, and popular culture. He is the author of the book, *Democracy in Twenty-First Century America: Race, Class, Religion, and Region* (Mercer University Press, 2012). He is currently at work on an untitled book on religion, masculinity, and hip hop.

**Xiumei Pu** is a Ph.D. candidate in Feminist Studies at the University of Minnesota. She will defend her dissertation "Imagining the Decolonial Spirit: Ecowomanist Literature and Criticism in the Chinese Diaspora" in the spring of 2013. Her forthcoming essay "Turning Weapons into Flowers: Ecospiritual Poetics and Politics of Bön and Ecowomanism" offers her understanding of Tibetan Bön and ecowomanism, exploring the meanings of ecospiritual ways of knowing and ecospiritual practice. Her current research studies premodern Chinese ecospiritual traditions and their implications for contemporary Chinese and diasporic Chinese women's literature, (post)modern life, and the global healing praxis.

**Arisika Razak** is Associate Professor and former Program Chair of the Women's Spirituality Program at California Institute of Integral Studies, San Francisco, CA. Her work integrates women's studies in religion, multicultural and postcolonial feminisms, and women's health. Her essays on Alice Walker and womanism have been published in academic journals in the United States and Great Britain. She leads spiritual and embodied workshops nationally and internationally. Her film interviews include *Alice Walker: Beauty in Truth* (2012), and *Fire Eyes* (1994), an African feature film on female genital mutilation.

**Roger A. Sneed** is Assistant Professor of Religion at Furman University in Greenville, South Carolina. He holds a Ph.D. in Ethics and Society from Vanderbilt University. His first book, *Representations of Homosexuality: Black Liberation Theology and Cultural Criticism*, was published by Palgrave Macmillan in 2010. He is currently working on a manuscript that explores masculine anxiety and the myth of black homophobia in African American religious and cultural life.

**Sharon D. Welch** is Provost and Professor of Religion and Society at Meadville Lombard Theological School (Unitarian Universalist). She is a Senior Fellow of the Institute for Humanist Studies, and a member of the International Steering Committee of Global Action to Prevent War. Welch is the author of five books: *Real Peace, Real Security: The Challenges of Global Citizenship* (2008), *After Empire: The Art and Ethos of Enduring Peace* (2004); *A Feminist Ethic of Risk* (1990), *Sweet Dreams in America: Making Ethics and Spirituality Work* (1998), and *Communities of Resistance and Solidarity* (1985).

# Introduction: Ain't I a Womanist Too?

## *Third Wave Womanist Religious Thought*

**Monica A. Coleman**

> *But what's all dis here talkin' bout? Dat man ober dar say dat womin needs to be helped into carriages and lifted ober mud puddles, and to have de best place every whar. Nobody eber help me into carriages, or ober mud puddles or gibs me any best place! And ain't I a woman? Look at me! Look at my arm! I have ploughed, and planted, and gathered into barns, and no man could head me! And ain't I a woman? I could work as much and eat as much as a man—when I could get it—and bear de lash as well! And ain't I a woman? I have bourne thirteen chilern, and seen 'em mos' all sold off to slavery, and when I cried out with my mother's grief, none but Jesus heard me! And ain't I a woman?*[1]

In her now famous 1851 speech at the Akron, Ohio women's rights gathering, Sojourner Truth critiqued the default understanding of womanhood with her poignant question, "And ain't I a woman?" Sojourner Truth noted the ways that the work and lives of enslaved black women departed from the Victorian standards of piety, purity, submission, and domesticity—more commonly referred to as the "cult of true womanhood." Having different experiences and perspectives from white middle- and upper-class women did not negate Truth's womanhood. Rather, Truth calls for a redefinition, or more aptly, an *expansion*, of what it means to be a woman. This refrain has served as a touchstone, first for black women, and eventually for women of all backgrounds, to ensure that no woman, no matter how different her experiences, was left oppressed.

Likewise, there is a third wave of womanist religious thought that asks a similar question, "Ain't I a womanist too?" In so doing, this movement redefines and extends, from within and without, what it means to place black women's religious experiences at the center of theological activity and religious reflection. This introduction will address womanism in general, and issues of identity politics. It will discuss how third wave womanism dovetails with third wave feminism and will give some markers for what constitutes third wave womanist religious thought. The final section will note how the essays in this volume variously reflect third wave womanist religious thought.

## History of "Womanist" and "Womanism"

### *Alice Walker*

Within religious scholarship, Alice Walker's description of "womanist" is often invoked as a definition, at the most, or as poetic inspiration, at the least, for the religious reflection by and about black women. Alice Walker initially uses the term "womanist" in her 1979 short story, "Coming Apart." Almost parenthetically, she writes, "The wife has never considered herself a feminist—though she is, of course, a 'womanist.' A 'womanist' is a feminist, only more common."[2] Walker gives greater explanation in her 1981 article, "Gifts of Power: The Writings of Rebecca Jackson." Ruminating on the writings of the nineteenth-century black female Shaker preacher, Rebecca Jackson, Walker reflects on Jean McMahon Humez's editing of Jackson's work where Humez refers to Jackson's decision to live with a close woman friend as a relationship that, in modern times, would have been referred to as openly lesbian. Walker rejects Humez's naming for many reasons with these concluding remarks:

The word "lesbian" may not, in any case, be suitable (or comfortable) for black women, who surely would have begun their woman-bonding earlier than Sappho's residency on the Isle of Lesbos. Indeed, I can imagine black women who love women (sexually or not) hardly thinking of what Greeks were doing; but instead, referring to themselves as "whole" women, from "wholly" or "holy." Or as "round" women—women who love other women, yes, but women who also have concern, in a culture that oppresses all black people (and this would go back very far), for their fathers, brothers and sons, no matter how they feel about them as males. My own term for such women would be "womanist." At any rate, the word they chose would have to be both spiritual and concrete and it would have to be organic, characteristic, not simply applied.[3]

There are hints to where Walker will go with the term, "womanist." Community will be important and the term will be spiritual and concrete, organic and characteristic. Walker continues to frame the term "womanist" in contradistinction to the separatist trends within the white feminism of the time.

We see Walker's fullest discussion of "womanist" in the prologue to her 1983 collection of prose, *In Search of Our Mothers' Gardens*. Here she writes of womanist, in definition format, in four parts. For the sake of space, I will abbreviate them:

> 1. From *womanish* (Opp. of "girlish," i.e., frivolous, irresponsible, not serious.) A black feminist or feminist of color. Interested in grown-up doings. Acting grown-up. Being grown-up. Responsible. In charge. *Serious.*
> 2. Also: a woman who loves other women, sexually and/or nonsexually. Appreciates and prefers women's culture, women's emotional flexibility (values tears as natural counterbalance of laughter), and women's strength. Sometimes loves individual men, sexually and/or nonsexually. Committed to survival and wholeness of entire people, male *and* female. Not a separatist, except periodically, for health. Traditionally universal. Traditionally capable.
> 3. Loves music. Loves dance. Loves the moon. Loves the Spirit. Loves love and food and roundness. Loves struggle. Loves the Folk. Loves herself. *Regardless.*
> 4. Womanist is to feminist as purple to lavender.[4]

Within religious scholarship, Walker's articulation has held the most sway. There are at least two significant challenges associated with Walker's understanding of womanism, and its use in religious studies. The first challenge is that Walker's "definition" is not really a definition. It is poetic in nature, which makes it attractive. It resonates. It has staying power. You want to read it aloud. And yet, as Layli Phillips writes in "Womanism: On Its Own," it is "theoretically slippery and frustrating."[5] Black feminist Patricia Hill Collins reminds us that the "definition" is both historical and visionary, and that it represents conflicting political ideologies of nationalism, pluralism, integrationism/assimilationism.[6] Even Floyd-Thomas notes that Walker coined the term "womanist," but "*womanism* became a movement [within black women's religious scholarship] when black women scholars of religion used their *logos*" to unite theological reflection with social transformation.[7] Within religious scholarship, few womanist thinkers incorporate the breadth of Walker's writings and activism into their reflection. Karen Baker-Fletcher,[8] Melanie Harris,[9] and Arisika Razak[10] are notable exceptions, and they do this in quite different ways. The notable point is that Walker's definition has served as an important starting point—and point of departure—for reflection on black women's religious lives. However, its poetic nature requires significant exposition, explanation, and construction on the part of any who invoke the term.[11]

The second challenge that womanist religious scholars face when relying on Walker's writings on womanism is the neglect—and near erasure from the scholarship—of the two other significant progenitors of the term: Chikwenye Okonjo Ogunyemi, whose perspective came to be known as African womanism, and Clenora Hudson-Weems's articulation of the term, which calls itself Africana womanism.

### *Chikwenye Ogunyemi*

First publishing on "womanism" in 1985, Ogunyemi works with African diasporan literature to articulate the differences she sees among white feminist, black feminist, and womanist writings. For Ogunyemi, an African womanist is best known by the fact that she is conscious of more than issues of sex and gender. Rather, a womanist "must incorporate racial, cultural, national, economic, and political considerations into her philosophy."[12] Ogunyemi defines her concept of womanism even more explicitly as a philosophy that "celebrates black roots [and] the ideals of black life, while giving a balanced presentation of black womandom [and] concerns itself as much with the black sexual power tussle as with the world power structure that subjugates blacks."[13] She notes the need to focus on an ethics of survival—a principle that would become, through quite different routes, an important feature of womanist theology. She also highlights the complexity of sexual and gendered relations by arguing that "matrilineal and polygynous societies in Africa are dynamic sources for the womanist novel."[14]

### *Clenora Hudson-Weems*

Clenora Hudson-Weems's description of Africana womanism draws explicitly from Sojourner Truth's famous speech, while being rooted firmly in a pan-African nationalist politic. In her 1993 essay, "Africana Womanism," Hudson-Weems states that her use of the term "womanism" recalls Sojourner Truth's

"Ain't I a Woman" speech "in which [Truth] battles with the dominant alienating forces in her life as a struggling Africana woman, questioning the accepted idea of womanhood."[15] Hudson-Weems describes Africana womanism as "an ideology created and designed for all women of African descent. It is grounded in African culture, and therefore, it necessarily focuses on the unique experiences, struggles, needs and desires of Africana women."[16] In her 1989 writings, unlike Walker and Ogunyemi, Hudson-Weems establishes priorities in Africana womanism, stating, "Africana people must eliminate racist influences in their lives first, with the realization that they can neither afford nor tolerate any form of female subjugation."[17] Hudson-Weems sees sexism as a secondary problem that arises out of racism and classism. She finds inspiration from Sojourner Truth, arguing that "before Sojourner could hope to address gender problems, she had to first overcome discrimination from her White audience. Clearly, gender was not her primary concern."[18]

Hudson-Weems is interested in the impact of Africana womanism within the field of Africana studies and Africana women's studies. She believes that Africana men and Africana women are and should be allies. Spirituality plays a smaller role in Hudson-Weems than in Ogunyemi's and Walker's expressions, and in another interesting departure from Walker, Hudson-Weems rejects homosexuality outright.

## Naming/Identity Politics

These early articulations of "womanist" and "womanism" are joined in their desire to differentiate themselves from a largely white feminist movement, as well as from those who identify as black feminists. At the risk of being reductionist, the critiques can be summarized in the following ways: feminism is often critiqued for being racist and classist with an implied "white and middle-class" positionality in all its activities. Black feminism is critiqued for having a singular focus or privileging gender issues, within the multiple oppressions that black women experience. Both "white" feminism and black feminism are charged as being separatist from men. Some womanists also critique and resist feminism's association with same-gender-loving women. I think this is a decent summary of the critiques, although like Beverly Guy-Sheftall, I think that many of these critiques represent mischaracterizations of white feminism and black feminism—even at the times that they were made.[19]

Feminism, black feminism, and womanism have all evolved significantly since the 1980s. Many of the critiques have been addressed in the growth and diversification of each movement. Nevertheless, Patricia Hill Collins notes that the terms black feminism and womanism connote different academic and political agendas. Collins is correct when she reminds readers that "the womanist/black feminist debate occurs primarily among relatively privileged black women."[20] Indeed, this navel-gazing over names and nomenclature becomes dizzying. Here's what I think matters:

What seems central to these conversations is that "womanism" signifies a kind of self-naming. Alice Walker indicates that she chose the word "womanist" (over "black feminist") because there "was more room in it for changes," and it was "more reflective of black women's culture, especially Southern culture."[21] She liked "the feel, the fit, the sound" of the word.[22] Likewise, Floyd-Thomas connects womanism with Sojourner Truth around the issue of naming: "More than a century and a half after Isabella Baumfree changed her name to Sojourner Truth, a small cadre of Black female scholars of religion claimed a similar power of naming and called themselves womanists."[23] In fact, Phillips reminds us that womanism "named something that had been in existence for some time, functioning below the academic and activist radar and outside dominant histories of consciousness."[24] Those who adopt and adapt the nomenclature of "womanist" and "womanism" are making a particular statement about how they want to be referenced and with whom and what they want to be associated. And as corollary, those with whom they do not wish to be associated.

So names matter. The words we use, the names we call ourselves, or are called by others, matter. And this naming matters. Some scholars are prepared to establish the criteria by which they are willing to wrangle over names. In "Is a Womanist a Black Feminist?" self-described black feminist religious ethicist Traci West states that "specifying the boundaries between feminism and womanism in [her] work is of little significance to [her], unless it furthers some form of woman-affirming social shift toward a more just and compassionate world, and gives special attention to those persons who are victimized by violence [. . . especially] wives, prostitutes, lesbians, gay men and transgendered persons."[25] In her essay, "What's in a Name? Womanism, Black Feminism and Beyond," Patricia Hill Collins concludes that the work we do is more important than our naming. She believes we need to shift the emphasis from "black women's oppression to how institutionalized racism operates in gender-specific ways . . . and how gender oppression works in tandem with racial oppression."[26] I most appreciate Phillips's view. She states: "Self-labeling is a psychologically and politically valuable process, yet labels and identities are socially negotiated through dialogue. People may or may not agree about how to name a thing, but the process of negotiating the label is healthy and inevitable."[27] Thus conversations about this naming are relevant because of what's at stake.

The first thing at stake is black women's ability to name themselves. In the "Gifts of Power" article, Alice Walker asserts that choosing the name "womanist" is connected to a sense of freedom. She writes, "I simply feel that naming our own experience after our own fashion (as well as rejecting whatever does not seem to suit it) is the least we can do—and in this society may be *our only tangible sign of personal freedom*" (italics mine). In this sense, the politics of identity are not just about politics, but they are about identity. I believe this is true of all people, but it can be particularly relevant to those individuals and communities who are so often named by other people in ways in which they would not name themselves. In the movie version of Alex Haley's *Roots*, the slave master tries to tell the protagonist that his slave name is "Tobey," while the protagonist insists that his name is "Kunta Kinte." The viewers witness a brutal scene as the slave master physically and publicly whips Kunta Kinte into submission until he responds to the name, "Tobey." What I'm trying to say is that naming is an important step in reducing a subject to an object, and self-naming is a critical step in the move back to one's own subjectivity.[28]

The second issue at stake in womanist naming is power. In my 2006 roundtable article, "Must I Be Womanist?" I was trying to raise *this* question of identity politics. Why is it that some scholars and activists refer to themselves as black feminist, while others prefer womanist?[29] What is the difference? And, more importantly, what do we do when a title designed to give black women the space to name themselves is imposed upon activists and scholars from without, as Traci West describes so poignantly in her essay "Is a Womanist a Black Feminist?"[30] I am not referring to the ways in which some might ascribe the label "womanist" or "feminist" to historical personages who did not have access to such naming, and thus did not name themselves this way. Rather, there are individuals and institutions in the academy, religious leadership, and publishing that declare who, what, and how black women pursue and name their work, holding them by the golden handcuffs of employment, tenure, publication, and access to leadership and community. When the words designed to promote personal freedom become bars to cage in and restrain, we need to have a conversation about the viability and usage of those words.

Likewise, black women are sometimes the ones with the power. Collins deftly reiterates that "talk of centers and margins, even the process of coining to voice itself, that does not simultaneously address issues of power leaves masses of black women doing the dry cleaning, cooking the fast food, and dusting the computer of the sister who has just written the newest theoretical treatise on black women."[31] In other words, we must also be aware of the instances and positionalities whereby we who write about black women, oppression, religion, and justice hold power over other black women by virtue of factors we either cannot or do not wish to control, such as class, color, sexual behavior, and geography, to name a few. That is, black women—especially black women in the U.S. academy—are not *all* at the bottom of the proverbial scale.

## Third Wave Feminism

In "Must I Be a Womanist?" I wrestled aloud with whether or not "womanist" was the most appropriate nomenclature for black women religious scholars. Could not "black feminist" be equally or perhaps more apt, depending on one's political and religious commitments? I think I made a legitimate argument for black feminist's historic and current ability to address issues I saw as shortcomings within womanist religious scholarship. With notable exceptions, I found black feminist work more strident in addressing religious pluralism, sexual difference, and global politics than womanist religious scholarship. Of course—and this is an important aside—there are many who feel that black feminism has been a rather secular movement, becoming post-Christian and post-religious early on. Or to say it in kinder tones, black feminism, as such, has not engaged black women's religiosity in the ways that those who name themselves "womanist" have. Nevertheless, I did not require an abandonment of the term "womanist" for those working within religious scholarship. Trying to highlight the heterogeneity of the scholarship on black women's religiosities, I suggested that there might be a third wave within womanist religious thought.

Third wave feminism is the name given to an eclectic group of young feminists with diverse issues and strategies of addressing injustice in contemporary society. The idea of a third wave within feminism depends on identifying the first two waves of feminism. The first wave is often identified in the women's suffrage and abolitionist movements of the nineteenth century. This wave is composed primarily of liberal, northern, white U.S. women, but could well include the efforts of Anna Julia Cooper, Sojourner Truth, Maria Stewart, and Ida B. Wells-Barnett. The second wave is identified with the sexual revolution of the 1960s. Often dated with the 1964 publication of Betty Freidan's *The Feminist Mystique*, with corollary movements in Europe, the second wave of feminism is often characterized by its push for equality and equity, reproductive rights, etc. Explicitly named black feminism and women-of-color feminisms, also referred to as "U.S. third world feminisms" in the late 1970s and early 1980s, serve as a bridge between the relatively white and middle-class second wave feminism and where third wave feminists see themselves.

Finding voice in the mid-1990s, third wavers often distinguish themselves as being members of a particular generation. In *Feminism and Christianity*, Caryn Riswold describes herself as a third wave feminist because she is "raised on the benefits of first- and second-wave feminist activism."[32] That is, third wavers are the "first generation for whom feminism has been entwined in the fabric of [their] lives."[33] Third wave feminists often see themselves as sharing particular generational experiences. They benefit from the gains of second wave feminism: women's studies programs in universities, feminist organizations, and publishing outlets, to name just a few examples. In *Listen Up!: Voices from the Next Feminist Generation*, Barbara Findlen says that third wave feminists have

> been shaped by the unique events and circumstances of [their] time: AIDS, the erosion of reproductive rights, the materialism and cynicism of the Reagan and Bush years, the backlash against women, the erosion of civil rights, the skyrocketing divorce rate, the movement toward multiculturalism and greater global awareness, the emergence of the lesbian and gay rights movements, a greater overall awareness of sexuality—and the feminist movement itself.[34]

Yet other third wavers believe that they are better identified as a political generation.[35] That is, membership in the third wave is not simply age or birth rite, but affiliation with similar issues and politics.[36] After all, some individuals might have the generational experiences that Findlen describes, but align themselves more closely with second wave feminist politics.

Thus another marker of third wave feminism is that it is a departure from the second wave. Rebecca Walker describes this best in her anthology, *To Be Real: Telling the Truth and Changing the Face of Feminism*, when she writes that her generation has "a very different vantage point on the world than [their] foremothers."[37] In fact, many third wavers have experienced the second wave as a dogmatic, demanding conformation to a status quo that takes particular stances on work, abortion, beauty, and family. Walker describes this second wave mythos thusly:

> In order to be a feminist one must live in poverty, always critique, never marry, want to censor pornography and/or worship the Goddess. A feminist must never compromise herself, must never

> make concessions for money or for love, must always be devoted to the uplift of her gender, must only make an admirable and selfless livelihood, preferably working for a women's organization.[38]

Angela Y. Davis concurs that such a feminist status quo, while never intended by its architects, does "establish strict rules of conduct" and serves to "incarcerate individuality."[39]

While there is a departure from the second wave, there is also significant continuity. In *Third Wave Agenda*, Lisa Heywood and Jennifer Drake distinguish third wave feminism from post-feminism. Unlike post-feminism, which defines itself against the second wave,[40] third wave feminism contains elements of the second wave—such as the critique of beauty culture, sexual abuse, and power structures—while "acknowledg[ing] and mak[ing] use of the pleasure, danger, and defining power of those structures."[41] These continuities are best seen in third wave feminism's commitment to activism—another principle that distinguishes a third wave from post-feminism. Apart from the personal and academic writings about third wave feminism, the most common association for "third wave" terminology is found in the Third Wave Foundation, co-founded by Rebecca Walker. The foundation funds projects proposed by women, transgender and gender nonconforming youth between the ages of fifteen and thirty years of age:

> Third Wave is a member-driven multiracial, multicultural, multi-sexuality national non-profit organization devoted to feminist and youth activism for change. Our goal is to harness the energy of young women and men by creating a community in which members can network, strategize, and ultimately, take action. By using our experiences as a starting point, we can create a diverse community and cultivate a meaningful response.[42]

The words that consistently emerge in relation to third wave feminisms are: contradiction, ambiguity, multiplicity, hybridity, individualism, and activism. Third wave feminists are individualistic and communitarian, academics, activists and stay-at-home moms, knitters and athletes, bitches, punks, riot grrrls, dykes, and ladies. The third wave cannot be known without touching on its engagement with popular culture and the media images of independent women. Third wave writings reference Courtney Love, Madonna, Meshell Ndegeocello, Dora the Explorer, "Sex and the City," Queen Latifah, Mary J. Blige, e-zines, and blogs.[43] Third wavers acknowledge that the battle has not been won, but they want to live out the rights for which the second wave fought. Personally, I like the way Jennifer Baumgardner and Amy Richards put it in their thorough third wave text, *Manifesta*. Third wavers say: "I'm not a feminist but . . ." and "I'm a feminist, but . . . ," to illustrate their connections and departures from feminist associations.[44]

Admittedly there are generalizations being made in this typology. I've drawn broad strokes and missed the notable exceptions in each designated wave. Most importantly, I've failed to mention that the typology of waves differs significantly when examining black feminism on its own. That is, the aforementioned Maria Stewart, Ida B. Wells-Barnett, Anna Julia Cooper, and Mary Shadd Cary could well constitute a second wave of black feminism wherein race women unite their resistance of racism and gender-based oppression; this is a "second wave" when considered with the resistance efforts of slave women in the antebellum period—well documented by Angela Y. Davis,[45] Deborah Gray White,[46] and Harriet Jacobs.[47] Black feminist Kimberly Springer believes that "the wave model perpetuates the exclusion of women of color from women's movement history and feminist theorizing."[48]

This is not to say that black feminists do not speak of something like a third wave. Springer notes that there *is* a movement of contemporary black feminists, not unlike the aforementioned third wavers, that are post–civil rights era, college-educated, and middle-class, enjoying the benefits of the black feminist efforts that preceded them.[49] They too reference popular culture icons like Lauryn Hill, India.Arie, and Erykah Badu. While Springer laments their lack of engagement with sexuality, she notes that these black feminists do not speak of radical departures from or conflicts with their black feminist foremothers. This generation has its own ways of encountering popular culture, history, activism, "strong black woman" syndrome, and male engagement. More often calling themselves "hip hop feminists," this endeavor includes the likes of Veronica Chambers,[50] Lisa Jones,[51] and Joan Morgan,[52] who, like W. E. B. DuBois and Delaney before them, are joined by male counterparts such as Michael Awkward,[53] Gary Lemons,[54] David Ikard,[55] and Marc Anthony Neal.[56] Springer rejects the terminology of "waves" and prefers to see the work of young (i.e., contemporary) black feminists as part of a historical continuum of black women's raced and gendered activism in the U.S. Still, black feminists like Beverly Guy-Sheftall prefer to work with the wave terminology, redrawing the boundaries of the waves to be more inclusive of the activism of black women and other women of color.[57]

Finding myself closer to Guy-Sheftall's position, I give attention to the typology of waves, and a third wave in particular, because (1) it is generally accepted as a fair description of the development of U.S. feminisms (although that's not a particularly compelling reason), and (2) I think it is a useful and instructive metaphor for describing what I see happening—and what I hope to see happen—in womanist religious thought.

As Sallie McFague so well reminds religious scholars, metaphorical language is powerful, but limited. That is, our engagement of metaphors says a lot about what we are trying to theorize, but it always loses something. There is, as she says, an "is" and "is not" to metaphorical language.[58] The metaphor of "wave" has been extended into a model, and there is another significant competing model when speaking of womanism and womanist religious scholarship: the generational model.

I've noted that third wave feminism plays hide-and-go-seek with its relationship to age and generations. Some identify third wave feminism directly with Generation X. Others, myself included, prefer to associate third wave feminism with its characteristics and politics, noting that a second-waver by age may well have third wave commitments and vice versa.

In womanist religious thought, Floyd-Thomas invokes the language of generations. After identifying womanist "matriarchs" Delores Williams, Katie Cannon, and Jacquelyn Grant, Floyd-Thomas goes on to describe and name a first generation of womanist religious scholars. The second generation consists of those who were taught by or "influenced" by the works of the first generation. In her categorizing, the third generation "emerged as Black women are able to study with first- and second-generation womanists and learn about womanist theories and methodologies in seminaries and universities throughout North America and extending to the Caribbean and West and South Africa."[59] The strength of this language is that it provides a kind of genealogy, or apostolic succession model, of mentorship and privilege. It acknowledges the gains of the early womanist religious scholars, and their living legacies.

Layli Phillips also uses family language to talk about the relationships among womanism, feminism, and black feminism. She refers to womanism and white U.S. feminism as cousins, and womanism and black feminism as sisters. I like the family resemblance revealed in Phillips's categorization. She well highlights that, despite our differences, we are family. I find this to be especially true in womanist religious thought. In womanist religious thought, the "first generation," or "first wave," is still living. No one has died. We are mentors, mentees, colleagues, students, teachers, and friends with one another.

The generational and family metaphors lose three things that I think "wave" language captures. Like waves, what I'm trying to describe about the scholarship on black women's religiosity has movement. Mimicking the ocean, it ebbs and it flows; there are seasons of high tide and low tide; and often, it even roars. You can ride a wave, jump in it, or watch it wash your sand castles, or even your own physical brick-and-mortar house, away. I argue that third wave womanist religious thought has these same characteristics. Second, with a wave, one is known by when and where one arrives, rather than when one is born and with whom one studied. While generational language says something about what has been achieved, as well as when and where one learned, it doesn't say enough about how one turned out. While I think there are some generational markers to what I'm discussing, when it comes to one's politics and perspective, age, however, is more relevant in terms of how long one lives, what one lives to see, and what one does with one's life—the specific time period in which that life began.

Third, and most importantly, articulating "waves" within womanist religious thought has the connotations of third wave feminism. I find this particularly salient in helping to maintain the connections among womanist religious scholarship, the academic study of religion, white women's feminism, women-of-color feminism, global feminisms, and women's studies—connections that, most times, are tenuous at best. In reinforcing these connections, we become more able to see womanist religious thought as part of larger, global movements for social transformation in and through individual and communal religiosity.

Considering a "third wave" within womanist religious thought also suggests that there are shared traits between third wavers. Perhaps like third wave feminism, third wave womanist religious thought is also characterized by contradiction, ambiguity, multiplicity, hybridity, individualism, and activism. Perhaps third wave womanist religious thought also invokes popular culture and media images. Perhaps third wave womanist religious thought is also known by the compulsion to say "I'm not womanist but . . ." and "I'm womanist, but . . . ," to illustrate their connections and departures from second wave womanist associations.

## Waves of Womanist Religious Thought

### *First Wave*

And yes, there is a second wave of womanist religious thought—and a first. I agree with Floyd-Thomas that there appear to be womanist matriarchs. These "first wavers"—Williams, Cannon, and Grant in theology and ethics—are named so because they were the first to engage the term "womanist" in relationship to their religious thought. One might also extend this wave to the scholars in every religious discipline who first make black women's religious experiences the starting point or center of their religious reflection. This is no small point. It reflects the larger trend in the U.S. academy wherein black women earning doctoral degrees in some critical mass during the 1970s and 1980s insisted that the histories, literatures, and experiences of black women were worthy subjects of study and study by those who considered themselves part of the community they studied. It also speaks quietly to the difficulty of doing so within the Western academy. When black female religious scholars attend the meetings of their disciplinary guilds, nine times out of ten they are outnumbered by the white men in their midst. Thus to not only validate and reference black women's religiosity, but to make it the center of one's theological and religious reflection is no small accomplishment, and one that honestly does not have universal support throughout the academy. It is also significant that Floyd-Thomas argues against language of definition or movement in relationship to womanism in religion and society. She names this womanist "intellectual revolution" an "epistemology." While I prefer the language of movement and wave, Floyd-Thomas and I agree that the centering of black women's religiosity constitutes a sea change in religious scholarship. This is an important first step, indeed the foundation of womanist religious reflection. There may still be first wave womanist religious thinkers on the horizon—in subfields of religious studies that have yet to interact with black women's religious experiences. Thus for many religious studies fields, this wave still roars.

### *Second Wave*

The second wave of womanist religious thought is known by both its development of its respective disciplines and its establishment of normative womanist discourse. The second wave takes the initiatives of the first wave and extrapolates them into descriptive and constructive work within its field. More than a mere extension of the first wave, second wave womanist religious thought digs in and builds upon this focus on black women's religious experiences. I can best describe this through my own professional discipline of theology. In the first wave of womanist theology, Delores Williams and Jacquelyn Grant identify how an examination of the multiple oppressions that affect black women lead to different theological conclusions than their black male and white feminist theological counterparts, respectively. For Williams, this was about understanding the role of "survival" and "quality of life" in the quest for liberation. For Grant, this was a Christological position focused more on redemptive activity than the maleness of Jesus. Second wave womanist theology begins to delve deeper into theological reflection based on black women's experiences. Thus we see more in-depth reflections on Christology, as in the early work of Kelly Brown Douglas, and the development of womanist soteriologies, doctrines of the trinity, etc. I give this example to also highlight the need for a continued second wave. There is still much work to do. Again, to return to my own discipline, there is, at this time, still no published book-length womanist systematic theology ecclesiology or pneumatology, for that matter. Womanist religious scholars are still articulating their preferred methodological approaches and perspectives on their subject matter.

This wave can rightly continue for generations. For one womanist perspective on a particular dimension of a religious studies discipline is not sufficient or corollary to the plethora of work established in the centuries of Western (Christian) religious reflection. The growth of the second wave is related to the constituency of the field. In some religious studies disciplines, we can still number, on one hand, those scholars whose work seriously and centrally engages with black women's religiosities.

The second wave also, intentionally or not, establishes normativity within womanist religious studies discourse. As the field is developing, it develops in particular directions with specific assumptions and interests. There is great value in this wave's activity because it is instituting a canon within this multidisciplinary field. Traci West names womanist canon-building work as the "naming [of] ideas in response to silences in prevailing cultural discourses [that] extends the dissemination of ideas beyond existing venues in the academy."[60] We see this kind of canon-building and naming in black nationalism, Africana and Black Studies, Women's Studies, etc. As womanist religious thought gains a foothold in the academy, this is harder to deny. After all, one can take a "qualifying" or "comprehensive" exam in womanist religious scholarship or womanist approaches to one's religious studies discipline. With the development of coursework, syllabi, examination readings, and frequently cited sources, womanist religious thought builds its own canon within the larger canon of the field. In "Structured Academic Amnesia," Katie Cannon laments the devaluation of this womanist canon by the predominantly white and male religious academy, noting that some individuals "go to great lengths to demand that our [womanist] intellectual concerns and canons of discourse be ignored in all matters of contract evaluation, tenure review, refereed endorsements for promotions, grants, fellowships and awards."[61] Cannon reminds us that the existence of a womanist canon challenges the existing norms and has real consequences, with issues of standards, power, and economics on the line.

This is an issue of contention for those who see diversity as a hallmark of canon-resistance. About the wider field of womanism, Phillips argues that the "open-ended, polyvalent, polyvocal, dialogic, noncentralized, and improvisational character of womanism, allow[s] it to resist canonization, academic appropriation and ideological subsumption."[62] Floyd-Thomas concurs, arguing that "womanism is a movement with multiple voices, cultures, and experiences, rather than a school or a canon that prefers one voice, culture, or experience of 'woman' or of 'the Black woman' over others."[63] I agree that there is a level of diversity within second wave womanist religious thought, and that people are still contributing to it. This makes for an open canon. I believe the aforementioned perspective mistakes the openness of the canon for the absence of a canon. That is, some individuals seem to resist the language of "canonization" because of how it has traditionally excluded black women's selfhoods and interests.

While there are multiple voices in the second wave, the diversity of perspectives exists within certain boundaries. As religious scholars invoke the work of the first wave and expand this work within the academy, they establish particular themes as normative. For example, second wave womanist religious thought still associates black womanhood with the experience of multiple oppressions—usually named as "racism, sexism, classism and heterosexism"—named and engaged in that order. Victor Anderson's *Beyond Ontological Blackness* offers a salient critique of the challenges of defining blackness, or in this case, black womanhood, around essentialized experiences of oppression.[64] Similarly, the connection to Alice Walker's articulation of the term "womanist" often leads womanist religious scholars to focus so intently on the "survival and wholeness of entire people, male *and* female," that it can fail to adequately critique male [religious] power that dominates, excludes, and selfishly names and violates. Traci West gives an excellent description of the circumstances in which the maintenance of black women's safety necessitates relinquishing commitment to the entire community.[65] In "Must I Be a Womanist?" I also described this second wave as largely Christian, heteronormative, and detached from local and global political movements. All this is to say that I do believe that there *are* classics and foundational works in the womanist religious thought, and that they have a certain tenor and tone to them. The moral value of this normativity is still up for debate because the existence of a womanist religious canon—especially in less than thirty years—is not a scandal, but a triumph of the field's staying power.

## Third Wave

Finally, there is a third wave of womanist religious thought. I understand the naming of this wave to be descriptive and constructive. That is, I am naming some trends and patterns of scholarship that I have seen emerging, while also developing my own marks of what this third wave may be.

To begin with, third wave womanist religious thought focuses away from the identity of the scholar to the ideology of the scholarship. Although I have argued for the value of engaging in identity politics, articulating just what is at stake in issues of naming, the third wave of womanist religious thought challenges the identity politics of the second wave. That is, I have noted that I am a black female religious scholar and asked if I have to be a womanist. Now I flip the question and ask if a womanist has to be a black female religious scholar.

Although Phillips asserts that people other than black women or women of color can be womanists, discussions within religious scholarship cohere around the opposing position. Phillips states that "there is a consensus among the main progenitors of womanism [by which she means Walker, Ogunyemi, and Hudson-Weems] . . . that people other than Black women or women of color can be womanists."[66] Stacey Floyd-Thomas states the opposite opinion by noting that "to be a womanist is to be a Blackwoman"[67] and "that students and scholars of all backgrounds can *do* womanism even if they cannot *be*womanists."[68]

Karen Baker-Fletcher is even more dogmatic in her insistence that womanists can only be black women. For Baker-Fletcher, "a womanist is never a white woman or a white feminist."[69] In fact, women of color can only claim "womanist" nomenclature if they are "in authentic relationships of mutuality, equality, and respect with black women."[70] For Baker-Fletcher, this is an issue of protection. She writes, "The world has cruelly placed black women at the bottom of the totem pole. This requires us to protect one of our few oases."[71] Although Baker-Fletcher believes that white women can learn from womanists and advocate womanism, they cannot be womanists. Baker-Fletcher connects a white woman's desire to be womanist to the historical practices among white Americans of "[stealing] the most creative, cultural productions of black people."[72] Dialogue, mutuality, and respect with white women are acceptable, even hoped for, but naming is not. Baker-Fletcher rejects arguments about inclusion with a hermeneutic of suspicion that asserts "that the deeper, unexamined issue at stake is power and ownership. We [black female womanists] will not be reenslaved."[73]

This is no small issue and one reiterated among third wave feminisms. In Heywood and Drake's discussion of third wave feminism, they note the delicate nature of appropriation between white women and women of color. That is, third wave feminists connect to the language and images of multiplicity and difference found in the works of bell hooks, Audre Lorde, Gloria Anzaldua, Maxine Hong Kingston, Ntozake Shange, Bharti Mukherjee, and Toni Morrison. Thus they must acknowledge how much they owe to women-of-color feminism. This influence is so profound, that white third wave feminism must tread gently around appropriation aware of how, to use Hazel Carby's words, "feminist theory has frequently used and abused [the writings of black women] to produce an essential black female subject for its own consumption."[74] Thus for Heywood and Drake, a definitive aspect of third wave feminism is "negotiating multicultural and antiracist standpoints amid the ongoing tensions between borrowing and appropriating."[75]

I understand the fear of appropriation, or rather misappropriation, of a term that was created for self-naming. Especially given the history of the relationship between black and white cultures in the U.S. in general, and the development of white feminism vis-à-vis black political struggles, in particular. Yet, it is important that all constituencies understand the history of feminisms and womanisms, and cite the work and scholars to whom they are indebted for the current state of the field.

On this point, I stand with Phillips who says that "the womanist idea is not owned by Black women and women of color, even if it was developed, launched, articulated, and elaborated primarily by Black women and other women of color."[76] I'd like to take the radical position that black women relinquished ownership of the term "womanism" when they published it and brought it into the academy, just as Walker loses definitional rights to her term "womanist" to the "womanisms" that developed from her term. Can black female religious scholars really "own" a term originally borrowed from Alice Walker? Shouldn't the idea of "ownership" bother people from communities whose selves and bodies have been bought, sold, bartered, and colonized? To claim ownership of a term seems to reinscribe the hierarchies and attitudes that feminisms and womanisms resist in the first place. Finally, should these black women, as Baker-Fletcher declares they have done, call the religious academy or any institution they didn't create an "oasis"?

Many womanists have tried to address the issue of membership by distinguishing between "womanist" and "womanism." I prefer a more substantial shift. I want to move the conversation away from the identity of the scholar that centers black women's religious experiences and onto the work that is grounded in black women's religious experiences. That is, a hallmark of third wave womanist religious thought is that it is more of an ideology politic, than an identity politic. "A womanist," if we should even speak in those terms, is one who does womanist work; "womanist" may be only one of many descriptors for one's work. To put it more constructively, if womanist religious thought relinquishes a sense of ownership around membership identity and consciously notes the connections among white feminisms, black feminisms, women-of-color feminisms, global and third world feminisms, it has the potential to link to various types of struggles and form unlikely but fruitful alliances in its pursuit of social transformation.[77] To push the envelope even further, when men and nonblacks understand the history of womanist religious thought, its nuances, developments, and politics and identify their work in this way, they may be better positioned to challenge oppressive power structures than if black women policed this term and concept.

Third wave womanist religious thought as an ideology does and does not espouse a certain politic. Like Phillips who talks about five "overlapping characteristics" of womanism,[78] or Floyd-Thomas who discusses four to five tenets of womanism,[79] I resist rigid definition of third wave womanist religious thought. I prefer to say that there are "marks" of third wave womanist religious thought. That is, third wave womanist religious thought: (1) engages the religious lives of women of African descent; (2) maintains a goal of justice, survival, freedom, liberation, and/or quality of life; (3) understands itself to both draw upon *and also depart from* a tradition of womanist religious scholarship; and (4) engages work and thinkers both inside and outside of black religious scholarship.

## Black Women's Religiosity

Third wave womanist religious thought includes and takes seriously the religious experiences of black women. In so doing, it questions what is meant by all of these terms: "religious," "black," and "woman." Third wave womanist religious thought expands upon what has become normative in second wave womanist reflection: that black female descendants of the U.S. slavery system are Christian and experience an interlocking tripartite—perhaps quad-partite—oppression.[80] Discussions in third wave womanist thought have made it increasingly acceptable to discuss black women's non-Christian religious experiences. Thus discussions of black women in New Thought, Buddhisms, African-derived religions, spiritualisms, and humanisms are marks of a third wave of womanist religious thought. That is, third wave womanist religious thought may have convictions, but it cannot be dogmatic. It is an advocate of religious pluralism and will not condemn anyone to hell, if it dares even confirm the existence of a hell.

But there are still assumptions to be questioned. In these postmodern times, we cannot assume we know what "Blackwoman" means. In the binary racial codes of the United States, "black" refers to descendants of enslaved Africans in the U.S., but also to certain immigrants and their descendants with significantly different cultural, geographical, and religious histories and experiences. Outside the U.S., third wave womanist religious thought may encompass the religious experiences of those in the Caribbean, South America, various continental African experiences, or even the diaspora and women of color in Asia and Australia. In those contexts, "black" and "color" and "ethnicity" are construed in relevant local terms with particular meanings and significations. "Black" is also problematized by the voices of self-identified multi- and bi-racial individuals with a level of black "African" cultural and geographic heritage, however far removed.

Lastly, we cannot make assumptions about what is meant by the signifier "woman." Third wave womanist religious thought makes room and accounts for individuals who are biologically female, intersex, and transgendered. It can speak of individuals who may not be biologically female, or who do not fit into binary biological classifications and, yet identify as woman. When using the signifier "woman," there is no room in third wave womanist religious thought for hints of heterosexism, assumed-monogamy, or homophobia. Honestly, to do otherwise is a betrayal of the evolution of womanism itself. Both third wave feminism and womanist religious scholarship are wholly dependent on the work, writing, and public lives of women-of-color feminists—especially black and Chicana feminists—who courageously and unapologetically identify as lesbian and bisexual. These experiences produced the writings that elucidate the challenges of being silenced, marginalized, hybrid, complex, and brave. Thus while one of the marks of this third wave of womanist religious thought is its occupation with black women's religiosity, it does not assume singular meanings of those terms, but troubles them in its scholarship and casts wide the net for the contemporary complex meanings of identity.

## Goals of Justice, Survival, Freedom, etc.

Third wave womanist religious thought also maintains a goal of justice, survival, freedom, liberation, and/or quality of life. In this way, the third wave is directional. There is an ethical telos to the work of this wave. While valuing academic reflection as a goal unto itself, third wave womanist religious thought does have normative dimensions that cohere around principles of freedom and health. It can resist multiple oppressions without defining itself in terms of those oppressions. It can well embrace what Victor Anderson refers to as the grotesqueries of lived experience, highlighting both the challenges and joys of history and culture while advocating a particular ethic.[81] Advocating a particular ethic is the activism of the third wave, but just as in the realities of survival, health, and freedom, it may have as many individualist tones as it does communal tones. Herein individualism and separatism are neither the counterparts to community, nor values to be shunned as eurocentric and destructive. Rather they are integral components of the journey to spiritual maturity, personal freedom, and a socially transformed academy and world.

### Relies on and Departs from Womanist Religious Scholarship Tradition

I hope by now it is clear that third wave womanist religious thought both relies on and departs from the second wave of womanist religious scholarship. Like the second wave, the third wave develops scholarship within the religious disciplines. This wave appreciates and stands upon the shoulders of the second wave of womanist religious thought with its interest in black women's religious lives—however we construe them—and its connection to activist and liberative efforts and ends. Yet it also sees itself as departing from the womanist religious tradition as it is established. The departures may arise as third wavers redefine black, woman, and religious. They may arise as third wavers challenge key ideas in the second wave canon. Thus third wavers may never be canonized. More importantly, when they start to become canonized, it may be time for a new wave.

Likewise, Alice Walker's articulation of womanist may not be the touchstone to third wave womanist religious thought. For religious scholars, Walker's articulation of womanist was the departure and source of inspiration. As second wavers begin to acknowledge, womanist religious scholarship or "womanism" exists quite independently—for better or for worse—of Alice Walker's writings, life, and politics, intersecting with Walker's work more like a tangent than a Venn diagram. Third wave womanist religious thought may refer to the first and second wave of womanist religious scholarship as a launching pad, *or* look to the other architects of womanism, *or* work with Phillips's understanding of womanism *or* take another direction altogether. Thus third waver womanist religious thought assumes its roots, but needn't be loyal to them for loyalty's sake, personal affection, or political expediency.

Why not, then, find new terminology? Why not thoroughly distinguish this third wave from the larger womanist religious discourse with other naming? It is because we are in the same "ocean"; there are continuities; and we are connected—in subject matter and in interpersonal relationships—to those from whom we differ.

French poststructuralist Jacques Derrida writes compellingly about ways to relate to one's academic and cultural forebears. There is a level of affirmation in relating to one's heritage. But to affirm "means not simply accepting this heritage but re-launching it otherwise, and keeping it alive."[82] One should not accept one's heritage literally or as a totality. Rather, how we relate to our past should be a matter of choice. Choosing one's heritage is not accepting everything or erasing everything. For Derrida, "the best way to be faithful to a heritage is to be unfaithful."[83]

Thus the third wave declares that there is no need to disown our history because of the differences. Third wave womanist religious thought does not need to be characterized by rejection, arguments, criticism, and academic chiding between waves. To question is not necessarily to disavow; to depart is not necessarily to reject. Questioning and departing, rather, are indications of growth and expansion. This growth and expansion is often done in directions that feel more true to an individual's passions and self—the personal freedom that is integral to the naming of "womanist."

Lastly, third wave womanist religious thought engages academics, activists, and researchers both inside and outside of black religious scholarship. Declaring this aloud is almost unnecessary, for as Katie Cannon says, "You can't get a PhD in the western hemisphere without knowing a lot about white men, whether you want to or not."[84] All too often, an academic's extensive and examined knowledge of the white Western male canon of one's field leads to a virtual lack of knowledge about marginalized scholarship. The first and second waves of womanist religious thought respond to this trend through their extensive reference to black women's literary, historical, cultural, and now religious scholarship. Even in her vigorous critique of womanist terminology, Cheryl Sanders admits how delighted she is to see the prevalence of scholarship by and about black women in the footnotes of the responding scholars, no matter their differences. Indeed, this is a hallmark of womanist religious thought—lifting up the important work of scholarship by and about black women—and not just for the sake of representation. Scholarship by and about black women is relevant to the scholarship of the religious academy as a whole, and increasingly available as black women's presence in the academy grows, and the academy becomes more receptive to work on black women's lives. This is no small task because, as I mentioned earlier, black religious scholars disproportionately and unjustly bear the burden of highlighting black religious scholarship. Including scholars who do not identify as black and female under the rubric of "third wave womanism" is one way third wave womanist religious thought encourages womanist knowledge across the religious academy.

Third wave womanist religious thought insists on a kind of cross-pollination that dialogues with and between areas of scholarship that do not normally interact. At times, this means citing dominant voices within one's field for their theoretical or constitutive contribution to one's argument. Thus there is no need to defend using one's knowledge of white male theorists because one's subject matter includes the religious lives of black women. Other times, this principle means engaging marginalized fields of scholarship with each other. Third wave womanist religious thought may engage fields that appear to be natural allies, and yet are rarely interlocuted with religious thought; i.e., African philosophy, Caribbean history, feminist theory, queer studies, Native American educational critiques, and disability studies, to name a selected few. The choice of scholarship invoked in third wave womanist religious thought is a reflection of what best makes an argument while also acknowledging the multiple influences and identities that a scholar maintains. For while womanist religious thought is an influence upon one's work, so perhaps are poststructuralism, pragmatism, transcendentalism, psychoanalysis, mysticism, and law. Third wave womanist religious thought does not ask us to prioritize or compartmentalize our identities, alliances, or scholarship into untouching silos.

Defining this third wave by content, rather than by form, breaks open the boundaries of womanist religious thought. Persons with varied gender and racial identities may conduct womanist religious thought. Likewise, some work by an individual may fall under the third wave of womanist religious thought, while other work does not. Or some work by a singular individual may fall into the second wave, while other work falls more aptly into a third wave. This wave is generational inasmuch and only as it sees itself as part of a larger tradition of womanist religious scholarship. This wave needn't fight as vigorously as the first wave to suggest that black women's religious lives are worthy of academic study.

And yet in a dialectical move back to identity, I want to suggest that there are two regulative qualities about the individual who engages in third wave womanist religious thought. First, a third wave womanist religious thinker has a community of accountability. The third wave must present itself and answer to a community. Presumably, this is the community of the thinker. While this proposition may initially sound like a principle of second wave that I have denounced, I want to add that the thinker gets to identify the community of accountability, and this community may shift with different pieces of scholarship. There's no reason to assume that the community of accountability is "the historic black church" as has commonly been expressed in black religious dialogues. The community of accountability may be a faith community, but it may also be an academic, cultural, gendered, nonprofit, political, ancestral, or grass-roots community. There is no hierarchy of value, no standard for what makes one a "legitimate scholar activist," because there is activism inside and outside of the academy. The community of accountability is no reflection of the depth of one's cultural and racial commitment. This community of accountability exists in part to ground the third wave thinker, but also to challenge and support the thinker in the production of new ideas. There is no reason that one should venture alone into uncharted waters.

Second, a third wave womanist religious thinker brings his or her whole self to one's work. This is more than a mere acknowledgment of one's social location. In some sense, this principle is manifest in the scholarship one engages and produces, and the community to which one is accountable. And while this may not occur in each article of scholarship, this should be true across one's body of work. More importantly, third wavers bring their whole selves to their work because they refuse to bear the ill-consequences of lives marked by silences of selfhood, betrayal of loved ones, compartmentalization, closets, or lives that are all-work-and-no-play. And yes, this is a privilege of being in the third wave. To be more personal about it, my work is no more or less womanist than it is process, constructive, postmodern, queer, black, feminist, American, Christian, pagan, and so many other things.

In conclusion, third wave womanist religious thought is a movement within the tradition of womanist religious scholarship, and larger global activist scholarship. To spend an article, a lecture, two days, and a couple of anthologies discussing womanist typologies is both a mark of academic privilege, and an insistent reminder that naming is about personal freedom and power—two things that must be monitored and revisited regularly if we intend to share them equally.

I was originally propelled to this idea because of my deep affinities with black feminism *and* womanism, and my sense that the power to name one's own work was being usurped by those who do not author said work. I do not know that I've undermined the power structures that try to decide who does what work and what they call it. Rather I've tried to acknowledge new sources of power within womanist naming as well as the factors that constrain radical impulses. I've tried to affirm the needed coexistence of different hopes for this field, even as they sharply disagree.

For this last reason I think it's fair to adapt Sojourner Truth's refrain to womanist religious thought. Just as Sojourner's question, "And ain't I a woman?" expanded the boundaries of work, race, and gender in the interest of inclusion, freedom, and power, so does the question, "Ain't I a womanist?" Although the context is much more circumscribed, the same issues are at stake. Third wave womanist religious thought includes scholars of varied gendered and racial identities who both affirm and problematize that which concerns the religious experiences of black women. Third wave womanist religious thought acknowledges the complexities of self-naming, other-naming, and the progression that occurs as one grows within, and from, a particular scholarly heritage. Third wave womanist religious thought learns from the developing canon and pushes back against it. Third wave womanist religious thought is a part of womanist traditions while exploring new directions. As a third wave, it is contradictory, ambiguous, multiple, hybrid, personal, and political. This is what it means to be faithful. To echo Derrida, "this faithfulness sometimes still takes the form of unfaithfulness and waywardness [by being] faithful to the differences; that is to say, one must go on with the conversation."[85] I consider this question, "Ain't I a womanist?" to be another part of the dialogue.

This volume includes colleagues whose work represents some of what can be considered third wave womanist religious thought. The third wave of womanist religious thought is not a mere proposition, but already contains lively and innovative scholarship. This volume is divided into four sections: religious pluralism, which is more aptly engagement with non-Christian religions; popular culture and media; gender and sexuality; and politics—grouped together under this rubric for the first time.

The section on religious pluralism reveals the third wave interest in the experiences of women and female deities in non-Christian religions. Debra Majeed's essay on the practice of polygyny in African American Muslim communities investigates the social, communal, and religious complexities of plural marriage among the single largest group of American Muslims. Stephen C. Finley explores the esoteric spiritual leadership of the Nation of Islam's Mother Tynetta Muhammad as she transformed herself from one of the Honorable Elijah Muhammad's secretaries, to a trusted member of Minister Farrakhan's inner circle. Pu Xiumei offers a womanist ecospiritual reading on Di Mu, an indigenous goddess in contemporary China. Such a reading allows Pu to interpret a medicine woman's engagement with Di Mu and Buddhism as a survival strategy for indigenous religions in an increasingly technological era.

In concert with the third wave engagement with media, the section on popular culture asserts that understandings of masculinity and feminist affect black women's religious and secular lives. Darnise C. Martin's essay examines how gospel house music culture functions as church for black gay men by deftly comparing the underground dance movement to the hush arbors of African American slavery. Elonda Clay's "Confessions of an Ex-Theological Bitch" plays on the popular memoir by hip hop music video dancer Karrine Steffans's "Confessions of a Video Vixen" to talk about the ways in which contemporary women continue to function in subservient roles in the media and churches. While examining the misogynist lyrics of hip hop artist Rick Ross, Ronald B. Neal argues against the prevailing notion that black males create sexism and homophobia in black America. Rather, Neal illustrates how the Abrahamic faiths construct and reinforce colonial concepts of masculinity that are echoed in contemporary hip hop.

Third wave womanist religious thought troubles categories of gender and sexuality as it explores their religious significance. In this section, Monica R. Miller problematizes both Don Imus's controversial statement about "nappy-headed ho's" and the black community's response to it. Noting the classism engrained in the response, Miller reclaims the deviant expression in an effort to highlight the diversity that exists within contemporary African American gendered communities. In "Dark Matter," Roger Sneed draws on neo-soul music and science fiction for useful constructions to describe the experiences of black queer individuals. This allows Sneed to construct a concept of liminality that is more appropriate for black queer life than the dominant theories of liminality. Nessette Falu wrestles with the ways that black lesbian identity is articulated in academic writings and contemporary film by interpolating postmodern theory with black lesbian activism and advocacy. Finally, EL Kornegay Jr. combines personal story with James Baldwin's writings for narratives on how men and women can redefine heterosexual masculinity. He finds answers in both narrative structure and the blending of the sacred and profane.

Third wave womanist religious thought has a political bent that advocates for justice and inclusion in global, American, and academic politics. In this final section Sharon D. Welch draws on womanist and Buddhist ideologies for global peace policies. Looking specifically at the political leadership of Ronald Dellums and Nelson Mandela, Welch finds new ways to embody the visionary pragmatism that black feminist Patricia Hill Collins proposed over twenty years ago. In "We'll Make Us a World," Barbara A. Holmes reads Michelle Obama's creative renegotiation of First Lady for clues to new options for engaging racism in a purportedly postracial society. The new model of empowerment is not limited to Christian themes, but utilizes embodied creativity, reflexive memory, and trickster resourcefulness to move toward an egalitarian future in religion and government. Victor Anderson uncovers the historic tones within contemporary struggles to define "black culture" within religious studies. Anderson excavates political movements and current academic strivings to reveal the ongoing power and problematic category of "blackness." Moving us even deeper into the academic classroom, Arisika Razak articulates a pedagogical approach that reflects the best of womanist striving. Razak finds that this is best done with a commitment to Alice Walker's writings, the incorporation of various postmodern and antiracist theories, a plurality of embodied movements, multiple religious traditions, and personal engagement.

This volume presents the work of theologians, philosophers of religion, ethicists, cultural critics, historians, a midwife-healer, and a psychologist. While there is no representation from those working in textual studies or the practical theology fields, this is not to say that there is no third wave within these areas. In short, I believe this volume offers a partial, yet compelling portrait of a third wave in womanist religious scholarship. In this way, the connections between womanism and postmodernism are again revealed. Like poststructuralism, womanism "unpack[s] complex oppressive processes and forms of violence, concentrat[es] on the circulation of power; and . . . promote[s] equality and democracy while respecting difference and freedom."[86]To find a way to draw from the past in constructive ways while moving boldly into the relevant concerns of contemporary society is nothing less than what process thinkers refer to as "creative transformation." And this, I believe is a universal calling.

## Notes

1. Sojourner Truth, *Narrative of Sojourner Truth: A Bondswoman of Olden Time, With a History of Her Labors and Correspondence Drawn from Her "Book of Life,"* Schomburg Library of Black Women Writers, ed. Henry Louis Gates Jr. and Jeffrey C. Stewart (New York: Oxford University Press, 1991), 134. Nell Irvin Painter notes that the phrase "ar'n't/ain't I a woman" ascribed to Truth is more rightly the words of Frances Dana Gage, who added them to a report made twelve years after the 1851 speech in Akron, where Truth is said to have given this speech. This expression has long been associated with Sojourner Truth, and even if the words are not hers, reveals the issues within black womanhood/black feminism highlighted in this volume. See Nell Irvin Painter, "Introduction," *Narrative of Sojourner Truth*, Penguin Classics (New York: Penguin, 1998), x; and Nell Irvin Painter, *Sojourner Truth: A Life, a Symbol* (New York: W. W. Norton, 1996).

2. Alice Walker, "Coming Apart," in *The Womanist Reader*, ed. Layli Phillips (New York: Routledge, 2006).

3. Alice Walker, "Gifts of Power: Rebecca Jackson," in *In Search of Our Mothers' Gardens: Womanist Prose* (New York: Harcourt Brace Jovanovich, 1983), 81.

4. A. Walker, *In Search*, xi–xii.

5. Layli Phillips, "Womanism: On Its Own," *The Womanist Reader*, ed. Layli Phillips (New York: Routledge, 2006), xix.

6. Patricia Hill Collins, "What's in a Name?: Womanist, Black Feminism, and Beyond," *Black Scholar* 26, no. 1 (Winter/ Spring 1996): 9–17.

7. Stacey Floyd-Thomas, "Writing for Our Lives: Womanism as an Epistemological Revolution," in *Deeper Shades of Purple: Womanism in Religion and Society* (New York: New York University Press, 2006), 4.

8. Karen Baker-Fletcher, "Womanist Journey," in *Deeper Shades of Purple: Womanism in Religion and Society*, ed. Stacey Floyd-Thomas (New York: New York University Press, 2006), 158–75; and *Dancing with God: The Trinity from a Womanist Perspective* (St. Louis: Chalice, 2006), ix–x, 6–7, where she correlates aspects of Alice Walker's work with the Christian holiness traditions.

9. Melanie L. Harris, "Alice Walker's Ethics: An Analysis of Alice Walker's Non-Fiction Work as a Resource for Womanist Ethics" (Ph.D. diss., Union Theological Seminary in the City of New York, 2006); Melanie L. Harris, "Loving the Spirit: Expressions of Paganism in Alice Walker's Non-Fiction" (paper presented at the annual meeting of the American Academy of Religion, Washington, DC, 20 November 2006); Melanie L. Harris, *Gifts of Virtue: Alice Walker and Womanist Ethics* (New York: Palgrave Macmillan, 2010).

10. Arisika Razak, "Her Blue Body: Alice Walker's Womanism," *Feminist Theology* 100, no. 1 (2009): 100–126, with ecological goddess/nature-based religions.

11. For two good summaries on womanism in religious thought, see Linda E. Thomas, "Womanist Theology, Epistemology, and a New Anthropological Paradigm," *CrossCurrents* 48 (Winter 1998–1999): 488–99; and Stephanie Y. Mitchem, *Introducing Womanist Theology* (Maryknoll, NY: Orbis Books, 2002).

12. Chikwenye Okonjo Ogunyemi, "Womanism: The Dynamics of the Contemporary Black Female Novel in English," in *The Womanist Reader*, ed. Layli Phillips (1985; reprint, New York: Routledge, 2006), 21.

13. Ibid., 28.

14. Ibid., 31.

15. Clenora Hudson-Weems, "Africana Womanism," in *The Womanist Reader*, ed. Layli Phillips (New York: Routledge, 2006), 48.

16. Ibid.

17. Ibid., 53.

18. Clenora Hudson-Weems, "Cultural and Agenda Conflicts in Academia: Critical Issues for Africana Women's Studies," in *The Womanist Reader*, ed. Layli Phillips (New York: Routledge, 2006), 42.

19. Beverly Guy-Sheftall, "The Evolution of Feminist Consciousness Among African American Women," *Words of Fire: An Anthology of African-American Feminist Thought* (New York: New Press, 1995), 1–22.

20. Patricia Hill Collins, "What's in a Name? Womanist, Black Feminism, and Beyond," *Black Scholar* 26, no. 1 (Winter/Spring 1996): 15.

21. Alice Walker, "Audre's Voice," *Anything We Love Can Be Saved: A Writers' Activism* (New York: Random House, 1997), 80.

22. David Bradley, "Alice Walker: Telling the Black Women's Story," *New York Times Magazine* (8 January 1984): 25–37.

23. Stacey Floyd-Thomas, 3.

24. Phillips, xx.

25. Traci West, "Is a Womanist a Black Feminist?," *Deeper Shades of Purple: Womanist Approaches to Religion and Society*, ed. Stacey Floyd-Thomas (New York: New York University Press, 2006), 292.

26. Collins, 16.

27. Phillips, xxxiii–xxxiv.

28. This is one of Clenora Hudson-Weems's strongest and most valuable points. She uses the African term/concept "Nommo" to refer to it in her text.

29. Monica A. Coleman, "Must I Be a Womanist?," *Journal of Feminist Studies in Religion* 22, no. 1 (Spring 2006): 85–96.

30. Traci West, 292.

31. Collins, 15–16.

32. Caryn Riswold, *Feminism and Christianity: Questions and Answers in the Third Wave* (Eugene, OR: Cascade Publications, 2009), 7.

33. Barbara Findlen, "Introduction," *Listen Up: Voices from the Next Feminist Generation* (Seattle, WA: Seal, 1995), xii.

34. Findlen, xiii.

35. Nancy Whittier, "Turning It Over: Personnel Change in the Columbus, Ohio Women's Movement, 1969-1984," in *Feminist Organizations: Harvest of the New Women's Movement*, ed. Myra Marx and Patricia Yancey Martin (Philadelphia: Temple University Press, 1995), 180.

36. Rita Alfonso and Jo Trigilio, "Surfing the Third Wave: A Dialogue between Two Third Wave Feminists," *Hypatia: A Journal of Feminist Philosophy* 12, no. 3 (Summer 1997): 7–16.

37. Rebecca Walker, "Being Real: An Introduction," *To Be Real: Telling the Truth and Changing the Face of Feminism* (New York: Anchor, 1995), xxxii–xxxiii.

38. R. Walker, xxxii.

39. Angela Y. Davis, "Afterword," in *To Be Real: Telling the Truth and Changing the Face of Feminism*, ed. Rebecca Walker (New York: Anchor, 1995), 281.

40. Leslie Heywood and Jennifer Drake, "Introduction," *Third Wave Agenda: Being Feminist, Doing Feminist* (Minneapolis: University of Minnesota Press, 1997), 1. They are referring to thinkers such as Danielle Crittenden, Rene Denfield, Camille Paglia, Katie Roiphe, Wendy Shalit, and Christina Hoff Sommers. It is an interesting aside to know that the term "postfeminist" was first used after the "first wave" in 1919. Cf. Susan Faludi, "Feminism Then and Now," Public Lecture, Radcliffe Institute for Advanced Study, Harvard University, Cambridge, MA (27 May 2010).

41. Ibid., 3.

42. Ibid., 7.

43. Laura Brunell, "The Third Wave of Feminism," *Encyclopedia Britannica*, http://www.britannica.com/EBchecked/topic/724633/feminism/280083/The-third-wave-of-feminism.

44. Jennifer Baumgardner and Amy Richards, *Manifesta: Young Women, Feminism and the Future* (New York: Farrar, Straus & Giroux, 2000), vii.

45. Angela Y. Davis, *Women, Race and Class* (New York: Vintage, 1983).

46. Deborah Gray White, *Ar'n't I a Woman: Female Slaves in the Plantation South*, 1985. Rev. ed. (New York: W. W. Norton, 1999).

47. Harriet Jacobs, *Incidents in the Life of a Slave Girl, Written by Herself*, 1861, Rev. ed. (Cambridge, MA: Belknap Press of Harvard University Press, 2009).

48. Kimberly Springer, "Third Wave Black Feminism?" *Signs* 27, no. 4 (Summer 2002): 1063.

49. Springer, 1064.

50. Veronica Chambers, *Mama's Girl* (New York: Riverhead, 1997).

51. Lisa Jones, *Bulletproof Diva: Tales of Race, Sex and Hair* (New York: Anchor, 1997).

52. Joan Morgan, *When Chickenheads Come Home to Roost: My Life as a Hip-Hop Feminist* (New York: Simon & Schuster, 1999).

53. Michael Awkward, "A Black Man's Place in Black Feminist Criticism," in *Negotiating Difference: Race, Gender, and the Politics of Positionality* (Chicago: University of Chicago Press, 1995).

54. Gary L. Lemons, *Black Male Outsider: Teaching as a Pro-Feminist Man, A Memoir* (Albany: State University of New York Press, 2008) and *Womanist Forefathers: Frederick Douglass and W. E. B. DoBois* (Albany: State University of New York Press, 2009).

55. David Ikard, *Breaking the Silence: Towards a Black Male Feminist Criticism* (Baton Rouge: Louisiana State University Press, 2007) and http://nationofcowards.blogspot.com.

56. Marc Anthony Neal, *New Black Man* (New York: Routledge, 2006) and http://newblackman.blogspot.com/.

57. Beverly Guy-Sheftall, "Response from a 'Second Waver' to Kimberly Springer's 'Third Wave Black Feminism?'" *Signs* 27, no. 4 (Summer 2002): 1092.

58. Sallie McFague, *Metaphorical Theology: Models of God in Religious Language* (Philadelphia: Fortress Press, 1982) and *Models of God: Theology for an Ecological, Nuclear Age* (Philadelphia: Fortress Press, 1987).

59. Floyd-Thomas, 4.

60. West, 292.

61. Katie G. Cannon, "Structured Academic Amnesia: As If This True Womanist Story Never Happened," *Deeper Shades: Womanism in Religion and Society* (New York: New York University Press, 2006), 22.

62. Phillips, xxi.

63. Floyd-Thomas, 7.

64. Victor Anderson, *Beyond Ontological Blackness: An Essay on African American Religious and Cultural Criticism* (New York: Crossroad, 1995).

65. Traci West, 294. West gives examples of black women who experience intimate violence from black men, black male clergy who sexually harass women congregants, and state- and church-sanctioned arguments against same-sex marriage.

66. Phillips, xxxvi.

67. Floyd-Thomas, 6.

68. Stacey Floyd-Thomas, *Mining the Motherlode: Methods in Womanist Ethics* (Cleveland: Pilgrim, 2006), 4.

69. Karen Baker-Fletcher, "A Womanist Journey," in *Deeper Shades of Purple: Womanism in Religion and Society*, ed. Stacey Floyd-Thomas (New York: New York University Press, 2006), 161.

70. Baker-Fletcher, 163.

71. Ibid.

72. Ibid., 164.

73. Ibid., 168.

74. Hazel Carby, "The Multicultural Wars," in Black Popular Culture, ed. Michele Wallace and Gina Dent (Seattle: Bay, 1992), 192.

75. Heywood and Drake, 10.

76. Phillips, xxxvi.

77. Vron Ware makes a similar point regarding white feminist appropriation of black feminist work: "[T]he extent to which this borrowing, or appropriating, is acknowledged obviously varies a great deal, but I think it can potentially provide an important link between different types of struggles . . . [leading] to forming alliances." *Beyond the Pale: White Women, Racism and History* (New York: Verso, 1992), 240.

78. Phillips names them as "anti-oppressionist, vernacular, nonideological, communitarian and spiritualized" in Phillips, xxiv–xxvi.

79. Floyd-Thomas names them as "radical subjectivity, traditional communalism, redemptive self-love and critical engagement" in *Mining the Motherlode*, 8–11. She adds "appropriation and reciprocity" in *Deeper Shades of Purple*, 7.

80. By quad-partite, I am referring to the interlocking oppressive systems of racism, sexism, classism, and heterosexism.

81. Ibid.

82. Jacques Derrida and Elisabeth Roudinesco, *For What Tomorrow . . . : A Dialogue*, trans. Jeff Fort, Cultural Memory in the Present (Palo Alto, CA: Stanford University Press, 2004), 3.

83. Derrida and Roudinesco, 2.

84. Katie G. Cannon, "Womanism and the Soul of the Black Community," public lecture, Bennett College for Women, Greensboro, NC (30 March 2005).

85. Jacques Derrida, "The Last Interview," *SV (Studio Visit)* (November 2004), 7.

86. Phillips, xxxi.

# PART I

# Religious Pluralism

# 1

# Muslim Marriage

## *A Womanist Perspective on Troubling U.S. Traditions*

**Debra Majeed**

The social and theological dynamics peculiar to the reality of African American Muslims continue to influence how they marry and organize their households. Indeed, the peculiarities of black life in America have historically distinguished the lived experiences of these Muslims from other practitioners of Islam regardless of their nationality or citizenship. That is, the absence of marriageable men (e.g., single, heterosexual, legitimately employed, living outside of prison walls, and free from drugs) within black America and the higher status routinely afforded married women have led some African American Muslim women to accept plural marriage.[1]Moreover, the educational and, often, financial strides that black females have achieved have created a related reality: Muslim women who prefer to knowingly share their husbands, regardless of the knowledge or consent of their husbands' other wives. Whether practiced within a Muslim-majority nation or non-Muslim state, this form of nontraditional marriage is contentious. Though few in number compared to the overwhelming number of heterosexual monogamous unions, plural marriage among the single largest group of American Muslims offers a fascinating, complex, underexplored, and often misunderstood teachable moment about Muslim marriage.[2]

### Polygyny and African American Muslims[3]

Plural marriage in Islam is equated with *polygyny*, the practice of a husband being married to up to four wives at the same time.[4] Unlike *polygamy*, which refers to more than one spouse—husband or wife—and thus is un-Islamic, polygyny is permitted by the Qur'an, the primary authority of the world's estimated 1.82 billion followers of Islam.[5] The guiding Qur'anic perspective on plural marriage, *Al Nisa*3, attempted to address an inequity concerning the rights and maintenance of women and children, and the existing customary practice that both became the property of men when they married in pre-Islamic Arabia.[6] While examinations of Islamic legal materials routinely promote this verse as a divinely inspired reform in Arab history that served to repudiate one expression of patriarchy and protect women and children from abuse and destitution, no consensus exists about how, where, or when *Al Nisa* 3 should be invoked today. Indeed, opponents of polygyny have declared that "the love between a husband and wife should not be divided."[7] Debate also surrounds the question of whether the intent of this "Qur'anic reform" was to "raise the status of women" and, if it did, what that means in the twenty-first century.[8] Indeed, both supporters and opponents of the practice within African American Muslim communities defend their positions with divergent interpretations of this verse. Even so, both sides agree that this verse addresses a personal and/or family matter that should be adjudicated in a way that privileges the Islamic legal position on marriage.

*Al Nisa* 3 was revealed following the deaths of about seventy Muslim men in the seventh century "as a concession to the prevailing social conditions" when "equal justice and impartiality were guaranteed."[9] It was, as Michele Alexandre has observed, "innovative and radical at the time, especially considering the laissez faire state of polygamy before the Qur'an was revealed to the Prophet. [He] was concerned that, in a time of great wars, wives not be left widowed and destitute and children not be left orphaned and homeless."[10] A popular English translation of this verse reads, "If you fear that you shall not be able to deal justly with the orphans, Marry women of your choice, Two or three or four; but if you fear that you shall not be able to deal justly (with them), then only one, or (a captive) that your right hands possess, that will be more suitable, to prevent you from doing injustice." In seventh-century Arabia's patriarchal, misogynistic society, the physical survival of women often necessitated depending upon provision from the men in their lives, through whom women also negotiated their legitimacy and social honor. Without recognition as autonomous moral agents, women who outlived their "protectors" could traverse few avenues to secure their own survival or the survival of their children. That is to say, women displaced by war without a husband or male relative were suddenly on their own "in a society that confused value with material wealth." Widows also were undervalued in a male-privileging society that not long before murdered female infants at birth. With the advent of the Qur'an, Muslim men were instructed to marry no more than four women, with the number dependent upon a man's ability to provide for and treat each woman with justice. Thus the revelation of the Qur'an did not accompany the introduction of polygyny, but with it, one form of plural marriage was regulated and restricted.[11]

Many African American Muslims, particular those who follow the teachings of W. D. Mohammed, view marriage as "the legal gateway to a vast array of tangible and intangible protections, responsibilities, and benefits, most of which cannot be replicated in any other way."[12] Routinely, they are taught to privilege marriage as superior to and opposite of singleness, though fully aware that polygyny is illegal in the U.S. and that the majority of the world's people consider polygyny akin to human slavery—that is, "[as] an institution whose past purpose was no longer acceptable to most people."[13] African American Muslims also are aware that perspectives of Muslims and others that the "original intent" of the Qur'an on this matter was to lead to its prohibition, as occurred with slavery.[14] Ultimately, like most Muslims, they recognize marriage as the only legitimate arena for sexual intercourse and procreation. Legalities aside, they also acknowledge a few realities highlighted in recent national polls, namely:

- "Black women born after 1950 are twice as likely as white women to never marry by age 45 and twice as likely to be divorced, widowed, or separated.[15]
- Only about 30 percent of black women are living with a spouse, compared with about 49 percent of Hispanic women, 55 percent of non-Hispanic white women. and more than 60 percent of Asian women."[16]
- Finally, "highly educated black women have increasingly fewer options when it comes to potential mates."[17]

## Black Theodicy and Womanism

Proponents of polygyny subscribe to the idea that the landscape of seventh-century Arabia is strikingly comparable with the context of twenty-first-century North America, whereby "war" has led to population imbalances in both regions. Then, as now, they say, the lack of available men, and/or the high number of female-led households, and the continued economic disparity experienced by mothers and their children, makes the practice of polygyny both mandated and permissible.[18] Unlike Arabia's first Muslim women, their contemporary counterparts in black America are often more financially stable than Muslim men. Thus African American Muslim women may—and often do—choose polygyny because they believe it to be the only way they authentically can practice their religion, live a morally good Muslim life, and sustain their communities. As these women demonstrate with their commitment to the continuation of community life and the superiority of marriage over singleness, they risk—and sometimes sacrifice fully—the legal rights afforded to wives in dual-partnered monogamous unions. Women married to polygynous men and those who approve of their family formations also are less likely to interrogate sexism in the primary setting they inhabit—the home.[19] Granted, as Donald McCrary has pointed out, the home is a challenging environment to analyze. Still, no other representation of the private sphere can claim the spotlight as "the place most people first acquire sexist attitudes."[20] With that line of reasoning, proponents of polygyny, I would argue, invoke two theoretical frameworks that are significant considerations for this issue: black theodicy and womanism. I will offer an analysis of the relationship of these frameworks to the lived realities of African American Muslims and to the "black family question."[21]

Throughout the history of the U.S., African Americans have experienced life in America as what William James labeled "multiple realities."[22] For them, one sphere consisted of the limitations of housing, educational, and other opportunities, along with characterizations of black life established and promoted by the dominant culture. This "reality," or *outside*world, was created by "white modes of cultural domination" that fostered, constructed, and reinforced knowledge about African Americans by encounters (or perceptions of the same) between them and white Americans.[23] In this world, as Michael Eric Dyson notes, "black men and women became sexual and economic properties" and "healthy black self-regard and self-confidence were outlawed."[24] More often than not, contradictions of this world were created solely by African Americans, who organized an alternate world about themselves and their experiences living in a racist society. In this "reality," parallel universe, or *inside* world, African Americans were freer to exercise control over their representations, the formations of their households, as well as their actual experiences and the meaning they and others derive from them. Still, this inside world was a multidimensional, complex sphere with boundaries (sometimes fluid) that African Americans traversed depending upon their viewpoints on such issues as religion, sexuality, marriage, and black identity as forms of resistance. African Americans interpret both worlds in relation to each other. Situated at the breach between them is the moral authority to acknowledge and respond to black suffering, even if doing so challenges civil law.

The contextualization of proponents of polygyny echoes Sherman Jackson's view of black theodicy as the theory of ethnic misery that "focuses on the problem of evil in the more specific context of the historical communal suffering of Blackamericans" and the implications of broken relationships.[25] In Jackson's world, this particular category of theodicy brings forth the question: How can African American Muslims—as self-determined, active agents—free themselves from the social evils perpetrated on the black family without questioning the justice, omnipotence, and omnipresent nature of Allah?[26] Black theodicy rejects the individual, "out-for-me" mentality in favor of a communal, "the good of the many outweighs the good of the one" framework that supports African American Muslim attempts to experience "the Islamic theological tradition speaking effectively to *their* concerns and realities."[27] Black theodicy also permits considerations of Muslim marriage as a response to black suffering and as a method of survival that links African American Muslims to their first-generation Muslim ancestors.

Second, proponents of polygyny hold perceptions about how best to organize their households that prompt an exploration of what Katie Cannon labels, "the womanist house of wisdom."[28] Indeed, this essay brings debates about Muslim marriage to bear on a section of "the house" that I label "Muslim womanism," a theologically infused cultural hermeneutic that "foregrounds" the lived reality of African American Muslim women as it challenges totalitarian understandings of marriage, partnering, and household organization.[29] Like my colleague Traci West, I am concerned about "those persons who are victimized by violence (sometimes lethal) that is too easily tolerated by society."[30] For this research project, society is African American Muslim communities. Potential victims are Muslim women, wives, and children.

Muslim womanism is grounded in the racist and patriarchal culture of the U.S., in the nuances of black struggles for justice, in acknowledgment of Islamic legitimacy and Qur'anic justice. This strategy challenges scholars to speak holistically about Islam and the diverse experiences of its female adherents by accomplishing for Muslim women what Katie G. Cannon and other Christian womanists have endeavored to achieve for their Christian subjects: documentation—and when necessary, problematization—of the agency, subjectivity, and moral formulas that African American Muslim women accept and construct. That is, Muslim womanism uses the works of Muslim (usually female) scholars to promote internal critiques on at least two fronts: first, as a challenge to followers of Islam to question limitations imposed on the role and/or agency of Muslim women in the private or public sphere, including a woman's rights in marriage; and second, as an analysis of the burden Muslim women tend to assume for the survival of the community.[31] Thus the discourse of Muslim womanism moves beyond the race analyses of black male intellectuals, the gender analyses of many feminist (predominantly white female) intellectuals, and the faith analyses of Christian womanists and Muslim (largely non-Western and nonblack) feminists in its interest in questions of knowledge production, history, and human existence that form African American Muslim family life and the life-world of African American Muslim women.[32]

Muslim womanism removes the scholarly and popular veil from the realities of African American Muslim life, giving public voice to and advocating justice for what has long existed privately, though misunderstood, due to two "parallel" and internal structures.[33] The first structure is cultural patriarchy, as expressed by some male Muslims and others who presume to dictate what are the embodied experiences of African American Muslim women in both the private and public spheres. The second structure, cultural exegesis, draws attention to the ways in which African American Muslims approach the Qur'an for theological insight, gender liberation, and communal survival, especially in their consideration of polygyny as a necessary form of Muslim marriage. In this regard, polygyny becomes a "language against oppression" and a tool for cultural survival in which the otherwise marginalized seize power from the dominant culture.[34] In other words, to use Muslim womanism as a theoretical lens for the exploration of Muslim family life is to particularize the experiences of the single largest group of American Muslims, and to promote the excavation of black reality from the perspective of the women who live it.

## The Practice of Polygyny

"We're at war," declared a male religious leader in the New York region, alluding to the battles and loss of life in the time of the Prophet Muhammad. "With the high incarceration of our men and other social challenges, we have to find some solution to save our community. When polygyny is practiced correctly and honestly, it has tremendous results for everyone involved. When it is not practiced correctly and honestly, the suffering and hurt can be devastating."[35] Women who share their husbands do not self-identify as polygynous; rather they speak of their unions as monogamous in that only their husbands are married to other spouses. Both women and men do, however, agree on the emotional strain polygynous households experience. In the words of one husband with two wives: "[Polygyny] has an emotional component. [For its success,] you would have to make sure that the sisters can afford the emotional ride that it will take. That's sometimes more important than the economics. There is no support system in our community. Even drug addicts have a system, an alcohol anonymous."[36]

While abuses do occur, data from more than 400 surveys and interviews of more than forty individuals currently or formerly in polygynous households suggest that the mistreatment of women and children documented recently in Mormon polygynous communities is far removed from the family life experienced by their Muslim counterparts. In fact, most of the sister wives I interviewed spoke of their homes as challenging but healthy environments, though they acknowledged that polygyny is not for everyone. "My husband isn't right if he doesn't have two wives," explained an Atlanta mother of four, who came into the marriage as the second wife.[37] By "right," this sister equated a peaceful existence with shared responsibility for the care of her husband. Thus she felt motivated to initiate conversations with women who might be interested in joining their family. Another southern sister reflected upon the pain that is inevitable. "It is not an easy thing," she said, referring to her life with her "sister" wife. "It is a challenge and it can be very hurtful. You are going to hurt the other sister or sisters involved—that is a reality. Your actions will cause them pain . . . but it can be worked through."[38]

A frequently shared example of polygyny becoming abuse is when a husband forces this form of marriage upon his current wife for reasons that appear more self-directed than representative of legitimate Qur'anic teachings.

"This was definitely not my idea," began Sister B, a fifty-year-old real estate broker from the Midwest. "My husband came home one day and told me that ours was to become a polygynous household. We had been married for fifteen years. Our children are adults. We work together. Nothing was missing in our relationship, yet he goes and gets a woman who was not a Muslim but who lived in a polygynous environment. She had no children so this wasn't an example of him helping out a single mother. He didn't ask my opinion. He said the Qur'an says he can take another wife and he wants to whether I like it or not. I'm trying to decide what to do. Sometimes I have to use an electric heater because he hasn't paid the utility bills, but I'm not in position to move just yet."[39]

Sister B initially accepted polygyny because she agreed with her husband's interpretation of the Qur'an. She also valued her position in her mosque, her social respectability, and the ease with which she was able to traverse the boundaries of gender. Her husband often accompanied her to *Jum'ah*, Friday congregational prayers, and other mosque activities. He usually took his second wife to programs in an adjacent community. Occasionally, however, both wives attended the same community event, well aware of the hushed conversations around them. Sister B did divorce the father of her children about a year after this interview. Today she is married again, but this time her marriage contract stipulates that polygyny will result in divorce.

By all accounts, some of my female subjects are comfortable with polygyny, though their "comfort" can be easily interpreted as "accommodation to gender norms."[40] Interestingly, even some of these women acknowledge that they once dreamed of living in traditional household formations, not because they thought the one-husband, one-wife convention was better, but because they had been socialized to value heterosexual monogamy. Too often, though, the peace that one sister possesses does not translate to the lived experience of her husband's other wife. Indeed, while all of the women I have interviewed who share their husbands say Muslim men have a right to determine the structure of their households, the majority of these women are clearly conflicted. During our sessions, they often spoke of the *security* they once felt among other women who no longer saw them as a threat. Today, they voice concerns about the *insecurity* they feel each time a new or unmarried sister joins their mosque.

While marriage for these women reflects conventional gender norms, it has also served to challenge their unquestioning acceptance of Qur'anic interpretations that force them to choose between their faith—as communally understood—and the value they attribute to marriage. With few exceptions, they publicly appear to faithfully "stand by their man," even as they hope he will stand by them and visibly ensure their rights in religious or civil matters. In private, however, they battle internal and external ideologies and realities that are increasingly at odds with each other. In some cases, this struggle has involved suicide attempts, sister-on-sister violence, foreclosure, and/or divorce. For other women, the struggle has caused them to dig deeper into the well of resolve from which they can more healthily live the saying, "I want for my sister what I want for myself." For most women, the battle has forced open the door to reflection about personal responsibility, communal accountability, and what the G'd of Abraham really expects of them in a patriarchal, sexist environment.

## Black Theodicy and Muslim Womanism: The Discourse Begins

Coupling black theodicy with Muslim womanism renders a production of knowledge that evokes the question, "To what extent must/should Muslim marriage be only (or primarily) a theological issue for African Americans?" In *Islam and the Problem of Black Suffering*, Jackson notes:

> Theology is ultimately a negotiated product, the medium through which religious communities conceptualize and talk about God *in the public space*, where the only valid form of knowledge is objective knowledge to which everyone has ostensibly equal access. This discourse serves the community by enabling it to settle on conceptual frameworks and concrete understandings that are broad and resonant enough to draw its disparate members into a common and commonly owned religious identity. . . . In this capacity, theology plays an indispensably crucial role in the collective life of religious communities.[41]

For Jackson, theology—in the classical or traditional sense—is limited. I read this limitation as one that invites Muslim womanism into dialogue as "another kind of knowledge: experiential knowledge."[42] From this perspective, theology is a "publicly negotiated construct" that "freezes" the divine message on plural marriage within static descriptions of *war*, *widows*, *orphans*, and the *lack of marriageable men*.[43] Thus those who interpret *Al Nisa* 3, the Qur'an's central message on polygyny, as one of permissibility and/or male privilege, could do so via time travel, "feigning imperviousness to variations of depth, awareness, or vantage point."[44]To them, the issue is simple: the lack of marriageable Muslim males means polygyny is permitted in twenty-first-century North America as it was in seventh-century Arabia. What this analysis does not feature—but Muslim womanism does—is integrated analysis of race, gender, situatedness, context, and lived experience.

Jackson describes experiential knowledge as a "complement to theology" that is "highly subjective, private, and hopelessly contingent on a live and personal *relationship*."[45] To interpret this in the language of Muslim womanism is to recognize the African American Muslim female experience as "ground for reflection" that elucidates the realities and complexities (and, perhaps, contradictions) of Muslim marriage in African American life.[46] That is, Islam is a religion that is best *lived* and *experienced* in relationship—in this instance, a relationship between humans and their Creator as well as a relationship between humans themselves. To be a Muslim is to be one who strives to live in submission to the Creator; one who recognizes that mates have been created for creation as a "sign" from the Creator.[47] More specifically, Islam views sexuality and the human longing to belong to another as significant aspects of our identity as human beings. Islam also characterizes procreation as a response to a divine mandate. Indeed, as Amina Wadud observes, [women open their bodies] "to receive the sperm of men" and after nine months, [open their bodies] "again in surrender to Allah's call."[48] Thus in Muslim womanism, experiential knowledge alerts us to the particularities of culture, gender, and context that African American Muslim women and men confront as they struggle to organize Muslim family life in a secular nation that promotes the sanctity of monogamous, heterosexual marriage. Muslim womanism also draws attention to different perceptions of reality to which Muslim women craft and cling as they tolerate, welcome, and/or peacefully contend with other women also married to their husbands.

For the majority of Americans, the presence of polygynous households "troubles" the institution of marriage as a social, and, for many, religious union between one man and one woman. Both Muslims and non-Muslims promote this traditional view of marriage as one that is scripturally sound and socially preferred. While monogamy also is the normative expression of marriage within African American communities, Muslims and non-Muslim women who reside within them struggle to build families and avoid the reality of "single motherhood and father absence" that has plagued Americans of African ancestry since the days of legalized slavery.[49] In this chapter I have demonstrated that how African American Muslims organize their households is largely dependent upon the manner in which they interpret the Qur'an, the availability of marriageable Muslim men, and the willingness of Muslim women to knowingly establish households with husbands married to other women. In no small measure, African American Muslim communities struggle today because they lack consensus on the appropriateness of polygyny and communal resources that support healthy family life—regardless of household formation. These deficits are not peculiar to African American Muslims, but they confirm that such deprivations ultimately undermine the extent to which Muslim marriage actually protects and benefits women and children. As a lens into marriage in Islam, Muslim womanism gives voice to the lived realities of women and thus brings Muslim family life into sharper focus. It can also raise questions that lead to solutions around justice and healthier living. This womanist perspective may trouble the conventional portrayal of marriage as a Western institution, but it equally contributes to an understanding of Muslim marriage in the U.S. in all its richness, complexity, and ambiguity.

# Notes

1. As late as 1996, government officials in Malaysia used data that suggested men outnumbered women as a rationale for the justification of polygyny. The data were later refuted. Roger Mitton, "The Polygamy Debate: Many Women Are Saying That One Is Enough," *Asiaweek*, December 20, 1996, 24.

2. At 35 percent, African Americans comprise the single largest group of American Muslims, according to a 2009 Gallup study. They are a part of a "native-born" community of converts that is a "characteristic unique to the U.S." Gallup's Center for Muslim Studies, "Muslim Americans: A National Portrait," Gallup, Inc., 2009, 20. http://www.abudhabigallupcenter.com/144332/Muslim-Americans-National-Portrait.aspx

3. The overwhelming number of books, journal essays, films, and television events mischaracterize family unions that feature a husband with multiple wives as polygamy. This work joins the growing number of academic and public works that label the practice more correctly. The other, less commonly practiced form of plural marriage is polyandry, a marriage of one *wife* to multiple husbands.

4. This type of plural marriage is also referred to as "multi-party unions" or "de facto polygamy" because of its illegal status. For example, see Michele Alexandre, "Lessons from Islamic Polygamy: A Case for Expanding the American Concept of Surviving Spouse so as to Include de Facto Polygamous Spouses, *64 Washington and Lee Law Review* 4; and Mark Holzer Henry, "The True Reynolds v. United States," *Harvard Journal of Law and Public Policy* 10 (1987): 43–46.

5. Population figures derived from "Muslim Population Worldwide," *Islamic Population Worldwide*, http://www.islamicpopulation.com.

6. See for example John L. Esposito, *Women in Muslim Family Law*, 2nd ed. (Syracuse, NY: Syracuse University Press, 2001), 12. In the 1930s, this region became known as the Kingdom of Saudi Arabia under the leadership of King Abdul Aziz Ibn Saud. Today, it is the largest Arab nation in the Middle East.

7. Roger Mitton, "The Polygamy Debate: Many Women Are Saying That One Is Enough," *Asiaweek*, December 20, 1996, 24.

8. Esposito 12.

9. Muhammad Abduh and Muhammad Rashid Rida, *Tafsir al-Qur'an al-Hakim*, vol. 4 (Cairo: Manar Press, 1930), 349ff., as cited in Esposito, 48.

10. See Alexandre.

11. As Jamal Badawi and others persuasively argue, associating polygyny with Islam continues to be a feature of the Western mythology of the Islamic religion and practice. See Jamal Badawi, *Gender Equity in Islam: Basic Principles* (Indianapolis: American Trust Publications, 1995).

12. E. Wolfson, *Why Marriage Matters: America, Equality, and Gay People's Right to Marry* (New York: Simon & Schuster, 2005).

13. John L. Esposito, *Women in Muslim Family Law*, 2nd edition, 101.

14. Ibid., 137.

15. Yale Center for Research on Inequities and the Life Course, "Marriage, family on the decline for highly educated black women," *PhysOrg.com*, Aug. 8, 2009, http://www.physorg.com/news168967339.html.

16. Sam Roberts, "51% of Women Are Now Living Without a Spouse," *New York Times*, Jan. 16, 2007, http://www.nytimes.com/2007/01/16/us/16census.html.

17. "Marriage, Family on the Decline for Highly Educated Black Women," *Yale News*, August 8, 2009, http://news.yale.edu/2009/08/08/marriage-family-decline-highly-educated-black-women.

18. Throughout human history, diverse societies have legalized or temporarily permitted the practice of polygyny after the deaths of males in "hunting and battle." For example, the ancient Greeks permitted the practice after they suffered huge losses in the Sicilian Expedition of 413 bce, and Socrates and Euripides reportedly took multiple wives under this temporary law. See A. E.

Zimmern, *The Greek Commonwealth: Politics and Economics in Ancient Athens*, 5th edition (New York: Oxford University Press, 1931), 30—as cited in Sebastian Poulter, *English Law and Ethnic Minority Customs* (London: Butterworth, 1986), 45.

19. Unlike most "immigrant" sisters, most African American Muslim women spend a significant amount of time in the mosque, making *salat* (ritual prayer) and organizing and/or participating in community activities. Thus the mosque would be the secondary locale of importance for them.

20. Donald McCrary, "Womanist Theology and Its Efficacy for the Writing Classroom," *College Composition and Communication* 52, no. 4 (2006): 545.

21. As a conceptual matter, the "black family question" first emerged following two controversial reports in 1965—research from Kenneth Clark that resulted in *The Dark Ghetto* (Middletown, CT: Wesleyan University Press, 1965) and Daniel Patrick Moynihan's "The Negro Family: The Case for National Action," Office of Planning and Research, United States Department of Labor (March 1965), http://www.dol.gov/oasam/programs/history/webid-meynihan.htm

22. William James, *The Principles of Psychology*, vol. ii (New York: Dover, 1890), as quoted in Norbert F. Wiley, "Marriage and the Construction of Reality: Then and Now," in *The Psychosocial Interior of the Family: A Sourcebook for the Study of Whole Families*, ed. Gerald Handel and Gail G. Whitchurch (Chicago: Aldine, 1967), 37.

23. Michael Eric Dyson, *The Michael Eric Dyson Reader* (New York: Basic Civitas Books, 2004), 138.

24. Ibid.

25. Sherman Jackson, *Islam and the Problem of Black Suffering* (New York: Oxford University Press, 2009), 4.

26. Ibid.

27. Ibid., 6. Italics are mine.

28. Katie G. Cannon, "Response," *Journal of Feminist Studies in Religion* 22, no. 1 (2006): 97. For a fuller exploration of the concept, see Cannon, Alison P. Gise Johnson, and Angela D. Sims, "Womanist Works in Word," *Journal of Feminist Studies in Religion* 21, no. 2 (2005): 135–46.

29. Thomas Friedman's writings on religious totalitarianism have influenced my theorizing on the subject. See Friedman, "Foreign Affairs: The Real War," *New York Times*, Nov. 27, 2001. One of the few (if only) other essays to connect womanist thought to Muslim women also claims that any form of feminism is least likely to meet the needs of Muslim women in the U.S. See Earl H. Waugh and Jenny Wannas, "The Rise of a Womanist Movement Among Muslim Immigrant Women in Alberta, Canada," *Studies in Contemporary Islam* 5 (2003).

30. Traci C. West, "Is a Womanist a Black Feminist? Marking the Distinctions and Defying Them," in *Deeper Shades of Purple: Womanism in Religion and Society*, ed. Stacey E. Floyd-Thomas (New York: New York University Press, 2006).

31. One of the early sayings of the Prophet that Muslim women are taught is "paradise lies at the feet of the mother."

32. I prefer the term *Muslim* to *Islamic* feminism. For me, the latter suggests validation from within divine revelation, or a reference to an act, practice, tradition, or structure maintained/suggested by or reflective of the teachings of Islam.

33. My conceptualization of parallel structures is drawn from the theoretical contributions of a first-generation womanist. See Marcia I. Riggs, *Awake, Arise and Act: A Womanist Call for Black Liberation* (Cleveland: Pilgrim, 1994).

34. This construction of polygyny represents my contextualization of the "contact-zone" teaching theories of Patricia Bizzell as quoted in D. McCrary, "Womanist Theology and Its Efficacy for the Writing Classroom," *College Composition and Communication* 52, no. 4 (2001): 526.

35. Interview by author, Brooklyn, May 20, 2003.

36. Brother A, interview by author, Tampa, June 12, 2004.

37. Fictitious names and/or other descriptives are used to protect the identities of both women and men who live in polygynous households. Telephone interview by author, July 23, 2003.

38. Sister B, interview by author, Tampa, June 12, 2004.

39. Telephone and email conversations with author, November 2002–April 2003.

40. Jamillah Ashira Karim, *American Muslim Women: Negotiating Race, Class, and Gender within the Ummah* (New York: New York University Press, 2009), 118. In fact, I have shared forums with at least two who joined their husband and me as facilitators of a summer workshop on polygyny that was well publicized and attended.

41. Sherman Jackson, *Islam and the Problem of Black Suffering* (New York: Oxford University Press, 2009), 161–62.

42. Ibid.

43. Ibid.

44. Ibid.

45. Ibid.

46. Emilie M. Townes draws attention to the experiences of black Christian women as appropriate intellectual "ground" for this discourse. See *A Troubling in My Soul: Womanist Perspectives on Evil and Suffering*, ed. Emilie M. Townes (Maryknoll, NY: Orbis, 1993), 3.

47. Al-Rum 22 (Qur'an, 30:22).

48. Amina Wadud, *Inside the Gender Jihad: Women's Reform in Islam* (Oxford: Oneworld, 2006), 125–26.

49. Sara McLanahan and Gary Sandefur, *Growing Up with a Single Parent": What Hurts, What Helps* (Cambridge, MA: Harvard University Press, 1994), 2.

2

# From Mistress to Mother

## *The Religious Life and Transformation of Tynetta Muhammad in the Nation of Islam*

Stephen C. Finley

Mother Tynetta Muhammad had been one of the numerous secretaries of the Honorable Elijah Muhammad (d. 1975) with whom he was engaged in what was interpreted at the time as extramarital relations.[1] Her status over the last four decades, however, has been transformed from putative "mistress" to one who is now seen as the "mother" of the Nation of Islam (NOI) and as one of the plural wives of Muhammad. Hence, as a member of the "royal family" in the NOI under the leadership of Minister Louis Farrakhan, Mother Tynetta, as she is affectionately called, is a trusted member of Minister Farrakhan's inner circle. In fact, she functions as a, if not "the," spiritual interpreter of some of the most consequential events in the NOI and in Minister Farrakhan's life.

Therefore, rather than an excursus on how the transformation from "mistress to mother" occurred, which has not been established in extant literature,[2] the major thrust of this paper will give attention to the substance of the transformation. In short, it will argue that the title and trope of "mother" function to give Tynetta Muhammad authority in the NOI, but more importantly, how she enacts this mothering serves to create a unique and authoritative religious space for her that is unrivaled within the organization. Some of the symbolic ways of mothering are similar to those that Layli Phillips indicates in *The Womanist Reader*, where she suggests:

> Motherhood as a womanist method of social transformation has its roots in African cultural legacies. Motherhood, here, however, must be dissociated from its purely biological connotation and even from

> its strictly gendered connotation. . . . In doing so, every individual has the ability to contribute to the ultimate goals of womanism: societal healing, reconciliation of the relationship between people and nature, and the achievement and maintenance of commonwealth.[3]

Though her biological son, Ishmael Muhammad, is a prominent member of the Nation, the form of symbolic mothering is consistent with what Phillips indicates. Furthermore, the manner in which she transcends traditional notions of mothering can be read as an implied critique of the male-dominated NOI in that she transgresses dominant notions of mothering and transforms them into an instrument of religious importance that is unrivaled in the NOI. Her lofty pronouncements that signify her exalted role in the NOI are seen most poignantly in her *magnum opus*, *The Comer by Night 1986*, and in her weekly column titled "Unveiling the Number 19," which is an extension of her interpretation of reality that is found in *The Comer by Night 1986* and continues to be produced.

Implied in this argument is that the life of Mother Tynetta, as a black religious woman, is instructive for womanist religious thought—as a woman whose life and voice may have been excluded from prior womanist discourses given that she was a member of the NOI (rather than a Christian church) and due to the salacious manner in which her relationship to the Messenger Elijah Muhammad has been framed (therefore, not a typical representation of "respectability"). Although the trope of mother does serve to sanitize and sublate the notion of mistress, Mother Tynetta makes a unique and ingenious move in that she strategically deploys the symbolic capital garnered from the transformation of her status to wife of the Messenger and mother of the Nation, and she recasts it as cultural capital in the form of religious knowledge (as cultural competence) that deflects and deconstructs prevailing notions of mothering.[4]

## Tynetta Muhammad as "Mother" to Louis Farrakhan

Nowhere can the performance of the trope of metaphorical motherhood be seen more poignantly than in Mother Tynetta's social and spiritual position in the life of Minister Louis Farrakhan and in the most significant event of his religious life. On September 17, 1985, Farrakhan reported having a vision of being taken into what the public would understand as an Unidentified Flying Object, which he recognizes as the Mother Wheel—a divine vehicle of destruction and regeneration that the Messenger Elijah Muhammad taught him would bring an apocalyptic end to the age of white supremacy and usher in a millennial era of peace on earth. Farrakhan delivers the most provocative version of this vision in a press conference at the J. W. Marriott Hotel in Washington, D.C. on October 24, 1989. In what is called "The Announcement," Minister Farrakhan relates his vision of the Mother Wheel, which he experienced concretely on Tepozteco Mountain in Tepotzlan, Mexico. Farrakhan declares:

> In a tiny town in Mexico, called Tepotzlan, there is a mountain on the top of which is the ruins of a temple dedicated to Quetzalcoatl—the Christ-figure of Central and South America—a mountain which I have climbed several times. However, on the night of September 17, 1985, I was carried up on that mountain, in a vision, with a few friends of mine. As we reached the top of the mountain, a Wheel, or what you call an unidentified flying object, appeared at the side of the mountain and called to me to come up into the Wheel. Three metal legs appeared from the Wheel, giving me the impression that it was going to land, but it never came over the mountain.[5]

Here, Minister Farrakhan is careful to point out the relationship between the topography and epistemology of his mountaintop experience as if to suggest that it was the apex of religious experience that had noetic qualities[6] that linked him symbolically to Quetzalcoatl. In other words, he wants to frame his experience as a religious one, and he desires that we connect his vision with the Christ figure, Quetzalcoatl, so that it is clear that the information he is about to transmit is transcendent in nature and not human in origin.[7] Tynetta Muhammad makes further connection between the topography and the mystical sense of the event in one of her columns, noting the mountainous terrain on one of her religious pilgrimages to Sedona, Arizona and its resemblance to UFOs reminded her of Tepotzlan, Mexico. Farrakhan also notes that he was with a few "friends" at the time of his vision, of which Mother Tynetta Muhammad was one, along with his wife Khadijah Muhammad and his colleague Jabril Muhammad.

Farrakhan explains the encounter in detail by suggesting that the public audience in attendance at the press conference would apprehend what he describes as a UFO abduction.[8] That is, he was carried into the Mother Wheel, he says, where he had an encounter with Elijah Muhammad. What this experience means is complicated and multifaceted. For instance, Farrakhan suggests that Muhammad gave him a message that was of critical importance to black bodies, the NOI, and for Farrakhan in particular. But this is not the only data he gleaned from Muhammad. He reports that Muhammad's words to him were intentionally cryptic in order to allow sufficient time and ambiguity so that Farrakhan could glean their full weight and implications. The message apparently had a double meaning. The initial implication was that President Reagan was planning a war on Muammar Qaddafi and Libya. Yet, the secondary content of the communication was devastating, as it pointed directly to President George Bush and his insidious scheme, according to Farrakhan, to destroy black people. Farrakhan says Muhammad told him to report:

> I am here to announce today that President Bush has met with his Joint Chiefs of Staff, under the direction of General Colin Powell, to plan a war against the Black people of America, the Nation of Islam, and Louis Farrakhan, with particular emphasis on our Black youth, under the guise of a war against drug sellers, drug users, gangs and violence—all under the heading of extremely urgent national security.[9]

According to Minister Farrakhan, the government was concealing a genocidal conspiracy to destroy black people within an ostensible campaign against drug sellers and users under the guise of "national security."

Several other implications of Farrakhan's Wheel vision would later be important for Mother Tynetta. For example, Farrakhan would come to believe that the event proved that Muhammad was still alive physically.[10] Furthermore, the encounter gave his religious life coherence. Hence, Farrakhan connected the UFO vision of 1985 to an earlier vision that he had in 1955 that convinced him to commit to the NOI, and the latter vision validated his life and choices as "true." The latter vision also directed his subsequent public and political activity including the Million Man March, which Michael Lieb suggests was one of many enactments of his experience with the Wheel.[11] The Wheel also crystallized his view, inherited from Elijah Muhammad, that "black" as a surplus category—as a term that meant more than its received meaning in the United States—signified Asians, African Americans, Latinos, and Native Americans as part of the Black Nation. They were all "black" in the theology and mythology of Muhammad. Built by the Japanese, according to Muhammad, the Wheel became a powerful metaphor for this notion of "black" as "hybridity" and interraciality, presupposing postcolonial notions of cultural hybridity.[12] Mother

Tynetta reinforces Farrakhan's inclusion of these groups in the meaning of the Wheel and in the work of the Nation, as well as a concern for "poor whites."[13]

Just as significantly, the experience of the Wheel validated Farrakhan's reconstitution and leadership of the NOI—given that several rival groups emerged after the death of Muhammad in 1975, each claiming legitimacy, and in some cases claiming that Farrakhan distorted and watered down Muhammad's teachings. As in the case of Muhammad's son, Warith Deen Mohammed, Muhammad was interpreted as pointed progressively to Sunni Islam as the appropriate religion for African Americans,[14] which is where he immediately directed the NOI, changing the name to the World Community of Islam in the West.[15] The claim of contact with Muhammad may have served as a powerful sign to those who would doubt the authenticity of Farrakhan's Nation and could function as a direct affront to those who were promulgating competing truth claims about the rightful heir to Muhammad's religious legacy. Delineating this sequence of events in detail is critical because it is within this narrative that Mother Tynetta establishes herself as a religious leader and speaks to all of the issues mentioned here. That is to say, it is vis-à-vis Farrakhan's encounter with the Wheel that Mother Tynetta emerges most movingly and powerfully *as mother* to him and through this remakes herself as religious sage.

First, Tynetta Muhammad enacts *mother as defender* of Louis Farrakhan, and she does so vociferously. For instance, the chapter in *The Comer by Night 1986* that focuses on Farrakhan's UFO experience and his subsequent defiance of a U.S. travel ban to Libya is her longest entry, and she addresses it unabashedly and without trepidation of any sort.[16] She proclaims:

> Minister Farrakhan was guided in his decision to go to Libya, by means of a Vision coming to him in much the same way as the Vision came to Moses in the Sacred Valley of Tuwa. He was guided in this Vision though the words of the Honorable Elijah Muhammad speaking from inside a great plane called the Mother's Wheel, which is described in Ezekiel's Vision, Chapters one and two. He was told to expose the military plans of President Reagan and his Joint Chiefs of Staff which was to be staged in some part of the globe. As a result of this vision he has warned the President to stay away from fanning the flames that can erupt into World War III. This he has done both at a Press Conference in Washington, D.C., and Libya, which a gentle word to Pharoah [*sic*] warning him that the time of our deliverance has come.[17]

Mother Tynetta strategically usurps the authority of the United States government by suggesting that Minister Farrakhan's mandate came, not from a mundane and temporal source such as the American government, but from Elijah Muhammad on the Mother Wheel. She goes further by making a reference to the biblical book of Ezekiel as if to suggest further evidence that he was authorized by a transcendent source that is infinitely beyond the limited scope, reach, and intellect of those who were attempting to constrain the political activity and international excursions of the Minister.

In so doing, she also makes a profound claim: the millennia-old *visio Dei* of the prophet Ezekiel in which he reports seeing a chariot or wheel in the heavens was in fact the same Wheel that empowers and sanctions Louis Farrakhan, thus connecting him to the prophet Ezekiel and beyond to the divine source of the Wheel.[18] She goes further still in illuminating the biblical connection when she says that Ezekiel 10 contains twenty-two verses that are "strikingly similar to the experience the Minister Farrakhan shared with us concerning his vision and his being taken on board one of these smaller wheels, which picked him up from the side of the mountain, in a small Mexican village, moving straight forward to dock into a much larger wheel."[19]

In referencing Farrakhan's press conference in which he made his "announcement" about the Wheel and in warning the government against actions that would potentially initiate a world war, she makes a subtle but significant alteration of Elijah Muhammad's and Farrakhan's nomenclature of "Mother Wheel," and she adds the possessive, rendering it "Mother's Wheel." While it is unclear exactly why she does this, what her grammatical creativity could intimate is that the collective attributes of the divine vehicle, namely, as protecting, avenging, life generating, abstract and secret knowledge imparting, transcendent and immanent, sanctity, and so on, are qualities that when aggregated she may believe are most appropriately associated with the feminine and more specifically possessed and captured by the trope of mother if not by the actual activity of motherhood. Nevertheless, she uses this term consistently throughout her text.

Second, Tynetta Muhammad performs *mother as affirmer*of Minister Farrakhan. To this end, she explicitly approves of his theological and political positions, and she reiterates these explicitly in her own writings. For instance, she maintains, in concert with Farrakhan's report of his experience on the Wheel, that Elijah Muhammad is "alive and in the company of his lord,"[20] thus supporting his claim that Muhammad only appeared to die but persists bodily in what she refers to as a "space craft."[21] At the same time, Mother Tynetta establishes her own productive space, which she stabilizes not by allusion to her historic relationship to Muhammad or Farrakhan but by her own generative religious activities. For example, she says that she has "dreams" and that these dreams are prophetic and insightful, suggesting that even while she alludes to Farrakhan as instructive, her own experiences independently confirm his teaching.[22]

Ultimately, her own dreams validate that Elijah Muhammad is "alive and well" and that "he is not dead."[23]Furthermore, although she clearly intends to support Farrakhan's vision, she asks if it is coincidence that these dreams have occurred "at a time when there have been unprecedented sightings of U.F.O.'s [*sic*] in the world including the Mediterranean, North Africa, the Persian Gulf as well as North, Central and South America."[24]What she implies here is that, even through affirmation of the Minister, her own functions as one spiritually adept are on full display, given the apparent connection between her dreams and the worldwide UFO sightings, whatever that connection may be. By approving of such positions, she also reinforces her status as one who has the right and authority to render such affirmation but also as one who is connected to a spiritual reservoir that elucidates her own religious epistemology. It is in her capacity as divine knower that her position *as mother* gains its full weight.

## Mother Tynetta Muhammad as Ultimate Interpreter of Reality

It would be insufficient to suggest that "mothering" entails a simple co-sign and defense of Minister Farrakhan. Rather, such "mothering" as an enactment of her position as a "Mother" of the Nation has created a space for her own unique interpretation of the world. In this role, she asserts her agency and humanity and performs *mother as interpreter of ultimate reality*. She does this most intensely without any hint of being constrained by sexism or assignment to domesticity that might limit or censor her language. It is in this capacity that she flexes her intellectual gifts, her confident candor, and her religious insight. She displays her gifts and insights through an expressive display of complex metaphysics in which she draws upon astronomy, mathematics, numerology, and arts such as music and dance as epistemological sources in the construction of a Gnostic system of knowledge that is hers and hers alone. Mother Tynetta has divine authority that comes from the manner in which she deploys cultural capital in the form of religious knowledge. Found primarily in her book *The Comer by Night 1986* but also in her weekly column "Unveiling the Number 19," Mother Tynetta argues that the key to unlocking the deepest and most profound truths of the universe are found in the recognition and strategic deployment of the number 19.[25] She claims and acknowledges, however, that the discovery of the importance of 19 was Dr. Rashad Khalifa's, "who was martyred on January 31, 1990 at the age of 54. He is [*sic*] also a citizen of Africa and our Brother who was born in Tanta, Egypt."[26]By claiming that Dr. Khalifa was a "citizen of Africa and our Brother," Mother Tynetta may be attempting to make an epistemological link between the mathematical code of 19 and the truth of the universe from the perspective of people of indigenous African descent, in particular the NOI. This would seem consistent with her stated future endeavor:

> We will focus on some of the new archeological and astronomical discoveries being uncovered by scientists who have been linked to the ongoing Revelatory Science of the 19-based Mathematical Code. Further evidence will be explored proving that the Honorable Elijah Muhammad brought to the Lost and Found Aboriginal Members of the Nation of Islam, the roots of Universal Knowledge and the Supreme Wisdom originating from the God of the Universe and the lord of all the worlds.[27]

So, while she gives Dr. Khalifa the credit for the discovery of the Code, she locates its origins with the God of the Universe, and Elijah Muhammad as the instrument through which the knowledge was disseminated.

She has in mind three points that she wants to communicate in her writings. First, she is concerned with unveiling the identity of God to the world, stating that "Almighty God Allah makes His Appearance in the world under the cover of Darkness, as *The Comer by Night*, to reveal His True Identity as *the Hidden One*, the One Wrapped Up in the Mystery of time that has lasted for thousands, millions and trillions of years of history until today."[28] She locates this concern in Surah 86, verses (or *ayah*) 1–17 of the Qur'an. Second, she maintains that it is time for the true identity of God to be revealed to the world, but not simply God's identity, but also God's "whereabouts." This would seem to implicate the Mother Wheel in the divine drama, given that it is the location of Master Fard Muhammad, whom she suggests is Allah, citing a passage from Elijah Muhammad's *Message to the Blackman in America* for support.[29]

Related to this, she is interested in the identity of black people, explaining their true place in the cosmos, interpreting the experience of black people in America vis-à-vis white supremacy, and she desires that their relationship to Allah be finally disclosed. Third, she intimates that this is secret knowledge. It is a gnosis, however, that will have its ultimate resolution in the number 19, in what she calls the "Miraculous Mathematical Code of the Holy Qur'an," apparently following Dr. Khalifa in the use of the term.[30] This is significant in that what was once hidden—God and the secret knowledge of the Universe—can now be absolutely known and expressed rationally through the mathematical and numerological code over which she has mastery. This results in the reconciliation of any possible tension between the idea of gnosis—that God is hidden and the universe is a mystery—and Elijah Muhammad's idea that God can be known because God was a living, breathing, and fleshly man, who could be known and experienced bodily.[31] Though Mother Tynetta fails to define the Code succinctly and sufficiently, she suggests that the nature of Islamic knowledge is ultimately mathematical, and she locates her contention in the earlier teachings of Master Fard Muhammad and Elijah Muhammad. Related to this, it was in 1975, the year of Elijah Muhammad's "departure," that the code was revealed.

Briefly, she maintains that the truths of the Qur'an can be divinized by a mathematical code of 19, as mentioned in Surah 74.30.[32] Knowledge of the cosmic significance of the number 19 can be used to decode the meaning of the Qur'an and historical, meteorological, and geological events. What makes her theory consistent with Western esoteric religion generally and how she understands the meaning of the NOI particularly is her objective to conflate religion and science and to reenchant nature as active and certain rather than arbitrary.[33] Mother Tynetta declares, "This makes science and religion wedded as one."[34] As a consequence, she aggregates the Mathematical Code, astronomy, numerology, science, and the arts to erect her own science of interpretation that fashions an aperture that only she inhabits and that gives her discursive privilege in terms of the events she interprets and the manner in which she appropriates such knowledge. For instance, she declares:

> In my continuing research on the Miraculous Mathematical Code of the Holy Qur'an and its meaning for us today, I would like to present further proofs of its Divine Expression in relation to the Divine Teachings of the Honorable Elijah Muhammad. There are exactly 14 letters in the spelling of the Honorable Elijah Muhammad's Name . . . also 14 letters in the spelling of the name, Louis Farrakhan. I had also noted that there are exactly 19 letters in the spelling of Wallace Fard Muhammad. When adding all three sets of letters, I came to the number 47. The 47th Surah of the Holy Qur'an is entitled Muhammad and contains all three sets of initials designated in the code. So it became very apparent, as evidenced in the Mathematical Code, that the name Muhammad, most surely is certainly Minister

> Farrakhan's true name as well. Louis Farrakhan Muhammad is a true spiritual son of the Honorable Elijah Muhammad.[35]

It is rarely clear exactly how she makes connections between words and the meanings of events, and it often seems arbitrary, but she will generally cite the number 19 as being key to her interpretation. Having done so, as in this case, she may then exercise privilege based on the truths that she alone has uncovered.

In her determination, for instance, that Muhammad was the true name of Minister Farrakhan, she exercised the license that being a "Mother," who interprets the universe, gives her. She explains that it was through the discovery of the meaning of the Code vis-à-vis the names of Elijah Muhammad, Fard Muhammad, and Louis Farrakhan that prompted her to introduce the Minister as "Minister Louis Farrakhan Muhammad" at the Saviour's Day convention in 1984: "It portended a sign of greater things to come, all significantly covered in the name 'Muhammad.'"[36] In this case, she exercised her prerogative as a mother who is the possessor and purveyor of esoteric knowledge to name Minister Farrakhan as a sign of meaningful future experiences based on her numerological calculations.

## Mothering as Religiously "Dangerous" in the Religious Life of Mother Tynetta

This essay has argued that Mother Tynetta *as mother* to the Nation of Islam and in particular her performance of motherhood vis-à-vis Minister Louis Farrakhan has opened creative spaces in which she carries out her own productive intellectual system of religious thought that she calls the Qur'anic Mathematical Code. Such mothering has also given her privilege with respect to her ability to act independently of historic and traditional constraints on black religious women, in this case within the NOI. Rather than a domestic category, which may be viewed as subjugated, Mother Tynetta acquired symbolic and cultural capital over time, which allows her to perform a dangerous "mothering" by way of being responsible to and for a religious interpretation of reality that had the capability to establish value and meaningfulness within the Nation. Her position as "Mother" is one of power and respect that she strategically stabilized, not only through her mothering relationship with Farrakhan *per se*, but by connecting it to his UFO vision—arguably the most significant and authoritative religious event in his life.[37] Such a relationship is strategic in a sense, but it fails to totalize mothering in the sense in which she practices it.

Traditionally, black feminist and womanist thought has struggled diligently in opposition to signifiers that perpetuate the subjugation of black women. From mammies, jezebels, welfare queens, and "strong" black women, their critical and constructive projects have wrestled with the naming of black women in ways that critique gendered oppression.[38] The use of the heuristic mother, in this essay, does not perpetuate but rather disrupts the myth of the strong black woman as the one who is expected to be the backbone of black religious institutions or even the vehicle through which it is passively reproduced, socially and biologically.[39]

What Tynetta Muhammad exemplifies, to the contrary, is a religiously embodied appropriation of symbolic capital that was converted to cultural capital vis-à-vis the religious authority by which, via two modes of mothering, she transforms what would otherwise appear to be traditional and problematic ways of mothering into a complex authorial placement as a religious producer, possessor, and purveyor of Gnostic and esoteric knowledge. That is to say, Mother Tynetta avoids the pitfalls of obsequious and oppressive forms of mothering by utilizing her symbolic status as "wife" of Elijah Muhammad and mother of the NOI to circumvent unhealthful meanings that may have been ascribed to black women's bodies. Thus her tactical deployment of cultural capital in the form of a unique variety of religious knowledge—of which she disseminates in accordance with her own autonomy and authority—eludes the fixity and objectification that befall forms of mothering that womanists and black feminists decry.

Consequently, her lived religiosity both critiques and resignifies the more traditional understanding of "mother" by making more active this otherwise passive-laden position. Moreover, her mothering contradicts Elijah Muhammad, who suggested that "[t]he woman is the man's field to produce his nation."[40] As enacted by Tynetta Muhammad, then, mothering becomes *dangerous* and deviant, not only over against traditional ways of viewing "mothering" but also over against the patriarchal structure and forms within NOI that it challenges. In this sense, her mothering challenges a system of domination within a larger American culture of oppression.[41] More than this, Mother Tynetta critiques the philosophical and theological systems that order and regard gendered relations and motherhood as fixed within the NOI, although this is a lived and embodied critique as opposed to an explicit engagement of its discourses. Again, this critique renders her dangerous to the existing *status quo* as she not only lives outside the norm but threatens the cosmology upon which the standard is constructed. She further threatens the unique claim on truth by the NOI and Islam when she proclaims that mathematics and the Code underlie all the great religions—thus making an ecumenical shift that critiques theological and racial partitioning.

What womanist religious thought can glean from the religious transformation of Tynetta Muhammad, as a "dangerous" mother, is that she is a woman who can religiously affirm or disavow, make or break, the Nation and its leader by her esoteric inclinations, proclivities, and interpretations. It is in that space that she becomes a divine oracle of sorts, by providing spiritual guidance, cosmic insight, and vision in a manner that may not have been afforded other women inside and outside the NOI. In some ways, even Minister Farrakhan is beholden to the weight of her religious authority and pronouncements as she often holds the solution to the meaning of the events, sounds, and sights both on earth and in the heavens.

## Notes

1. Karl Evanzz, *The Messenger: The Rise and Fall of Elijah Muhammad* (New York: Vintage, 2001), 57–82. Mother Tynetta was known as "Tynetta Nelson" during this period.
2. Evanzz, *The Messenger*, 374, 423, 435; Mattias Gardell, *In the Name of Elijah Muhammad: Louis Farrakhan and the Nation of Islam* (Durham, NC: Duke University Press, 1996), 125.
3. Layli Phillips, "Womanism: On Its Own," in *The Womanist Reader*, ed. Layli Phillips (New York: Routledge, 2006), xxix.
4. Pierre Bourdieu, *Outline of a Theory of Practice*, trans. Richard Nice (Cambridge: Cambridge University Press, 1977), 186–87.
5. Louis Farrakhan, *The Announcement: A Final Warning to the U.S. Government* (Chicago: FCN, 1989), 5–6.
6. William James, *The Varieties of Religious Experience: A Study in Human Nature* (1907; reprint, New York: Modern Library, 2002), 414–15.
7. Michael Lieb, *Children of Ezekiel: Aliens, UFOs, the Crisis of Race, and the Advent of the End Times* (Durham, NC: Duke University Press, 1998), 205–6.
8. Farrakhan, 5–6; Brenda Denzler, *The Lure of the Edge: Scientific Passions, Religious Beliefs, and the Pursuit of UFOs* (Berkeley: University of California Press, 2001), 33–55.
9. Farrakhan, 10.
10. Jabril Muhammad, *Is It Possible That the Honorable Elijah Muhammad Is Still Physically Alive???* (Phoenix: Nuevo, 2007), 5–8.
11. Lieb, *Children of Ezekiel*, 202–4.
12. Homi Bhabha, *The Location of Culture* (New York: Routledge, 1994), 256.
13. Tynetta Muhammad, *The Comer by Night 1986* (Chicago: The Honorable Elijah Muhammad Educational Foundation, 1986), 34–35, 42.
14. Warith Deen Mohammed, *An African American Genesis* (Calumet City, IL: M.A.C.A. Publication Fund, 1986), ix, 68.
15. Clifton E. Marsh, *The Lost-Found Nation of Islam in America* (Lanham, MD and London: Scarecrow, 2000), 157.
16. Tynetta Muhammad, *The Comer by Night*, 45–56.
17. Ibid., 55.
18. Ibid., 55; Lieb, *Children of Ezekiel*, 198, 206–7.
19. Tynetta Muhammad, 58.
20. Ibid., 55.

21. Ibid., 81; cf. Tynetta Muhammad, "The Romans, the Passion of Christ, and Saviour's Day 2004." *Unveiling the Number 19*, 9 March 2004, http://www.finalcall.com/artman/publish/printer_1328.shtml.

22. Tynetta Muhammad, *The Comer by Night*, 85; cf. Gardell, *In the Name of Elijah Muhammad*, 128.

23. Tynetta Muhammad, *The Comer by Night*, 84.

24. Ibid., 86.

25. Gardell, *In the Name of Elijah Muhammad*, 178–81.

26. Tynetta Muhammad, *The Comer by Night*, viii.

27. Ibid., xii.

28. Ibid., 53.

29. Elijah Muhammad, *Message to the Blackman in America* (Atlanta: Secretarius MEMPS Publications, 1965, reprint 1973), 294; Tynetta Muhammad, *The Comer by Night*, 53.

30. Tynetta Muhammad, *The Comer by Night*, 102.

31. Elijah Muhammad, *Message to the Blackman in America,* 1–15.

32. Tynetta Muhammad, *The Comer by Night*, 102.

33. Wouter J. Hanegraaff, *New Age Religion and Western Culture: Esotericism in the Mirror of Secular Thought* (Albany: State University of New York Press, 1998), 388, 397.

34. Tynetta Muhammad, "In Search of the Messiah—King Solomon Examines the Queen of Sheba." *Unveiling the Number 19*, July 17, 2003, http://www.finalcall.com/artman/publish/printer_903.shtml.

35. Tynetta Muhammad, *The Comer by Night*, 102.

36. Ibid., 102.

37. Ibid., vi, 85–88.

38. See, for example, Kelly Brown Douglas, *Sexuality and the Black Church: A Womanist Perspective* (Maryknoll, NY: Orbis Books, 1999), 35–44; Anne duCille, *Skin Trade* (Cambridge, MA: Harvard University Press, 1996), 81–119; Patricia Hill-Collins, *Black Feminist Thought: Knowledge, Consciousness, and the Politics of Empowerment*, 2nd ed. (New York: Routledge, 2000), 69–96; Delores S. Williams, *Sisters in the Wilderness: The Challenge of Womanist God-Talk* (Maryknoll, NY: Orbis, 1993), 42–45, 62–64, 70, 78–80.

39. Stephen C. Finley and Margarita Simon, "'That Girl Is Poison': White Supremacy, Anxiety, and the Conflation of Women and Food in the Nation of Islam," in *Women in New and Africana Religions,* ed. Lillian Ashcraft-Eason, Darnise L. Martin, and Oyeronke Olademo (Westport, CT: Greenwood, 2010), 3–27; Elijah Muhammad, *Message to the Blackman in America*, 58.

40. Elijah Muhammad, *Message to the Blackman in America*, 58, 60.

41. Williams, *Sisters in the Wilderness,* 34–59.

3

# Nature, Sexuality, and Spirituality

## *A Womanist Reading of Di Mu (Earth Mother) and Di Mu Jing (Songs of Earth Mother) in China*

**Pu Xiumei**

*Tree mother*
*Watch over the child*
*Send her where she should be*
*May safety and peace be with her*

–Adapted from a prayer to a tree when a sick child is adopted by the tree (Meishan, Sichuan Province, China)

### Introduction

Mu, Earth Mother, is an indigenous[1] goddess in Chinese spiritual tradition. I am unable to find an English term that is the exact equivalent of "Di Mu." The English term "Earth Mother" is closest to the meaning of "Di Mu." In Chinese, the term for mother is "mu qin." The character "mu" in "Di Mu" is the same character as "mu" in "mu qin." Although the character "Mu" in "Di Mu" is translated into "mother," its meaning is larger in scope than "mu qin," or mother. Mu means the origin of Creation, of which the mother is a part. While the term "mu qin" in contemporary Chinese is used metaphorically to mean origin, it implies an anthropomorphic view of mu, in other words, mu is personified and reduced to the role of a biological mother, and thus the philosophical and cosmological meanings of mu are lost. To use "mu qin" to mean "origin" reverses the order of language creation. Indeed, "mu qin" is a term created from the root word "mu." I mention the difficulty in finding an English term that is the exact equivalent of the Chinese term "Di Mu" to remind my readers that the English term "Earth Mother" may not capture the meanings of Di Mu in its entirety.

In spite of Di Mu's indigenous goddess status, she has been gradually overshadowed by male deities and has fallen into oblivion in contemporary mainstream religions in China. The scripture *Di Mu Jing*, or *Songs of Earth Mother*, has been classified as apocrypha.[2] In this essay I reread Di Mu from a womanist ecospiritual perspective. I explore how the original conceptualization of Di Mu offers a holistic worldview that simultaneously embraces nature, sexuality, and spirituality. I contend that Di Mu embodies a womanist ecospirituality that acknowledges an alternative sexuality and meanwhile has a keen concern for environmental well-being. In a time of rapid social changes that pose threats to the natural environment and indigenously inclined spiritual belief systems in rural China, it is vital to reevaluate the Di Mu tradition. My analysis is based on my field research on women's spirituality conducted in southwest rural China from January to August 2009.

## Nature, Sexuality, Spirituality, and Womanism

The womanist perspectives used in this essay are based on Alice Walker's womanism and Layli Phillips's womanism. To focus on Walker's womanism and Phillips's womanism is not to exclude or to minimize the value of Africana womanism by Clenora Hudson-Weems, African womanism by Chikwenye Okonjo Ogunyemi, and womanism as understood by a host of womanist scholars. I agree with Layli Phillips that womanism is a collective tapestry woven organically together with different threads of womanisms. The reason I have chosen Walker's womanism and Phillips's womanism is that their distinctive and keen awareness of nature and spirituality closely pertains to my research interest in womanist ecospirituality.

To be sure, Hudson-Weems's Africana womanism and Ogunyemi's African womanism do have an awareness of spirituality and the nature-spirituality tie. However, they have not explicitly elaborated on the connection between nature and spirituality.[3] The significant nature-spirituality bond has been expounded on in Walker's and Phillips's womanisms. I use the term "womanist ecospirituality" to glue womanist ecological sensibility and spiritual consciousness together. By using the term "womanist ecospirituality," I intend to indicate the inseparability of spirituality from nature. Womanist ecospirituality recognizes the interdependence between nature and people, the relationship between environmental health, societal health, physical health, and spiritual health. As Layli Phillips points out in her essay "Womanism: On Its Own," an individual's bodily health is "an indicator of and conduit of societal and environmental health."[4] Here I wish to add that bodily health is also perceived in some indigenous spiritual belief systems as an indicator and conduit of balance in the spiritual world. I agree with Phillips that health and healing involve "rebalancing the world socially, environmentally, and spiritually."[5]

The relational view of health and healing is commensurate with the womanist idea of community. The womanist community is imagined by Walker and Phillips as a space that encompasses not only humankind but also the natural and the spiritual beings. A womanist community is an ecospiritual-cultural community. I imagine that in such a space, humankind, like a tree, a bird, an ant, a particle of dust, and a spirit is a participant, not the master, of the universe. There is no hierarchy. The universe is a network. Everything has its own purpose in the network. Everything influences and is influenced by one another. Having such understanding, womanist ecospiritualists are what Alice Walker would call universalists.

Womanist ecospirituality encourages ecospiritual epistemology. Ecospiritual epistemology invokes an ancient way of knowing, that is, we come to know through knowing nature. This concept is also referred to as "The Book of Nature" in the West.[6] This way of knowing in contemporary life is illustrated in Walker's 1983 four-part definition of "womanist." In the definition, the daughter asks: "Mama, why are we brown, pink, and yellow, and our cousins are white, beige, and black?" The mother answers: "Well, you know the colored race is just like a flower garden, with every color flower represented."[7] The diversity of colors in the flower garden helps the daughter to understand the diversity of races in the social garden. The fact that it is the diversity of colors that makes the flower garden beautiful teaches the daughter that it is racial diversity that makes the social garden lovely. The knowledge the flower garden reveals to the daughter protects her from suffering a sense of racial inferiority. More importantly, through learning from the flower garden, the daughter develops a womanist ethics of universalism, committing to "survival and wholeness of entire people."[8] Here the flower garden, and by extension nature, produces knowledge. Contemplation upon nature, speech, and writing bring that knowledge into light. The process of thinking nature and articulating its meaning is the process of transmitting knowledge from nature to the heart on a profound spiritual level. Knowledge transmission, in this case, is a deep ecospiritual communication.

Womanist ecospiritual epistemology is different from modern dualist epistemology. While modern dualist epistemology tends to emphasize hierarchy and boundaries between the human species and natural species, womanist ecospiritual epistemology acknowledges oneness between humankind and nature. Such acknowledgment is best exemplified in two novels by Walker, including *The Temple of My Familiar* (1990)[9] and *Now Is the Time to Open My Heart* (2005).[10] In *The Temple of My Familiar*, Walker suggests that Miss Lissie's familiar is not only her true social self but the animal and the plant sides of her. To seek the temple of her familiar is to reclaim not only her true social self, which is racialized, gendered, sexualized, and pushed underground by subjugating devices, but also the animal and the plant sides of her, which is disassociated from her and unrecognized by her male counterparts. The idea that nature is an integral part of a person gestures toward a womanist ecospirituality.

Womanist ecospirituality challenges the modern conceptualization of humanness based on evolutionist thoughts, one of which is the mis/belief that what distinguishes humans from animals and plants is the higher intelligence that only humans have, and that the higher intelligence has enabled humans to evolve into a higher and superior life form on the evolution chain. In accordance, a hierarchical pyramid[11] has been established between humans, animals, and plants with humans on top, animals beneath humans, and plants beneath animals. The stratification of species partially reflects how humanness has been defined. Humanness is also a racialized and gendered construct. Women and people of color were classified as lesser humans who were closer to nature. It is not surprising but disturbing that earlier colonists and explorers who went to Africa and the Americas described indigenous peoples as apes. Scientific racists propagandized that certain groups of people had less intelligence. Likewise, scientific sexists believed that women had less intelligence than men. Reduction of women and ethnic peoples to animals and nature was employed as a tactic to strip women and ethnic peoples of their power and human rights. In history, subjugation of nature, women, and ethnic peoples went hand in hand.

*The Temple of My Familiar* begs us to be aware of the wounds and dismemberment that sexism, colonialism, and racism have inflicted upon people. It urges us to see Lissie's disassociated parts—the feminine side, the animal side, and the plant side, among other identities—as a whole. The representation of Lissie as woman, lion, monkey, and plant refutes colonialist and racist notions of humanness. Here I do not suggest that species differences should be conflated but rather our view of humanness be reconceptualized. It needs to be recognized that the human body is also a natural body; in other words, the human body is a form of biological organism—it lives, decomposes, and transforms into other life forms.[12] To disassociate humankind from nonhuman nature and view the former as superior to the latter is a denial of nature, of the animal and the plant sides in us. Likewise, to disassociate masculinity from femininity is a denial of a significant part in each individual, as femininity and masculinity constitute two complementary essences in each individual. I invite my readers to consider that we are simultaneously human and nature, female and male, and feminine and masculine.

Reclaiming the subjugated feminine side is necessary not only for women but also for other sexes. I side with the Yoruba[13] and Taoist idea that each individual despite sex simultaneously has elements of masculinity and femininity. To prioritize either element results in imbalance. Imbalance creates personal problems. On a larger scale, societal gender imbalance creates social disharmony. To restore balance, each sex and society has to acknowledge the simultaneity of masculinity and femininity within a corporeal body and culture. Likewise, power imbalance constructed between humanity and nature, in other words, disassociation of humanity from nature and humanity's superiority to nature leads to the misconception that humanity can triumph over nature. This misconception has resulted in the serious environmental issues we face today. To tackle such issues, we have to rely on not only environmental technology but also a new way of relating to nature. We have to realize that we are part of nature and each corporeal body is natural. There is no hierarchy between nature and humanity.

Walker's recent novel *Now Is the Time to Open Your Heart* offers another example of how to think of womanist ecospirituality. Kate, the story's protagonist, obtains spiritual healing through her reunion with Grandmother. Grandmother is multidimensional. She is a corporeal character, a spirit, and an herbal remedy called "Yagé." By drinking the "Yagé," Kate sees snakes, symbol for sexuality and source of energy for life and creativity. Kate's healing is complete only when she realizes that she is Grandmother herself. The flow of healing energy from Grandmother as woman and goddess in ancient time to Grandmother as herb to Grandmother as snake to Kate as Grandmother in contemporary time deconstructs the dominant Western dualism of nature/human, body/spirit, spirituality/sexuality, and past/present. Womanist ecospirituality offers a fluid way of thinking perceived boundaries.

Womanist ecospirituality deconstructs not only dualism of spirituality/sexuality but also dualism of queer sexuality/heterosexuality. The term "womanist" was coined by Walker to describe an alternative sexuality practiced by Rebecca Jackson. In Walker's 1981 book review essay "Gifts of Power: The Writings of Rebecca Jackson,"[14] Walker disagrees with Jean McMahon Humez on Jackson's sexual orientation. Humez labels Jackson a lesbian simply because Jackson left her husband and lived with a woman intimately for the rest of her life. Walker's own term for women like Jackson is "womanist." Walker argues that Jackson's practice invoked an African tradition of woman-bonding, in which women who loved women sexually or nonsexually rarely thought of lesbianism; instead, they referred to themselves as "whole" women, or "holy" women. Walker's argument offers a more fluid understanding of women's sexuality. If this alternative sexuality has to have a name, it would be womanist sexuality. Womanist sexuality challenges the binaries between queer sexuality and heterosexuality, vocabulary constructed in Western sexology.

It is worth noting that Jackson's sexuality is discussed inseparably from her spirituality, her quality of being "holy." More importantly, nature is a significant catalyst for her spirituality. Her spiritual awakening came with thunder and lightning, and by extension, nature. The intricate weaving of nature, spirituality, and womanist sexuality resonates with an ancient Chinese tradition of understanding nature, woman's sexuality, and spirituality. Di Mu tradition is one example.

## Di Mu

My interest in Di Mu, or Earth Mother, has been revitalized by the womanist notions of community and health as I discussed before. The womanist notions of community and health have inspired me not only to be more aware of social and environmental issues, but also to rethink alternative spiritualities in China, especially nature- and woman-oriented spiritualities that are labeled "primitive," 'backward," and "superstitious" and excluded by mainstream religions in China. My study informed by a womanist consciousness has retrieved my memories of animistic spiritual beliefs and practices in southwest rural China where I grew up. Being viewed as "feudal," "superstitious," and "backward," these animistic beliefs and practices in that area are rapidly disappearing because of modernization and urbanization.

The contemporary processes of development have drastically changed the material and spiritual life of people in southwest rural China. Horticulture is endangered by the emerging economic agriculture; vast areas of fertile land are lost to newly constructed highways, suburban real estate, markets, and factories;

and people's health is threatened by toxins from air pollution, contaminated water, and agricultural products infested with pesticides and herbicides. Riverside Village, one of the places where I conducted my research, reported its first case of breast cancer in 2008. Although I have no intention to romanticize rural life and rural spiritualities, I posit that environmental degradation and the disappearing of animistic beliefs and practices are closely related to incursions of contemporary development. It is urgent to reevaluate beliefs labeled as "backward feudalist superstition," one of which is belief in Di Mu. I contend that rather than "backward" and "feudalist," Di Mu belief reflects a complicated way of understanding nature and woman, and thus by extension, humankind. Di Mu belief also invites us to think alternatively of woman's sexuality.

Who is Di Mu? Di Mu is one of the earliest female deities in Chinese spiritual history, dating back to the Stone Age. Di Mu is a multidimensional, transcendental, and primal goddess. Di Mu is corporeal; she is a woman, a female archetype, a human mother. Her West African counterpart is Green Lady.[15] Di Mu is chi;[16] she is an omnipotent principle of life. Di Mu is simultaneously nature, woman, goddess, and chi in one. The simultaneity of sacredness, humanness, and nature-ness in her is not contradictory but organic. Womanist characters like Kate, Lissie, and Rebecca Jackson are contemporary African American counterparts of Di Mu. Like Di Mu, they embody holiness, humanness, and nature-ness simultaneously.

Nonetheless, in today's spiritual belief system in China, Di Mu might have transformed into other identities. Some Chinese scholars of folk religion speculate that Tu Di Gong, or Earth Father, is a variation of Di Mu.[17] I think this speculation holds water to a certain degree. The transformation of Di Mu from a female to a male might have happened in the process of patriarchalization of Chinese culture in early Chinese history. She was replaced by Tu Di Gong (Earth Father) to make space for Sky Father, whom Chinese emperors used to legitimize their ruling of the subjects in the name of Sky Son. To aggrandize the power of Sky Father and his Sky Sons, Tu Di Gong was reduced to the size of a dwarf. Whereas Di Mu is a supreme goddess, Tu Di Gong was relegated to the role of a local deity. When Buddhism was introduced to China, Tu Di Gong was assimilated to the Buddhist faith. His altar is placed either outside the temple (usually near the front entrance) or in a small corner inside the temple. In the long process of identity transformation and religious assimilation, Di Mu's status has been diminished and her true identity has been lost.

The etymology of Di Mu offers us a useful clue to imagine Di Mu. Di Mu is composed of two Chinese characters, including "di" and "mu." "Di" constitutes two components, "tu" and "ye." According to *Explanation of Chinese Characters* by Xu Shen,[18] "tu" resembles the way a plant grows out of soil, and "ye" the female genitalia. The character "mu" means origin, primal chi, and mother. The two dots in "mu" resemble breasts.

There are different ways to read Di Mu's etymology. Seemingly, woman's biological features are salient, which seems to insinuate woman's sexuality and reproductive capacity. Numerous archeological excavations have attested to the fact that Di Mu was portrayed as a woman whose breasts, abdomen, and genitalia were highlighted.[19] Therefore, there is a great temptation for traditionalists to read Di Mu as a goddess of fertility, and woman, or Di Mu in human form, as a means to reproduce. A goddess of fertility is often read as necessary for primitive societies in which production forces were low and people's knowledge of nature was limited. Thus they had to rely on supernatural power to pray for abundance and good harvest. Likewise, woman's reproduction is read as essential for primitive tribes whose survival depended on reproduction of offspring to continue the ancestral line. I would argue that such a reading is reductive. The reduction of Di Mu to a goddess of fertility, and a woman to her reproductive role, is, as a matter of perspective, not what Di Mu and woman really encompass.

A womanist ecospiritual perspective inspires new interpretations of Di Mu's etymology. "Tu," the foundational and essential component of "di," or the way a plant grows out of soil, signifies the capacity for recycling life, which does not necessarily involve sexuality. When it does, it is an alternative sexuality, or plant sexuality, which is different from, and more diverse than, human sexuality as constructed in our contemporary time. The component of "tu" and plant sexuality in imagining woman and woman's sexuality invites us to think of an alternative sexuality, the meaning of which cannot be conveyed by the contemporary vocabulary of human sexuality. The explicit association of woman's sexuality with Di Mu challenges the dualism of sexuality/spirituality.

Furthermore, the etymology of Di Mu illustrates the idea that the boundary between woman and nature collapses. Although some contemporary Euro-American feminists tend to read the nature/woman bond as essentialist, I would argue that the nature/woman bond is essential but not essentialist. The reading of nature/woman bond as essentialist is a reactionary dialogue with patriarchal dualism. It would be read differently from a womanist ecospiritual perspective. Walker's *The Temple of My Familiar* reminds us that the nature side is actually that which is disassociated from us in a sexist, racist, and colonial context. The inseparability of woman from nature, or nature from woman, begs for recognition of the interdependence between humankind and nature. The desire to separate humans from nature reveals a rationalist patriarchal anxiety to seek superiority and dominance over nature, woman, and those who are feminized, and the anxiety to seek the legitimization of the excessive use of woman, nature, and those who are feminized. Rationalist patriarchal ideology and practice has had serious material consequences that people worldwide have to face today. Di Mu belief challenges such rationalist patriarchal ideology and practice.

The most amazing legacy Di Mu has left us is a body of nature-oriented knowledge. My field research revealed that ordinary villagers in Riverside Village and Dragon Bone Village have a decent level of knowledge regarding medicinal herbs. Thanks to their generosity and help, I was able to collect numerous herbal remedies, including eye ailment treatment, postpartum bath, kidney disease, asthma, cystitis, otitis media, detoxification, fever, dysentery, and prickly heat. Among these remedies, the one for mal-acclimatization is interesting. Migrant workers usually carry a handful of dirt with them to the cities where they work. They mix the dirt with water and drink it. The question is not to ask how effective this remedy is, but to see how veneration for land, or Di Mu, has become part of the remedy for the anxieties and contingencies of migration and cultural transplantation. Villagers who remain in the countryside usually prefer not to go to the hospital for regular ailments. They gather wild herbs for the preparation of homemade concoctions to prevent or to cure disease.

Veneration for Di Mu has evolved into numerous variations, one of which is veneration for trees. In Riverside Village, there is a distinctive custom of looking for a tree godmother. It is believed that a sick child whose level of water element is disproportionate to his or her five elements[20] can be healed when a tree godmother is found. In both Riverside Village and Dragon Bone Village, it is common to see trees decorated with red cloth prayer ties. Each piece of cloth represents a sick person and a wish for healing that person. Over the years, villagers have also developed complicated tree-planting rituals and taboos. They believe when, where, and how to plant a tree around the house will influence the health and future of their family members. Villagers seek guidance by observing the condition of trees and plants around their house. The benefit of having such a tree veneration tradition is evident. The great number of surviving thousand-year-old trees I saw in southwest China testifies to the environmental legacy of tree veneration.

Villagers are grassroots environmentalists without knowing the term environmentalism. For example, a self-taught herbalist in Riverside Village consciously rescues disappearing medicinal herbs and plants them in her vegetable garden. She makes flu prevention remedies for her family and neighbors. She exchanges herbs and remedies with other local women. By doing so, she helps to preserve the endangered medicinal herbal species and the knowledge of healing. Grassroots environmentalism is especially important because it will be too late when environmental organizations finally make efforts to reach down to the villages. When external interventions are actually available, local knowledge systems are often at risk of being appropriated and commercialized.

Despite the fact that the Di Mu tradition is ingrained in everyday life, it is facing tremendous challenges today. Knowledge of herbs is disappearing. The older generation of herbalists has either died or has had a hard time surviving in an era of science-based medicine. In addition, it is getting more and more difficult for village herbalists to find successors. The majority of their children are migrant workers in cities. Their grandchildren have to go to school in towns or cities. Being removed from the country, the younger generation does not have enough time to learn the way of wild herbal plants. Even if they have, there are fewer and fewer wild medicinal herbs for them to know. Wild medicinal herbs are disappearing because of the overuse of herbicides, modern agricultural technology, and construction of cement roads. In a time of crisis, there has recently been a revival of Di Mu belief; in particular, there has been an increasing interest in *Di Mu Jing*, or *Songs of Earth Mother*.

### *Di Mu Jing, or Songs of Earth Mother*

My encounter with *Di Mu Jing* was accidental and miraculous. I was guided to a shrine for Di Mu before I was introduced to *Di Mu Jing*. The granddaughter of my host in Dragon Bone Village told me there was a ghost house near her school. Out of curiosity, I asked her to take me there. It turned out that the ghost house was a shrine dedicated to Di Mu, which is rare to see nowadays. The girl believed it was a ghost house because her classmates, friends, and parents told her there was a ghost living in the shelter. She never dared go there.

How did Di Mu turn into a scary ghost in the Dragon Bone Village where there has been a long tradition of nature and ancestor worship? To think through the question, I consider the larger social context into which the contemporary spiritual practice in Dragon Bone Village is situated. Like many other villages in southwest rural China, Dragon Bone Village has gone through a series of social changes and turmoil in the past century. Among those social upheavals, the construction of New China and the Cultural Revolution seem to have been the most detrimental. During the course, almost all temples and shrines were destroyed; villagers were taught to believe that belief in Di Mu and other nature deities was superstition. The few resilient practitioners had to go underground. In the meantime, mountains were deforested. It was not until late twentieth century that religious policies have loosened up.

The current spiritual belief systems in the village are juxtapositions of vernacular Buddhism, Catholicism, and indigenously inclined spirituality, such as ancestor worship and nature worship. Whereas Buddhism and Catholicism are legitimized religions, indigenously inclined spirituality is the underlying belief system. People who practice indigenously inclined spirituality often self-identify themselves as Buddhists. Meanwhile the revival of spirituality often accompanies struggles with officially listed cults like Fa Lun Gong and Men Tou Jiao. Villagers have a hard time deciding what is good spirituality and what is a cult. They are especially cautious and careful not to be associated with a cult. It was in such a messy context of social change, along with the consequent disbelief, doubt, and the latent interest in spiritualities, that Di Mu was turned into a scary ghost for the little girl.

Youth of the little girl's generation are introduced to modern education with an emphasis on math, science, and westernized modernist intellectual thoughts. Indigenous spirituality practiced by villagers is neither part of the curriculum nor part of everyday conversation among youth. Older generations of villagers keep silent about their practices in fear of being viewed as "backward" and "ignorant." It even took my host, who considered himself open-minded, weeks to open up to my inquiry. He introduced me to a Yin Chuan Yi Sheng,[21] or medicine woman in the village.

It turned out the shrine for Di Mu was built by this medicine woman. She showed me *Di Mu Jing*. *Di Mu Jing* has different versions; the version she has is circulated among self-identified Buddhist believers and practitioners in the rural area in Wushan, Chongqing Autonomous Region. This version is also circulated online among people who search for alternative spiritualities. This version is for chanting. Another version of *Di Mu Jing* is known as *Huang Di Di Mu Jing*. *Huang Di Di Mu Jing* was part of *Huang Li Tong Shu* and used as a guidebook for agriculture and divination. *Huang Di Di Mu Jing* comprises sixty stanzas, representing a temporal cycle of sixty years. Each stanza is composed of a poem and a divination. The poem and divination together predict the climate, conditions of farming, fishing, husbandry, natural disasters, and war that may happen in a particular year. *Huang Di Di Mu Jing* is beyond the scope of this paper. Undoubtedly *Huang Di Di Mu Jing* itself is a subject of study.

To go back, the online participants roughly fall into three groups. One group believes in Di Mu piously and embraces *Di Mu Jing* wholeheartedly. Another group considers belief in Di Mu as the legacy of feudalism and superstition. As a result, they vehemently condemn *Di Mu Jing* as apocrypha.

The third group has a more balanced understanding of *Di Mu Jing*. They recognize both its significance and limitations, reading it as a positive Chinese cultural heritage whose value has been undermined by feudalist traits embedded in the text. I side with this group, but depart from them by reading *Di Mu Jing* from a womanist ecospiritual perspective. I read it as a protest against war, materialism, and gender discrimination.

*Di Mu Jing* is composed of two parts: *Di Mu Zheng Jing*, or *Songs of Truth from Earth Mother*, and *Di Mu Miao Jing*, or *Songs of Witticism from Earth Mother*.[22] *Di Mu Zheng Jing* tells stories regarding the birth of Di Mu, the care Di Mu gives to the world, and undue disrespect for Di Mu. It calls for recognition of Di Mu as equal to Tian Di, Sky Father. It reminds readers that yin and yang are supplemental instead of oppositional to each other and that Di Mu and Sky Father have different but cooperative roles to sustain life cycles. To privilege Sky Father over Di Mu only results in masculine governance characterized by generations of kings' greed for materials and power, involvement in wars, and abuse of land. It warns us that the violence inflicted upon Di Mu, by extension nature and woman, results in environmental and social disasters. It foretells the environmental and spiritual crises we are experiencing today as a result of militarism, sexism, and excessive use of natural resources.

*Di Mu Miao Jing* persuades people to respect her. It also gives instructions of when, where, and how to venerate her. Compared with *Di Mu Zheng Jing*, this part seems to be aimed at folk believers and practitioners. The instructions are centered on veneration and reward, as well as disrespect and punishment. For example, it is instructed that if you venerate Di Mu properly, you will be healthy, wealthy, and enjoy a long life; otherwise, you will run the risk of spitting blood, contracting incurable disease, having droughts, floods, and no harvest. Although I do see a correlation between abuse of women and land, and the consequences, I find the strategy of fusing fear in believers questionable. While I remain critical of the strategy, I see this weak point as a problem resulting from the limitation of the author who was historically and socially situated and thus circumscribed by limited understanding of Di Mu in a historical time period. Therefore, it is unreasonable to pour out the baby with the bathwater.

In contemporary practice, to chant *Di Mu Jing* is usually to pray for blessing. To pray for blessing is probably the most common incentive among contemporary folk believers and practitioners of Di Mu. For example, on the front gate of the Di Mu shrine built by the medicine woman in Dragon Bone Village, there hang two scrolls that read: "May there be good weather for the crops; May the country prosper and the people be at peace." The personal story attached to this shrine also reflects such a positive incentive. According to the medicine woman, she was chosen to be a healer. However, she refused in the beginning because it was not an easy task to be a healer. Being a healer involves constant physical pain, dream talks with the Pu Sa, and the risk of being treated differently by fellow villagers. Her rejection ended up in a series of physical and emotional punishments. She finally came to terms with her mission. She agreed to chant *Di Mu Jing* and build a shrine for Di Mu. By doing so, she was rewarded with blessing and endowed with curing power for herself, her family, and the people who come seeking her consultation.

It is interesting to note that in the shrine, Di Mu, attired in gowns and a headdress that Tu Jia[23] women wear, sits next to Fu Ye and Guan Yin. While Di Mu and Fu Ye are the contemporary versions of indigenous deities, Guan Yin is a Buddhist bodhisattva. The juxtaposition of Guan Yin, Di Mu, and Fu Ye in the same shrine indicates that spirituality practiced by this medicine woman is indigenous spirituality blended with folk Buddhism. This blending is then creatively localized by dressing Di Mu the way local women dress. What this medicine woman did reminds me of what Rebecca Jackson did. Jackson started her spiritual journey with Christianity, but she constantly challenged the mainstream interpretation of Christianity and redefined it from her womanist perspective. Similarly, this medicine woman adopted Buddhism, a legitimized religion, and blended indigenous elements into Buddhism. She demonstrates a creativity that is vital to enabling indigenously inclined spirituality to survive in an era of scientism.

Another eye-catching element of her shrine is the tree growing in front of it. The tree was decorated with pieces of red cloth. The tree and red cloth invoke a tradition of veneration for the tree spirit, as I have previously discussed. This tradition is now considered by some Chinese environmentalists as the earliest form of Chinese environmentalism. In recent years, with an increasing concern for the environment, Di Mu tradition has achieved more visibility and legitimization. However, there is still a long way to go. The path will be difficult but hopeful.

## Notes

1. What I mean by "indigenous" in my text is different from the construction of the "indigenous" as "the other" in a colonial context. By "indigenous" I mean 1) native to a particular location, land-based, nature-oriented; 2) ancient, passed on generation after generation for a long time.

2. Yin Guang Fa Shi listed *Di Mu Jing* as a piece of apocrypha that Buddhists and lay Buddhist practitioners should not chant. He recommended *Ban Ruo Bo Mi Duo Xin Jing* [Prajna Paramita Hrdaya Sutra] instead. See Yin Guang Fa Shi, "Fu Li Zhonghe Jushi Shu" [Letter to Lay Buddhist Li Zhonghe].

3. See Clenora Hudson-Weems's *Africana Womanist Literary Theory* (Trenton, NJ: Africa World Press, 2004), her *Africana Womanism: Reclaiming Ourselves* (Troy, MI: Bedford, 1993), and Chikwenye Okonjo Ogunyemi's *Africa Wo/man Palava: The Nigerian Novel by Women* (Chicago: University of Chicago Press, 1996). In both *Africana Womanism* and *Africana Womanist Literary Theory*, Hudson-Weems lists "spiritual" as one of the womanist characteristics. In *African Wo/man Palava*, Ogunyemi elaborates the role of Yoruba spirituality in Nigerian womanist literature.

4. Layli Phillips, "Womanism: On Its Own," in *The Womanist Reader*, ed. Layli Phillips (New York: Routledge, 2006), xxx.

5. Ibid., xxx.

6. I thank Layli Phillips for pointing out to me the concept of "The Book of Nature."

7. Alice Walker, "Womanist," in *The Womanist Reader*, ed. Layli Phillips (New York: Routledge, 2006), 19.

8. Ibid., 19.

9. Alice Walker, *The Temple of My Familiar* (New York: Pocket, 1990).

10. Alice Walker, *Now Is the Time to Open Your Heart* (New York: Ballantine, 2005).

11. When I did my field research in Ngari, Tibet, Tibetan pilgrims told me that they never thought of summiting the sacred mountain because that would insult the mountain. Instead, they circled the sacred mountain on foot. Their practice is in contrast with the extreme sports of mountain climbing as a test of human capacity. For me, a sportsman on top of a sacred mountain is a contemporary symbolism of the hierarchal biocultural pyramid.

12. Rosemary Radford Ruether has a similar idea about the bio-nature of humans. She argues that humans, like plants and animals, are "finite organisms." As humans, we are also part of "a continual cycle of growth and disintegration." For a fuller discussion, see her essay "Ecofeminism: Symbolic and Social Connections of the Oppression of Women and the Domination of Nature," in *Ecofeminism and the Sacred*, ed. Carol J. Adams (New York: Continuum, 1993), 22.

13. See Chikwenye Okonjo Ogunyemi, *Africa Wo/man Palava: The Nigerian Novel by Women* (Chicago: University of Chicago Press, 1996).

14. Alice Walker, "Gifts of Power: The Writings of Rebecca Jackson," in *The Womanist Reader*, ed. Layli Phillips (New York: Routledge, 2006), 12–18.

15. See Malidoma Patrice Somé, *Of Water and the Spirit: Ritual, Magic, and Initiation in the Life of an African Shaman* (New York: Arkana Penguin, 1995), 217–24.

16. There is a line in *Songs of Earth Mother* that says "zhen qi wei mu mu shi qi," meaning chi is the primal essence of life.

17. See Xiao Dengfu, "Houtu yu dimu shilun tudi zhushen ji dimu xinyang" [Houtu and Di Mu: On the Family of Earth Deities and Belief in Di Mu] *Shijie zongjiao xuekan* [*Journal of World Religion*] 4 (December 2004): 1–14. Also see Ye Shuxian, "Zhongguo shanggu dimu shenhua fajue jianlun huaxia shen gainian de fasheng" [Legend of Di Mu and the Origin of Shen in China], *Minzu yishu* [*Ethnic Arts*] 3 (1997): 29–45.

18. Xu Shen, *Shuo Wen Jie Zi* [Explanation of Chinese Characters] (Kashi: Kashi Weiwuer Press, 2002).

19. See Du Zhengqian, "lun shiqian shiqi dimu guannian de xingcheng jiqi xinyang" [On the Conceptualization of Di Mu in Prehistory and Belief in Di Mu] *Nongye kaogu* [*Archeology of Agriculture*] 4 (2006): 109–10.

20. The five elements include mineral, wood, water, fire, and earth.

21. "Yin Chuan Yi Sheng" is a term villagers in the Dragon Bone Village use to call shamans and healers. The term means doctors who are bestowed with healing power by bodhisattvas or deceased healers. The heritage is not necessarily passed on through blood line, from a male to a male, or from a female to a female. The medicine woman I met with is considered a "Yin Chuan Yi Sheng" by the villagers. According to her, her healing power has come from Di Mu and Guan Yin. Healers like her are called "Pu Sa" in Riverside Village where I conducted my research. Villagers also use the same term to call Bodhisattvas.

22. The text I examine is the version the medicine woman gave to me.

23. Tu Jia is an ethnic group in China. They disperse in a number of provinces in China. Dragon Bone Village is next to Enshi and Jianshi in Hubei Province where Tu Jia resides. The older generation of Tu Jia women still wear ethnic clothing. I spotted women wearing headdress and upper outer garments like Di Mu's in the farmer's market in Da Miao, the town where Dragon Bone Village is located.

# PART II

# Popular Culture

4

# Is This a Dance Floor or a Revival Meeting?

## *Theological Questions and Challenges from the Underground House Music Movement*

Darnise C. Martin

I join with womanist voices that articulate a beloved community inclusive of all, exclusive to none. Womanist theology makes a claim for wholeness and inclusivity, transcending differences of gender, class, race, sexuality, and politics. Thus I am interested in expanding womanist notions of love and community not only to give voice to voiceless women as has been its tradition, but also to include men who are marginalized due to heterosexism. Womanists have described a type of community that thrives upon the inclusion of women and men, straight and gay, privileged and disadvantaged existing together in just and healthy ways. I join them in their understanding of the need for a whole community in which all are welcome, and none are marginalized. However, the womanist discourse has fallen short in at least two areas in particular: (1) by not addressing non-Christian African American persons, and (2) which is the focus of this work, an absence of an actual, practiced inclusion of homosexual people and their legitimate roles within African American community and spiritual life.

Understanding the context of the emergence of womanist theology as distinct from black theology and white feminism, I know that these African American women have demanded and created theological and communal spaces for our voices, but also with an intention for all members of the community who have been marginalized. As Linda E. Thomas writes, "womanist theology demands a God talk and God walk which is holistic, seeking to address the survival and liberation issues of women, men, children, workers, gays and lesbians, as these relate to local and global economies and the environment."[1] It is from this intention that I join with the voices of the third wave as I push the womanist envelope to live up to its promises of inclusivity and justice.

I have to admit that I come to writing this essay out of somewhat selfish desires. In the first place, I am an African American female religion scholar whose own spirituality lands me outside the realm of mainstream Christianity. My scholarship has largely been in the areas of New Thought and metaphysical religions, leaving many theology scholars wondering how or where to situate my work. My first book, *Beyond Christianity: African Americans in a New Thought Church*, is an ethnographic study of an Oakland, California church of African American New Thought believers. The second volume to which I have contributed as co-editor is *Women and New and Africana Religions*, a work intentional about presenting the religious diversity among women, including African Diaspora women, and the ways in which their spiritualities are expressed in their lives throughout the world. Thus I have an interest in religious diversity joining the conversation of womanist theology so that African Americans like me are not rendered theologically invisible.

In the second place, I write this essay out of another personal interest, and that is music. I am an avid fan of underground dance music known as house music. I will say more descriptively about the genre of house music shortly. However, suffice it to say for now that it is my love of house music that has led me to observe and intimately come to know the subgenre of gospel house music and the many facets of its emergence and continuing manifestation. I have come to learn, see, hear, and feel gospel house music as a socially and theologically critical form of protest music. I have come to know it as a life-affirming, humanizing art that functions as a form of religious identity construction and meaning system for gay black men as they seek to reclaim and reshape their religious beliefs in an alternative space that permits them freedom to be wholly themselves and still unequivocally loved by God. Many of these gay black men are also Christian, and they believe on Jesus Christ as lord, but the Christian church has shunned them, has dehumanized and marginalized them. Feeling the sting of excommunication, these men have not given up on their faith, but have creatively and intentionally relocated the worship space to the dance floor of the nightclub where they feel free to sing, dance, and worship in their own sanctuary with new and rearranged hymns of liberation and inclusiveness.

This is a phenomenon from which I have learned for nearly twenty years. I have danced and Sunday-shouted right along to house music anthems that are now considered classics of the genre. Thus this essay is a participant-observation, a labor of love testament to those black gay men who have carved out an alternative religious space when the Christian church folk they know have turned their backs on them, and label them sinful and ungodly.

Thus I propose to examine the complexities of the underground dance music movement known as house music in an effort to lift up the theological reflections, challenges, and commentaries found specifically within gospel house music, a subgenre of the larger house movement. This paper will describe a brief history of house music, contextualizing it within its own sets of norms and club culture, and attempt to represent the gospel house experience as a performed spiritual expression of a marginalized segment of the population. I will offer a social and theological critique of marginalized black gay men through an examination of selected lyrics, the dance floor environment, and the role of the DJ as important components that create a club atmosphere conducive to free personal expression and worship.

## Not Everyone Understands House Music

House music is an underground form of dance music made popular in the nightclubs of Chicago and New York City in the waning days of the disco era of the late 1970s and early 1980s. While disco imploded and attracted mass media scorn and ridicule, the impulse to dance and the accompanying music played in nightclubs continued to evolve, eventually taking on the more generic title of "dance" music to distinguish it from disco and the negative baggage associated with it. This dance music combined disco, funk, and rhythm and blues music, and took on a specific blend under the skill and style of each particular DJ who played it. Musically, it is described as rhythm-driven music created with electronic synthesizers and drum machines. It is music intended to be "felt" within the body, not just heard. Indeed, house music is often referred to by fans, DJs, and producers as being "a body thing, a soul thing, a spiritual thing."[2]

House music is enormously diverse and has developed many subgenres, such as deep house, soulful or vocal house, trance, electronica, euro, acid, techno, tribal, and (the subject of this paper) gospel house music, just to name a few within this narrow but deep well. These terms may also be substituted by reference to geographic region such as Chicago, New York, Detroit, Jersey, or euro-style "house" as these locations have become associated with particular styles that regular club-goers understand. Notably absent are West Coast cities.

While San Francisco has earned some recognition in the genre, it is comparatively minimal, and the rest of California barely registers at all on the scene.[3] The term "house" is a reference to one of the most famous dance clubs in 1980s Chicago, the Wherehouse, where this music was created and played by DJs on turntables into the late-night and early-morning hours. A similar following was happening in New York City at the legendary but now defunct club called the Paradise Garage. "House" became a type of shorthand for the style of music that came from the Wherehouse, even as it has spread and evolved around the world. Typically, much of the clientele of these clubs were and continue to be black and Latino gay men who had been part of the disco era, but found a new form of expression with house music. Thus much of the aesthetic of this music reflects a mix of African American and/or Latino culture and music, and a recognized gay sensibility espousing freedom of expression, pride, and self-reliance.

This is music that has emerged from, and is still largely maintained by, marginalized people and their cultures. As a result, it continues to exist as a largely underground phenomenon, in contrast to "mainstream," that which is widely recognized and accepted. Underground dance music refers to music, a lifestyle, a culture, and an aesthetic that is little known by the masses, functioning successfully below the radar of media attention, and therefore not played on radio or sold in common music outlets. House music enthusiasts must intentionally seek out the music, the clubs, and community networks in order to stay abreast of relevant news and information. What is known or at least supposed by the larger society tends to be stereotypical generalizations that house is "gay music" or for drug users tripping out on ecstasy.

House culture provides an alternative space and field of expression within which one finds a number of spiritual references, one of which is gospel house songs. House music clubs represent safe spaces where gay men and those straight folks sympathetic to them could find a place to be themselves in an affirming community and dance to the music they loved. Out of this context arose the sub-subgenre of gospel house music. In this form, DJs and producers create remixes of established gospel songs or create new songs with a gospel musicality, but with lyrics that actually replace some of the sin-oriented language with words of God's unconditional love and acceptance of everyone. Like the blues, some of these songs are written to critique the so-called "good Christian," who is found to be hypocritical, overly judgmental, and exclusive in their own personal behavior. Gospel house music has become a refuge for those gay men who still value their Christian faith, and the clubs allow them to create their own family connections and worship spaces. The music allows them to maintain their connection to God, but bypass the tension caused by oppressive teachings that generally ostracize and marginalize them.

## Lyrics and Theological Reflections

Let us now consider the lyrics of some gospel house songs and the theological reflections or critiques therein. The critical lyrics speak of the hypocrisy of so-called "good Christians" who are judgmental and exclusive in their faith expressions. As a counter to anti-gay Christian messages, gospel house lyrics emphasize a view of God as all-loving, accepting, and inclusive. These lyrics subvert the dominant Christian hermeneutical paradigm that God hates gay people or hates homosexuality, with self-affirming and God-affirming messages to the contrary. These messages are carried out musically as a combination of a heavy bass line and 4/4 dance tempo, soulful vocals, and lyrics that both praise God and deliver a social critique.

One of these songs, "You Don't Even Know Me," describes the singer's feelings of being harshly criticized but not actually known for the type of person he is. While it is not explicitly stated that the lyrics represent a statement about sexuality, I have witnessed that the song has been enthusiastically appropriated by gay audiences as representing their own situation in relation to homophobic communities. The lyrics are as follows, "You don't even know me. You say that I'm not living right / You don't understand me so why do you judge my life? / Who are you to say that I'm living wrong / always telling me what do? / It's my life, it's my life, and I'm living it now," followed by a soaring falsetto male voice widely imitated by the club-goers on the dance floor.[4]

Other songs are straightforward praise songs directed to God the father and/or Jesus as redeemer of all humanity, but without going through the Christian church as mediator. Some of these titles include "We Lift Our Hands in the Sanctuary," where the sanctuary is actually the club where the "worship" is happening on the dance floor. This song is not to be confused with the traditional gospel song of the same name by Kurt Carr. This song is a gospel house praise song where it has become an anthem sung from the dance floor. The lyrics state, "No pressure, no fear, nobody's in your business, nobody really cares . . . we rejoice, we lift our hands, love is alive in the sanctuary, I feel alive in the sanctuary, everybody dance in the sanctuary, people come to dance at the sanctuary, we clap our hands in the sanctuary, so hear our voice in the sanctuary, we rejoice in the sanctuary."[5]

We can also refer to a song titled "He Reigns," in which God is recognized and praised as a loving, omnipotent creator of all. As with many house songs, there are sometimes minimal lyrics, even a short phrase looped over and over.

This is such a song, wherein the phrase, "We pray to you because you deliver us, he reigns from heaven above, he reigns. He's an awesome God, he's glorious. He reigns we praise you. He reigns, he reigns, he reigns, forever and ever," which is looped repeatedly over a bass-heavy, rhythmic dance beat.[6] Again, because many gay men have lost their family connections and church affiliations due to their sexuality, the dance clubs have become spaces for reclaiming fragments of their traditional faith in alternative ways, ways that celebrate their humanity. A song like this one reveals a traditional vision of God as all-powerful deity, or one may say it is expressive of a neo-kingdom theology in which God rules as sole monarch over his kingdom. While it may seem surprising to encounter this type of traditionalism, it reinforces the concept for these men that it is God who is supreme, and God who will do the judging, not one human being over another. The critique remains against the one who takes on God's role as judge, and then marginalizes and oppresses others. This type of song actually functions for gay men in this context to solidify their devotion to God directly, despite the Christian church's effort to circumvent it. Gay men who celebrate with this song are subversively affirming their right to relationship with God despite what others might have to say about it.

## God Is a DJ[7]

To add to the complexities of understanding house music, I add that many varieties of the music and culture embody a generalized spirituality, a type of metanarrative of spirituality that gets disseminated through the description or names of clubs, specific parties, song titles, and a cultural aesthetic that is often determined by the DJ. The cultural aesthetic to which I refer is one that recognizes the music as generating a spiritual experience, and house enthusiasts often use the phrase "house is a spiritual thing" to describe the music whether in ordinary conversation with one another, or printed T-shirt graphics, posters, or included in song lyrics, there is a general understanding of the transcendent or spiritual feeling that house music stimulates. One song, called "House Music," states the following: "Not everyone understands house music; it's a spiritual thing, a body thing, a soul thing."[8] Another example comes from the song, "Spiritual Groove," which states, "This is the sound of a spiritual groove. When I hear this sound, I feel like dancing."[9] Other songs include "House of God,"[10] which is a clever critique of a minister's requests for money looped throughout the song; "God Is a DJ"; and yes, even "Inspirations from a Small Black Church on the Eastside of Detroit,"[11] where as one might imagine the already-fuzzy line between sacred and profane is further blurred with sounds of a church piano and a foot-stomping dance beat merged into the perfect juke joint song. Other areas in which we see this is in the names of clubs such as the Sanctuary and the Buddha Lounge. We also see the blurring of the sacred and profane in themed parties such as "Sunday Mass," a house music party taking place over the past year and a half at a well-known San Francisco club called The EndUp.

Likewise, some DJs have made their respective spiritualities a part of the atmosphere they create, complete with burning incense and a raised DJ booth reminiscent of a raised pulpit. Some, like Osunlade and Joe "Joaquin" Claussell, have come to be associated with syncretic African traditional religions. The DJ Bodhi Sattva mixes Asian and African elements to his eclectic sessions. The musical styles of Osunlade, Claussell, and Bodhi Sattva are representative of Latin, or tribal house subgenres in that they bring in an ethereal element complemented by African drumming or forest sounds of monkey and bird calls. Other DJs, while not embodying a particular spirituality themselves, create a spiritual atmosphere, by shifting the party into an intentional time of worship. Club-goers often refer to this as "the DJ took us to church." Internationally renowned house DJ Frankie Knuckles (aka Godfather of House) refers to "the disco as a church for the children fallen from grace." Music scholar Kai Fikentscher, in his book "You Better Work!," makes many connections between the rituals of the black church and the ritualism displayed on the dance floor of the club. He draws a parallel between the sacred and secular roles of DJ and preacher, both engaged in call-and-response that drives the crowd to an emotional and physical frenzy imbued with a larger meaning about who they are.

Moreover, Fikentscher quotes a club-goer from the days of the legendary Paradise Garage nightclub in New York, under the direction of iconic DJ Larry Levan. Consider the following comment:

> On Sunday mornings around 7:00am, Larry would stop all the dancing by putting on Aretha Franklin singing "Mary Don't You Weep." We knew he was giving us church. But then he would take us from [a black] church to his church! After Aretha [Franklin] was done with her song, he would serve us fiercely! And he didn't do this just once, but for several weeks.[12]

Thus the role of the DJ is critical for how the music is delivered and how or whether the space is successfully transformed into a safe, spiritual sanctuary. It is not unusual for African American house DJs to close their Saturday night into Sunday morning sets with gospel music as "the children" are sent out into a new day.

All of these cultural components reflect the general, syncretic spiritual metanarrative, and function as cues and reinforcement helping the underground house club-goer navigate the genres and subgenres of the music. If these signals are misread, a club-goer could end up at the wrong type of party. By this, I refer again to the many types of house music in the underground scene. If one did not understand the specific language code of what anthropologist Clifford Geertz might call a cultural native, he or she could end up at a party of another type of house such as electronic or trance, which are aesthetically and culturally very different from deep or gospel house.[13] As one who has made this mistake, it can be quite unsettling and disappointing. Since this is an underground movement, information is generally passed within the community through in-group language codes. Even with the extensive network now available on the Internet, getting to the desired house community remains a challenge for the outsider or casual fan. YouTube represents a public forum where one is able to observe comments and responses between the true "househead" and the so-called "wanna-be," who is perpetrating or faking it as a DJ or commentator in their video postings. This is made evident by the person's misuse of genres, lack of pertinent historical knowledge, or just poor DJ skills. The critiques in this case can be excoriating, drawing a distinction between the purist and the neophyte or dilettante. What emerges as important currency in perhaps any underground movement, but certainly here, is correct knowledge, language, and skills.

## The Underground and the Hush Harbor (or Hush Harbor as Underground)

Finally, I would like to offer a parallel for our consideration, between the underground house music club scene as alternative, safe space where spirituality is reconstructed by the marginalized people it serves, and the hush harbor practices of enslaved African Americans confined to plantation life and subjected to oppressive Christian messages. Scholars such as Albert Raboteau, C. Eric Lincoln, Lawrence Mamiya, and Deborah Gray White have given us historical accounts of American slave life.[14] In Raboteau's classic text, *Slave Religion: The Invisible Institution in the Antebellum South*, he vividly describes the secret religious practices of enslaved African Americans. He poses this alternative religion as a creative and life-affirming response to the slave-making and slave-keeping form of Christianity imposed upon them. As oppressed people living under constant threat and terror, enslaved populations of African-descended people understood the concept of a God who liberates, hermeneutically reenvisioning Christianity, infusing it with the remnants of Africa, and creating a hidden-in-plain-sight worship space where they were free to be themselves, loved and cared for by God. This worship always involved music and dance. For the African person, even in diaspora, to dance is to invite in the gods. Historical accounts describe for us the dancing and the singing, and the appropriation of the Christian message embodied in dance and the protest music we now call Negro spirituals. Again, we have a musical language that could be made public, but coded in such a way that only the insiders grasped the true meaning. These early spirituals are known to offer social critique, often veiled, but nonetheless proclaiming their own humanity despite all societal messages to the contrary. We find lyrics that reinforce that God is indeed on their side. While this may have seemed entirely absurd to the larger society, the enslaved African Americans knew differently, holding onto this knowledge as truth that would eventually be manifest.[15]

Moreover, accounts of slave religion, and later works on the black church and black Christ, reveal an intimate relationship between African Americans and Jesus. He was and still is often understood as co-sufferer, friend, comforter, and savior—not only in the afterlife, but as divine liberator from present-day suffering. Thus African American Christians have constructed a very specific relationship with Jesus throughout the struggle for dignity and civil rights. Indeed, in *A Black Theology of Liberation*, James Cone emphasizes that in terms of the historical Jesus, a marginalized minority is a more meaningful example than even the kerygmatic Jesus in the struggle for black civil rights. The kerygmatic is important, he says, for the ultimate salvation of humanity, but a practical application of theology to the specific conditions of black Americans requires an appreciation and emphasis upon the historical Jesus, a despised and marginalized minority person.[16]

Thus I draw a parallel between the special role of Jesus for African Americans in slavery and the civil rights struggle, hidden hush harbor religious worship, and the contemporary underground house music club scene. Here, marginalized gay black and Latino men have reconstructed an alternative spiritual space where they understand God to be for them, despite what the dominant society and the Christian paradigm assert against them. Underground, then as now, takes on a dimension of safety, freedom of expression, and radical inclusivity. Gospel house emerges as a new canon of freedom songs sung as they always are from the mouths of the oppressed, who nevertheless proclaim their humanity and right to be. The Christological point is illustrated by the house song "He Is," in which the claims of the Negro spirituals are heard once again in lyrics that report, "[Jesus] is my friend, my brother, oh yes he is."[17] As ethnomusicologist and Sweet Honey in the Rock founder Bernice Johnson Reagon has said, every generation must create their own freedom songs.[18] I assert that gospel house music represents a branch of that tradition.

### Conclusion

If we are to take seriously the womanists' challenge toward inclusive, healthy, and just communities, then the challenge stands to include all people regardless of gender identity or sexual orientation. The founding womanists such as Katie Cannon, Delores Williams, Jacquelyn Grant, et al., have opened a way for such inclusion to happen not only in the work they have done for black women, but in their vision for what can be done for people marginalized by heterosexism. If we are free to adjust our hermeneutical lenses of Scripture and church doctrine to overcome racism, sexism, and economic exploitation, then surely we are able to do so to liberate people from oppressive beliefs and systems around sexuality. If we understand that God's request that we "love one another" is the highest of teachings, then we already have a methodology to accomplish such a goal.

## Notes

1. Linda E. Thomas, "Womanist Theology, Epistemology, and a New Anthropological Paradigm," *CrossCurrents*, 48, no. 4 (Winter 1998–99): 493.

2. Eddie Amador, "House Music," released March 1999, on *International Club Union Session*, Vol. 2; compact disc.

3. A notable exception is the Deep House Music scene founded by Los Angeles DJ Marques Wyatt, who has been an active and prominent DJ for at least twenty years, and founder of the weekly party Deep: Where House Lives. As well as L.A. DJ Tony Powell who is the founder of Dirty Dirty House Club (DDHC).

4. Duane Harden, vocal performance of "You Don't Know Me," by Duane Harden, Armand Van Helden, Kossi Gardner, released July 2001, on *Filtered: The Best of Filtered Dance*, Tommy Boy; compact disc.

5. DJ Oji & Una, "We Lift Our Hands in the Sanctuary" (Ron Trent's Shelter Mix), by DJ Oji, released 2002, on *Sancsoul Sessions EP*, Sancsoul Records—SS002 (written for Strong Black Man Music); vinyl, 12", EP, 33 1/3, RPM.

6. Yass, "He Reigns," by Sebastien Grand and Yass, released 2007, on *I'm Free*, Purple Music, mp3.

7. Faithless, "God Is a DJ," by Catto, Maxi Jazz, Rollo, Sister Bliss, released 1998, on *Sunday 8pm*, Arista Records, 1998, compact disc.

8. "House Music."

9. Sound of Soul, "Spiritual Groove (Hard Steppin' Dub)," lyrics by Marcel Scooler; written, produced, and arranged by Mark Zehnder and Christian Kistler, released 2000, on the compilation CD *Lazy Dog: Deep House Music* by Ben Watt and Jay Hannan, Astralwerks, compact disc.

10. Dimensional Holofonic Sound, "House of God," by D.H.S., released 1991, on *House of God*, Hangman Records, vinyl, 12".

11. Dimensional Holofonic Sound, "House of God," by D.H.S., released 1991, on *House of God*, Hangman Records, vinyl, 12".

12. Kai Fikentscher, *"You Better Work!" Underground Dance Music in New York City* (Middletown, CT: Wesleyan University Press, 2000), 105.

13. Clifford Geertz, *The Interpretation of Cultures* (New York: Basic Books/HarperCollins, 1973), 11.

14. See Albert J. Raboteau, *Slave Religion: The Invisible Institution in the Antebellum South* (1978; reprint, New York: Oxford University Press, 2004); C. Eric Lincoln and Lawrence Mamiya, *The Black Church in African American Experience* (1985; reprint, Durham, NC: Duke University Press, 1990); Deborah Gray White, *Ar'n't I a Woman?: Female Slaves in the Plantation South*, rev. ed. (New York: W. W. Norton, 1999).

15. Raboteau, 243–66.

16. James H. Cone, *A Black Theology of Liberation*, 25 anniv. ed. (1970; reprint, Maryknoll, NY: Orbis Books, 2001), 110–28.

17. Copyright, "He Is" (Ferrer & Sydenham Inc Vox Mix), by Sam Holt and Gavin "DJ Face" Mills, remix by Jerome Sydenham and Dennis Ferrer, released 2006, on *Copyright feat. Song Williamson—He Is* (Ferrer & Sydenham Inc Vox Mix), Independence Records, vinyl 12".

18. Bernice Johnson Reagon, "The Songs Are Free," documentary by Bill Moyers conducted in 1991, *Bill Moyers Journal*, PBS, November 23, 2007, http://www.pbs.org/moyers/journal/11232007/profile3.html.

5

# Confessions of a Ex-Theological Bitch

## *The Thickness of Black Women's Exploitation between Jacquelyn Grant's "Backbone" and Michael Eric Dyson's "Theological Bitch"*

**Elonda Clay**

Hi, my name is Elonda.[1] I am an ex-theological bitch. I am in recovery from being a strongblackwoman[2] who was theologically restrained, socially silenced, and physically sacrificed. Yesterday, I was silent, "respectable," expendable. Today I "talk back" and take back the power of my own Pussy and voice. I liberate them both from being treated like a bitch. And these, these are my confessions . . .

Inspired by Karrine Steffans's *Confessions of a Video Vixen*,[3] I attempt here to break the silence on the ways that black liberation and womanist discourses can reinforce a "missionary position"[4] Christian identity. In writing this essay, I confess that I have kept my thighs closed or worse, covered my scuffed-up knees with the lap scarf of pretense that purports to speak *for* black women but denies the power of the Pussy and the resolve of black women on the bottom to do for themselves what no respectable theology will do: speak from a "woman on top" point of view.

This chapter flows in four sections. I begin by discussing black women and black churches, drawing from the works of Jacquelyn Grant and Michael Eric Dyson. Turning attention to the gender metaphors of "backbone" and "bitch"—particularly how they function within and outside of the texts—I seek to find links between these two metaphors, touching on their historical usage and what they signify about black women. Drawing also from the works of philosopher Michel Foucault, music artist Jill Scott, theologian Laurel Schneider, and others, I seek to problematize Christianity as a "confessional" religion. The thickness of gender oppression in Christianity is not only what is said (confession), but it is also what is not said (silence) about gender injustice. I conclude by imagining what black women and men's religious lives might look like if they challenge the "missionary position" of their Christian identities and practices, and move toward a transformation in sexual politics.

## Gender Metaphors for Black Women in Black Religious Thought (USA)

Jacquelyn Grant and Michael Eric Dyson have written on the collective silences in churches and communities on the oppression and exploitation of black women. Although they critique sexism and sexual segregation practices, they present the "backbone" and "bitch" statuses of black women as a tragic, inevitable fact. Therefore, they remain silent on the heterosexist bias of their metaphorical concepts.

In her essay "Black Women and the Black Church," Jacquelyn Grant brings attention to the well-worn adage that women are the "backbone" of the church.[5] Grant states that while backbone is a metaphor for the function of women in the black church, the word also refers to their location—the back. She observes, "What they really mean is that women are in the background and should be kept there; they are merely support workers." Grant goes on to say that women are accorded greater participation in decision making at smaller rather than larger churches. She proposes that women are penalized for trying to move from the backbone to the head position—the leadership of the church.[6]

There is another image conveyed by the backbone metaphor related to labor; one of carrying the weight of others, bearing the bulk of others' share of work on your back. So the multiple meanings of "support" not only work in and around the metaphor "backbone" to reference the supporting role and spatial regulating of women to the background, as Grant argues, but they also point to the internalized expectation of black women's self-sacrifice on behalf of "the body," whether "the body" represents their church, black communities, employers, families, or partners.

Michael Eric Dyson, in his 2003 Boardman Lectureship in Christian Ethics titled "Religion and Terrors," brings attention to the reality that while some blacks are outraged at the explicit expression of misogyny in hip hop culture, especially the use of words like "bitch" and "ho," they are silent concerning the routinization and banalization of misogyny in everyday life. Recognizing interconnections between speech and silence as they are operational within black churches concerning misogyny, Dyson states, "So you haven't been called a bitch, but you dangum been treated like one!"[7] He has also publically described this as being treated like a "theological bitch" within the institutional power hierarchy of black churches. He continues,

"You are granted no say in and ultimately no position of power all over the church where you give most cash, most money, or tithes . . . hegemony means that I dress it [domination] up so deep that I just dominate you and have you standing in line coming back for more. The cultural expressions of seduction through which complicity with power are secured. This is Hegemony 101. That form of terror is not interrogated, expressed, dialogued about and opened up as a form of solidarity between black women and men against their children in the hip-hop culture who are conveniently stigmatized."[8]

Dyson's comparative example is revealing. He argues that the exploitative intent and actions toward black women that are present in entertainment industries such as hip hop and the exploitative intent and actions that can flourish inside black religious institutions are similar in kind and similar in outcome. The thin veneer of innocence that separates morally sanctioned exploitation and mistreatment of black women within religious cultures and morally renounced exploitation and mistreatment of black women in entertainment forms is thus an illusion: one form of exploitation is institutionalized and normalized while the other is reviled and stigmatized, yet both environments potentially produce forms of terror and violence. In Dyson's example, being treated like a bitch by church leaders or members points to the investment black women make mentally, physically, and institutionally to heterosexism and patriarchy even though their contributions are undervalued, hidden, sometimes mismanaged, or even patronized.

The word "bitch" is meant to be pejorative and degrading. To be treated like a bitch is to be treated as an expendable nonperson and sex object. To be perceived as a bitch is to be feared or reviled because you are assertive or because you dare to withdraw your consent to being oppressed. To be called a bitch is an oppressor's attempt to claim the power to name and dominate someone else. The exercising of female power in a heterosexist patriarchal society not only points to gender nonconformity but also to bodies that are out of their proper place, displacing the order of racial and gender hierarchy[9] and thus "contaminating" that which is pure—male domination and entitlement, and dick-glorifying ways of performing and acting that benefit heteropatriarchal males sexually and financially.

The words "backbone" and "bitch" relate to animal metaphors, historically signifying a "similar in kind" relationship between black women and animals; black women as beast of burden or representative of an animalistic wild sexuality.[10] These animal metaphors convey a residual notion of ownership of black women as property and chattel as well. "Backbone" and "bitch" can be viewed as one side of the taken-for-granted binary constructions of womanhood and gender roles within black culture. The Imus media scandal[11] of 2007, where radio host John "Don" Imus referred to the female athletes on the Rutgers basketball team as "nappy-headed ho's" and "rough girls with tattoos" serves as a revealing event that exhausted the enduring binary of black women as either ho's (whores) or sistas. Within responses from the African American community, the "deviant" representations of nappy-headed ho's were consistently contrasted with the preferred, normative representations of sistas or ladies. No one said that nappy-headed ho's didn't exist; instead respondents generally agreed that Don Imus had called the wrong black women ho's. The women on the Rutgers basketball team were not ho's; they were valued educated achievers, respectable women, even role models!

The sista/bitch binary so deeply embedded in everyday black life made the black women on the Rutgers team "respectable victims,"[12] whereas common ho's and bitches clearly are not seen as worthy of respect. Women on the opposite side of the binary, poor or sexually objectified women like Karrine Steffans—an abuse survivor and self-identified video "vixen" who confesses her sexual encounters with powerful men and exposes the underside of the entertainment industry—are viewed as "bitches that get what they deserve."[13] "Respectable victims" are necessary agents within what feminist, lawyer, and civil rights activist Flo Kennedy describes as the "circularity of oppression." The circularity of oppression requires women's consent to oppression and their acceptance of second-class treatment within institutional and sexual politics. In exchange for their complicity, institutions provide selected women with some status by ennobling their suffering and sacrifice, particularly their sacrifices made on behalf of men.[14] Black sistas or ladies, as "respectable victims," gain superior status by accepting their license to oppress someone else, namely youth, poor people, bitches and ho's, queers, or anyone labeled socially inferior or noncompliant within heteropatriarchal systems.[15]

What both Grant and Dyson miss in their critiques of misogyny, sexist practices of male clergy, and institutionalized oppression within the hierarchical structures of black churches is that heterosexism and hypermasculinity are pervasive in religious traditions and organizations; both men and women consent to institutionalized oppression in certain ways, exercising power differentially in these spaces. In order to transform the circularity of oppression in black churches and communities, we have to withdraw our own consent and cooperation with oppression and stop gliding "serenely through the bullshit as though it was a field of daisies."[16]

Now we will move from the letter of the gender metaphors, to the spirit in which the metaphors were being applied. In other words, our discussion of gender metaphors leads to an exploration of black women's internalized gender roles and gender injustice and violence within black churches, with a particular description of how these processes can influence the religious lives of U.S. Christian black women.

## Confession, Silence, and Thickness in the Operational Theologies and Institutional Practices of Black Churches

In everyday conversation, the word "confess" means to acknowledge something wrong. When one confesses, they "speak fully on one's sins to a person with authority to hear and absolve sins."[17] A confession may or may not be private, but it always has public consequences. The confession is a product, the outcome of an interrogation process as well as a social activity, riddled with contradictions between inner freedom of the individual and external requirement of the law that enforces the social order.[18] Increasingly confession has become popular entertainment, especially in the form of "tell all" books. In Christianity, we can make a distinction between collective confessions, public confessions, and private confession.

Continental philosopher Michel Foucault describes Christianity as a salvation religion and as confessional religion, that is, a religion that requires the subject to speak truthfully.[19] But for Foucault, the practice of confession is not merely the result of personal conscience, it is a result of historical processes of surveillance and subordination as exercised within the hierarchical structure of Christian power relations—institutional, theological, and physical—in terms creating technologies of the self and systems of discipline.

Confession, therefore, is not an activity that functions by itself; as a speech act it is inseparably linked to silence or silences. Foucault scholar James Carrette notes that to understand Christianity as solely linked to speech is to operate with a narrow understanding of the relationships between speech and silence.[20] For Foucault, silence "functions alongside the thing said, within them and in relation to them within over-all strategies," dissolving the binary partitions normally built between what has been said and what has not been said.[21] Foucault posits that, "There is not one but many silences, and they are an integral part of the strategies that underlie and permeate discourse."[22]

Neo-soul music artist Jill Scott has a song called "Thickness."[23] In the song, she describes the encounters of a young black woman whose body is developed enough for her to be sexually objectified by men of all ages in the neighborhood, men who "never bother to see how big her mind is." For Scott, the thickness not only refers to the beautiful roundness of a black woman's body, but also the process of coming of age in an environment where black women's bodies are only seen as objects that, willing or not, are made for the sexual pleasure of men.

The "thickness" also represents the messiness of societal, communal, and family situations that support women's disempowerment or exploitation. Historian of science Evelynn Hammonds describes this as the problematic of silence on black women's sexuality, "where black women's bodies are always already colonized."[24] Thickness is a black woman's attempt to negotiate sexualities and spiritualities in that social reality where she is unappreciated, perceived as inferior and invisible outside of her legs and thighs, hips and tits. In contexts that champion heterosexist desire and masculine displays of bravado, a woman's usefulness is based on her willingness to be named and tamed by forces outside of herself. Lyrically, music artist Scott observes that imposing meaning upon bodies and silencing voices are core practices that construct young women as sexual objects. She sings, "They like her quiet and eager, sweet and meager . . . shhh, don't you complain about my other women, just drop that big thick ass on my stiffness . . . cause I ain't your tribesman no more. I ain't your friend . . ."

Thickness is commonly used as a metaphor for social conditions, embodiment, size, external events, and situations that constrict personal choices, or the sexy messiness of two bodies intertwined as they move toward ecstasy. Thick conditions require decision making under uncertainty and risk. These decisions are often bounded by cultural and gender norms or economic necessities, with risks or consequences that cannot be calculated, but that instead have to be journeyed through. Thickness is that which you cannot ignore, sidestep, or get around. It is a halting, emotionally bare moment that transports you immediately back into embodiment. Thickness is cumulative, multilayered, textured, emergent, and complex.

Silence, as a response to women's exploitation and oppression, is an established pattern for black women's religious lives. The thickness between the "backbone" and the "bitch" statuses for black women's religious lives is this: disempowerment, harassment, humiliation, exploitation, and gender-based violence are experienced by black women who sit in the pews on any given Sunday.[25] Black women are expected in some black churches to be invisible, except for their working hands, open pocketbooks, and occasionally when the opportunity arises, available pussies to be persuaded, conquered, and silently tossed aside as hussies afterwards.

Black women in black churches are sometimes restricted to and complicit with taking on the missionary position as their Christian identity; men are on top and active, women are on the bottom in a supporting, passive role. Feminist theologian Laurel Schneider, in her lecture "Changing the Missionary Position,"[26] discusses how the social position of active male dominance over passive female submission became the official Christian sexual position. Initially codified as the proper social order during the Greek and Roman empires, the social order of women on the bottom and men on top was baptized as a divinely sanctioned social hierarchy by theologians such as Saint Thomas Aquinas, and categorized by scientists within the vertical great chain of being.[27] This white supremacist logic, as practiced in colonial Christianity, still informs the practices and operational theologies within many black churches, where the gender hierarchy of dominance is taken for granted as the normal order of things. The silent strongblackwoman and "entitled because he's heterosexual" black man are gender stereotypes that draw not only from white supremacy and colonial logics, but also from homegrown black sexual politics of respectability.

Implicit in the use of "missionary position" as a trope to explore gender politics is a heterosexual model of sex. While such can be used to get at phallic and patriarchal processes of domination, the imagery of the missionary position, as invoked here, still reinforces the normalizing, and indeed hegemonic discourse of heterosexual intercourse. In this sense, "missionary"-style sexing is seen as a form of "normal" sexual engagement, therefore rendering all other expressions of sexuality as deviant, or "Other." The fluid range of what we call sexuality challenges what is recognized as sexually normative and therefore calls for a deconstruction of dominant sexist and heterosexist assumptions that inform gender stereotypes more generally.

On the economic front, women often receive no pay or less pay than their male counterparts who perform the same labor. When women clergy/laypeople speak up and ask for the same pay, they are often coerced through theological rhetoric to be self-sacrificing when it comes to a salary while males expect and demand higher pay. Female clergy are often expected to be "cleanup women"; that is, to untangle and set right the mess left behind by poorly performing, abusive, or career-ladder-climbing male clergy. Women often do much of the work and handle most of the details of church activities, while the men publicly receive credit without acknowledging they had assistance.

Both men and women participate in the perpetuation and maintenance of rape culture, even inside of religious institutions.[28] Rape culture is described as "a complex of beliefs that encourages male sexual aggression and supports violence against women . . . a society where violence is seen as sexy and sexuality as violent."[29] The editors of the book, *Transforming a Rape Culture*, further explain:

> In a rape culture both men and women assume that sexual violence is a fact of life, inevitable as death or taxes. This violence, however, is neither biologically nor divinely ordained. Much of what we accept as inevitable is in fact the expression of values and attitudes that can change.[30]

Even if they are religiously active, some people still feel entitled to full access and control over the bodies of others. An internalization of rape culture is reflected in the belief of some that sex with the "man of God" endows the receiver with more grace. Rape culture is not limited to opposite-sex expressions, but may also have same-sex expressions. Doing sexual "favors" for the pastor, including becoming a "holy hospitality escort" for visiting preachers, can be deceptively justified as part of women's religious duty to provide for and protect men. In cases of sexual assault, some survivors of clergy abuse take the fallback positions of self-blaming, self-sacrificing, or leaving everything to divine vengeance/restitution.

Attitudes and actions that protect sexual and domestic predators instead of survivors of violence by maintaining silence extend to vulnerable communities and families, where sexuality and gender norms also become very messy and complicated. One of the most taboo topics in black churches, families, and communities is gender-based violence in various forms such as rape, incest, stalking, domestic violence, and sexual or peer-to-peer violence involving youth at school. Some young people experience sexual assault by someone they know as their first sexual encounter. This is especially true for youth who live in vulnerable communities. Also, the popularity of the Internet and social media has led to a recent increase in the use of mobile technologies and online communications to facilitate cyberbullying and online invasion of privacy.[31] Online violence often mirrors the values and ideas of a rape culture.

## Conclusion: Scandalous Lessons and Unfinished Confessions

How do we learn from scandalous lessons and move on to what must be done? Are black churches so complicit with rape culture that they are unable to challenge it? How can people more successfully negotiate the thickness of gender roles and gender oppression in religious institutions without falling back into the bad habit of silence?

I propose that this would call for Christians to take a different position for their religious identity that rocks the boat (I hear Aaliyah in the background singing, "new position, new position"[32]), like the "woman on top" position. Now, I know many of you might think this is a mere inversion or reversal of power that maintains the oppressed/oppressor binary; however, being on top is not always a position of power. Others of you might be drifting off into a memory of being on top . . . wait for it . . . ahh there it is. But I am not merely referencing sexual intercourse here. An "on top" position is one that advocates for a panoramic view of sexuality and spirituality from "the top," where the wider social landscapes of desire, power, contradiction, sexual politics, and pleasure have the potential to converge in ways that transform rather than perpetuate rape culture. On top allows for the power of position, not just the positioning of power.

Transformation involves efforts to revise our own perspectives and practices as well as action to change social structures.[33] Black feminist bell hooks argues that efforts toward transformation demand that we give up set ways of thinking and being, shift our paradigms, and open ourselves to what has been previously unfamiliar.[34] I believe that this is also true if we are to engage gender and religion, sexuality and spirituality, in ways that are affirming and empowering, not hidden, painful, destructive, and disempowering. Above all else, love is the root politic for the transformation of black sexual politics. Men and women already work together to resist gender oppression. We need to find ways to encourage this "solidarity in the midst of difference" to continue.

Transformational sexual politics would help us to engage in critical reflection on womanist religious practices. It would also help us to rethink and challenge the politics of respectability that tend to fuel the conservative sexual politics that support continued silence and invisibility. Transformational sexual politics also assist black men in their struggle to resist masculinities built on dominance and violence as manhood-redeeming qualities. Four areas of unfinished confessions are briefly discussed below: Breaking the Silence, Self-Care and Health, Don't Be Seduced by Violence, and Rethinking Tradition.

### *I. Breaking the Silence*

Breaking the silence on the same old status quo requires speaking up and acting when you see gender injustice. Inappropriate jokes, touching, images or text messages, and bullying should not be tolerated or encouraged. The success of black churches depends on the financial and labor contributions of women; this should not be taken for granted as a given—or worse, exploited through unethical conduct.

While there is debate over involving the legal system in clergy misconduct, gross infractions of trust and claims of abuse must be addressed. Several actions that can be taken by survivors of clergy misconduct and sexual abuse include: (1) Keeping a record of each encounter when necessary. If necessary, file lawsuits against denominational bodies that do not respond to allegations of sexual misconduct of clergy. (2) File criminal charges against clergy who have committed sexual assault/abuse. Sadly, this is a seldom-pursued response to gender-based violence such as incest, rape, sexual abuse of youth (male and female), stalking, and domestic violence. (3) File for child support for any child fathered by clergy, whether they are married or not. Having a position of religious leadership is not a reason to deny or avoid parental responsibility.

### *II. Self-Care and Health*

Women and men need to engage in conversations about sexuality and health in spaces where conversations can be more open, honest, and holistic instead of judgmental and repressive. Black women need to resist being silent "respectable victims" of sexual harassment and sexual violence at school, church, family, and work. For some people, self-care has meant leaving their inherited religion and practicing spiritualities outside of institutions, as writer Alice Walker and many other women have demonstrated.

When necessary, we need to protest institutional nonresponse to sexist behavior or sexual violence. One example of raising awareness concerning sexual violence is the 2007 campus protest organized by the Feminist Majority Leadership Alliance at Spelman College for Morehouse College's nonresponsiveness to several incidents of alleged sexual assaults.[35] Survivors of assault and abuse should include professional help and community in their healing processes. If for any reason you experience your church as abusive, take action and find a different house of worship.

### *III. Don't Be Seduced by Violence*[36]

Heterosexual men need to consider what it means to be sexual; their hard-on does not mean that a woman either wants to or has to have sex with them. Women have a right to say "no," regardless of the circumstances. And no means no; I ain't talking no Destiny's Child–induced male sexual fantasies of women saying "no, no, no, when they mean yes, yes, yes."[37] Forcing yourself on someone sexually is rape, whether you know them or not.

Queer people need to consider how they can unlearn heterosexist-based eroticisms that dehumanize queers because of their sexual orientation or condone violent attacks on GLBTQ individuals. Unfortunately, some queers internalize the homophobia and heterosexism present in society, culture, and religious traditions, which can have a detrimental effect on their self-esteem and psychosocial well-being.

Heterosexual women need to consider how they are complicit with "dick-glorifying" or "real man" masculinity. Does she say that she is looking for a "conscious brother" who is sensitive to her needs, but ends up with the thug who could care less about her because he "acts like a real man" by behaving in a controlling, degrading manner?

### *IV. Rethinking Tradition*

Liberatory practices include the affirmation and holistic development of everyone's talents. Our capacity to move collectively and politically does not depend on competent leadership that is exclusively male. Denominations and individual churches need to create gender justice statements if they do not have them, and be held accountable for meeting those standards. Clergy and congregations can also connect with nonprofits that are advocates for gender justice. Lastly, we can challenge the politics of respectability and conservative sexual politics that maintain silence and shame about sexual and domestic violence in black communities.

Critiques of misogyny and disrespect of women in the greater community and media, accompanied by silence about abuse and oppression within churches, are prophetic yet hypocritical simultaneously. As they say in the hood, "game knows game." In other words, no one is deceived by the contradictions of the situation. Women and men do not need to watch music videos to observe misogyny; they can watch misogyny playing out much closer to home. We can begin by addressing the gender issues we face in the places we live; starting with our families, our schools, our churches, our communities, and our workplaces. I commend Monica A. Coleman's service work as an advocate to help churches help survivors of rape and sexual assault. Her book *The Dinah Project* provides an exemplary template of what an advocate for gender justice can do in the church and the community.[38]

We need to create holistic approaches to gender identities, power, language, institutional practices, and cultural practices that equip us for the present and the future. Our commitment to growing alternative ways of relating as spiritual and sexual persons and avoiding the perpetuation of gender-based violence in its various forms begins by engaging in dialogue on theology, religion, gender, and sexuality—and by "talking back" to their silences as well.

Hi, my name is Elonda. I am an ex-theological bitch. I am in recovery from being a strongblackwoman who was theologically restrained, socially silenced, and physically sacrificed. Yesterday, I was silent, "respectable," expendable. Today I "talk back" and take back the power of my own Pussy and voice and liberate them both from being treated like a bitch. And these, these are my confessions . . .

## Notes

1. The author would like to shout out her wonderful sisters, Kelly, Charlene, Meredith, Jennifer, and Adorno, for their laughter, support, fantastic feedback, and critical engagement during the writing of this piece.

2. "Strongblackwoman" as used here describes the stereotype and mythological construction of the black superwoman as sacrificed by others or as always self-sacrificing her own well-being for others. Strongblackwoman as an idealized (and ideological) representation and performance of black womanhood has been discussed at length by scholars Marcia Ann Gillespie, "The Myth of the Strong Black Woman," in *Feminist Frameworks: Alternative Theoretical Accounts of the Relations between Women and Men*, ed. Alison Jaggar and Paula Rothenberg (New York: McGraw-Hill, 1984); Michele Wallace, *Black Macho and the Myth of the Superwoman* (1979; reprint, London: Verso, 1999); Joan Morgan, *When Chickenheads Come Home to Roost: A Hip-Hop Feminist Breaks It Down* (New York: Touchstone, 2000); Juliette Harris and Pamela Johnson, eds., *Tenderheaded: A Comb-Bending Collection of Hair Stories* (New York: Pocket Books, 2001); Cheryl Townsend Gilkes, *If It Wasn't for the Women . . .: Black Women's Experience and Womanist Culture in Church and Community* (Maryknoll, NY: Orbis, 2001); Gwendolyn Pough, *Check It While I Wreck It: Black Womanhood, Hip-Hop Culture, and the Public Sphere* (Boston: Northeastern University Press, 2004); Patricia Hill-Collins, *From Black Power to Hip Hop: Racism, Nationalism, and Feminism* (Philadelphia: Temple University Press, 2006); Tamara Beauboeuf-Lafontant, *Behind the Mask of the Strong Black Woman: Voice and the Embodiment of a Costly Performance* (Philadelphia: Temple University Press, 2009).

3. Karrine Steffans, *Confessions of a Video Vixen* (New York: HarperCollins, 2005).

4. The missionary position, a sexual position in which the man is on the top and the woman on the bottom, is named because it is thought to be the preferred position that colonial missionaries sought others to conform to as the only "proper" position for sex. It has a subtext of normalizing heterosexual intercourse.

5. Jacquelyn Grant, "Black Women and the Black Church," in *All the Women Are White, All the Blacks Are Men, but Some of Us Are Brave . . . Black Women's Studies*, ed. Gloria T. Hull, Patricia Bell-Scott, Barbara Smith (New York: Feminist Press, 1982), 141.

6. Ibid.

7. Michael Eric Dyson, "Religion and Terrors." 2003 Boardman Lectureship in Christian Ethics, University of Pennsylvania. Boardman Lecture XXXIX, ed. Adam Graves http://repository.upenn.edu/boardman/1/.

8. Ibid.

9. Kimberly Springer, "Divas, Evil Black Bitches, and Bitter Black Women: African American Women in Postfeminist and Post–Civil Rights Popular Culture," in *Interrogating Postfeminism: Gender and the Politics of Popular Culture*, ed. Yvonne Tasker and Diane Negra (Durham, NC: Duke University Press, 2007), 272.

10. Kimberly Wallace-Sanders and Brittney Cooper, "NippleMania: Black Feminism, Corporeal Fragmentation, and the Politics of Public Consumption," in *Women in Popular Culture: Representation and Meaning*, ed. Marion Meyers (Cresskill, NJ: Hampton, 2008), 76–78.

11. Maria Newman, "Rutgers Women to Meet Imus over Remarks," *New York Times*, April 10, 2007, http://www.nytimes.com/2007/04/10/business/media/10cnd-imus.html?hp.

12. Neal defines a "respectable" victim to the black community as a black female who is perceived as morally superior and deemed a good representative for the strategy of "black respectability." Rape victims, sex workers, lesbians, single mothers, poor and homeless women, and pregnant teenagers are bodies that fall outside of the sphere of respectable victims. See Marc Anthony Neal, "*(White) Male Privilege, Black Respectability, and Black Women's Bodies," The Black Commentator*, April 20, 2006, *http://www.blackcommentator.com/180/180_white_male_privilege.html.*

13. Jennifer McLune, "You Told Harpo to Beat Me?": How Hip Hop Music Defines and Divides Black Women," *Smash Crew*, 2008, http://www.smashcrew.com/Home/Featured_Post/details/params/object/6040/default.aspx.

14. Florynce Kennedy, "Institutionalized *Oppression* vs. The Female," in *Sisterhood Is Powerful: An Anthology of Writings from the Women's Liberation Movement*, ed. Robin Morgan (New York: Vintage Books [Random House], 1970), 438–42.

15. Julia Penelope, "Do We Mean What We Say? Horizontal Hostility and the World We Would Create," in *Call Me Lesbian: Lesbian Lives, Lesbian Theory* (Freedom, CA: Crossing, 1992), 60.

16. Kennedy, 441.

17. Mike Hepworth and Bryan S. Turner, *Confession: Studies in Deviance and Religion* (London: Routledge & Kegan Paul, 1982), 5.

18. Hepworth and Turner, 155–56.

19. Michel Foucault, "Technologies of the Self" (University of Vermont Seminar), in *Technologies of the Self: A Seminar with Michel Foucault*, ed. L. H. Martin, H. Gutman, and P. H. Hutton (London: Tavistock, 1988), 40.

20. James Carrette, *Foucault and Religion: Spiritual Corporality and Political Spirituality* (New York: Routledge, 2000), 27, 36.

21. Michel Foucault, *The History of Sexuality, Volume 1: An Introduction* (London: Penguin, 1976), 27.

22. Foucault, *The History of Sexuality*, 17ff.

23. Jill Scott, vocal performance of "Thickness," by Jill Scott, recorded August 25–26, 2001, released November 2001, on *Experience: Jill Scott 826+*, Hidden Beach, compact disc.

24. Evelynn Hammonds, "Black (W)Holes and the Geometry of Black Female Sexuality," in *Theorizing Feminisms: A Reader*, ed. Elizabeth Hackett and Sally Haslanger (New York: Oxford University Press, 2006), 555.

25. Charisse Jones and Kumea Shorter-Gooden, "Can I Get a Witness?: Black Women and the Church," in *Shifting: The Double Lives of Black Women in America* (New York: HarperCollins, 2003), 259–78.

26. Laurel C. Schneider, "Changing the Missionary Position: Facing Up to Racism, Sexism, and Nationalism in the L(GBT) Liberation Movement" 10th Anniversary of the Gilberto Castaneda Lecture, LGBTQ Religious Studies Center, Chicago Theological Seminary, May 3, 2007, http://www.vimeo.com/6753878.

27. Ibid.

28. Marcia W. Mount Shoop, *Let the Bones Dance: Embodiment and the Body of Christ* (Louisville: Westminster John Knox, 2010), 59.

29. Emilie Buchwald, Pamela R. Fletcher, and Martha Roth, eds., *Transforming a Rape Culture* (Minneapolis: Milkweed, 1993), v.

30. Ibid.

31. "The Rise in Cyberbullying," *National Public Radio*, September 30, 2010, http://www.npr.org/templates/story/story.php?storyId=130247610.

32. Aaliyah, vocal performance of "Rock the Boat," by Steve Garrett, Rapture Steward, and Eric Seats, recorded 2001, released 2007, on *Aaliyah*, Blackground, compact disc.

33. bell hooks, "Feminism: A Transformational Politic," in *Talking Back: Thinking Feminist, Thinking Black* (Boston: South End, 1989).

34. Ibid.

35. Laura L. Rahman, "Breaking Silences: Spelman College Student Protest," March 20, 2007, http://www.youtube.com/watch?v=iEQYqCtWVd8.

36. bell hooks, "Seduced by Violence No More," in *Outlaw Culture: Resisting Representations* (New York: Routledge, 1994).

37. Destiny's Child, vocal performance of "No, No, No, Part 1," by Calvin Gaines, Mary Brown, Rob Fusari, Vincent Herbert, Barry White, in *No, No, No, Part 1* single recorded and released 1997, Sony, compact disc.

38. Monica A. Coleman, *The Dinah Project: A Handbook for Congregational Response to Sexual Violence* (Cleveland: Pilgrim, 2004).

6

# It's Deeper Than Rap

## *Hip Hop, the South, and Abrahamic Masculinity*

**Ronald B. Neal**

> *Music has been and continues to be the most significant creative art expression of African Americans. Blacks sing song and play music (in their churches and at their juke parties) as a way of coping with life's contradictions and of celebrating its triumphs) . . . Singing is the medium through which we talk to each other and make known our perspectives on life and the world . . . Today a new form of musical discourse has emerged in the black community called "rap" music. It is a musical talk, extremely popular among young people who are searching for meaning in a world that has no place for them.*
>
> –James H. Cone, *The Spirituals and the Blues*, 1991[1]

> *People presume that because I'm a feminist thinker they know that I'm gonna trash rap, especially gangsta rap. I can challenge the sexism and misogyny of it, but I can embrace the rage that is implicit in it and*

> *the sense of powerlessness that undergirds it.*
>
> –BELL HOOKS, *BOMB MAGAZINE*, 1994[2]

The title of this essay is taken from the title of a recent rap album *Deeper Than Rap* by Miami-based rapper Rick Ross.[3] Rick Ross is a rapper whose music narrates a precarious, complicated, ridiculed, and despised condition that exists among too many black males in the United States. With stories of drug dealing, gun play, sex, death, and intoxication, Rick Ross, like many rappers before him, claim that his music is the stuff of fact and not fiction, that his music is based on real-world lived experience. According to Ross, in order to understand his music one must go behind the music. One must probe the circumstances and human conditions, blasphemous human conditions, that fuel the language of "money, ho's, and clothes." Like most black male rappers who give such a rationale for their craft, Rick Ross's lyrics and his very character are subject to endless condemnation and rebuke. Charges of misogyny, female exploitation, homophobia, and overall youthful corruption single out Ross and other young black males, especially those who have come of age with hip hop as their soundtrack, as the most woman-hating, gay-bashing, and dangerous population in America. To be very dramatic, one can easily assent to some feminist, queer, and most conservative critiques of young black males and conclude that black males are not simply the perpetrators of sexism, homophobia, and misogyny in America but that black males are the very creators of sexism, misogyny, and homophobia in America.[4]

In light of such criticism, what I seek to do is complicate gender analysis. My aim is to engage and go beyond rap music and the way it has come to represent masculinity through hip hop. By going deeper than rap, I wish to add more material and more flavor to the way in which race, masculinity/gender, and religion are engaged. In the long scheme of things, I wish to disrupt all forms of gendered thinking that casts black males in categorical terms, especially those modes of gendered thought that cast black males in categorically demonic terms. This disruption calls for a thorough reexamination of gender and masculinity, black masculinity in particular, in the American context. This examination calls for an analysis of masculinity as it has been construed historically in the United States. Because gender does not exist in a historical vacuum, it is necessary to probe the historical contexts and historical experiences that have contributed to the construction of gender and masculinity, especially where black males are concerned.

## The Historical and Global Legacy of Abrahamic Masculinity

The form of masculinity that young black males are chided for exuding is a kind of masculinity that cuts across race, class, and ethnicity. Asian males, Latino males, Irish males, Middle Eastern males, Indian males, Italian males, and males from ethnic groups with roots in Europe, all in some way or another display sexist, misogynistic, violent, and homophobic tendencies and behavior. Because feminism has made limited forays into most of these cultures, our knowledge of the depths of sexism, misogyny, and homophobia within these groups in the United States and beyond is very limited. Every ethnic group in this country, especially those groups that have immigrant roots, have been shaped by religious and cultural traditions that extol the dominance of men over women. This is especially true for those groups whose religious and cultural heritages are Protestant, Catholic, Jewish, and Islamic. Although Protestantism, Catholicism, Judaism, and Islam are diverse in how they are expressed among these immigrant populations, they all share a common masculine origin. The dominant form of masculinity that unites these traditions and unites all men regardless of race, class, and ethnicity is Abrahamic masculinity.[5]

The Ancient Near Eastern legend of Abraham is the pillar and ideal form of dominant masculinity that governs the world and American society, including black communities. The global power of Christianity, Judaism, and Islam is indicative of the extent to which Abrahamic masculinity pervades the world. What is more, our current global conflicts involving each of these traditions—for example, conflicts involving Christians and Jews, conflicts involving Christians and Muslims, and conflicts involving Christians and Christians (Catholics and Protestants and Protestants and Protestants)—all point to the masculine ideal evidenced in the legend of Abraham. All of these traditions extol the virtues of Abrahamic masculinity. The most pronounced picture of such virtue is found in the Hebrew Bible (commonly referred to as the Old Testament). In the book of Genesis, especially chapters 12–22, there is a picture of a dominant male, a male who is selected and chosen, for religious purposes, to be a founder of the nation of Israel. In the Hebrew Bible, he is portrayed as a property owner whose possessions include land and slaves. He is portrayed as a husband and father whose relations with women and children are paternalistic and benevolent in orientation. Being surrounded by slaves, a subordinate wife, and a subordinate male relative, Abraham displays an exalted level of masculinity and social status that is legitimated and ordained by Yahweh, the deity who is the dominant character in the text. Through Abraham, a tradition of patriarchy is established that is extended through his male progeny. Ultimately, this Abrahamic masculinity will develop, expand, and lead to a full-blown empire, an empire that entails a succession of kings whose powers and authority are legitimated on theological grounds. Empire is the ultimate end of Abrahamic masculinity.

Over the last generation, feminist and womanist biblical scholars have pointed to the subordinating and oppressive quality of Abrahamic masculinity. They have pointed to the manner in which it perpetuates and legitimates inequality between men and women.[6] They have also pointed to the manner in which it thwarts the emotional lives and psychological development of children. However, Abrahamic masculinity continues to represent a dominant masculine ideal that continues to inform American society, including black communities. Historically, African American males have been judged by this religious standard of masculinity. This religious standard of masculinity, which has secular expressions, has informed the male identities of too many males. Males who do not exude or embrace the virtues that have been established by this dominant ideal of masculinity are often viewed in pathological terms. They are perceived as inferior, immoral, and criminal. Males who are not property owners, males who do not actively pursue marriage and procreation, males who are not in dominant relationships with women, children, and other males, and males who do not engage in projects of nation building are viewed as toxins, lethal viruses, and cancers that ruin the fabric of civilization.

## Black America and the Abrahamic Ideal

The Abrahamic ideal finds it greatest expression in popular expressions of religion and popular culture. The most visible representatives of religion in black communities are bishops, pastors, and ministers in general. These leaders extol, through sermons, media, and masculinity movements, the Abrahamic masculine ideal and chastise males who reject or have not attained this ideal.[7] At the very end of the twentieth century, during the mid- to late-1990s, the depths of Abrahamic masculinity as a normative male ideal were publicly expressed in profound ways. Nearly three decades after the emergence of second wave feminism and nearly a decade after the emergence of womanism, a variety of men's movements with Islamic and Christian instigators emerged from black communities. These movements paralleled and occurred simultaneously with the men's movements that emerged from predominately white evangelical institutions. The Million Man March led by Nation of Islam leader Louis Farrakhan, the Promise Keepers movement in 1995, and the Manpower movement in 1999, led by famed Pentecostal minister T. D. Jakes, gave expression to the supremacy of the Abrahamic ideal. From these efforts the most visible movement was that associated with the Million Man March.[8] The Million Man March symbolized the depths of Abrahamic masculinity in America, particularly among African Americans. The Million Man March was extraordinarily successful in communicating the Abrahamic ideal and in conveying the notion that the plight of black males was due to their failure and inability to live up to it. It communicated a pathological view of black males that was consistent with the longstanding views of black males held by white males, powerful white males in particular, whose masculine identities are informed by the Abrahamic ideal. What is more, the efforts of Farrakhan were, in an ironic and strange fashion, applauded by white males who publicly criticized him as being a racist black man. Notwithstanding such criticism, powerful Reaganite white males such as William Bennett, Pat Buchanan, and Rush Limbaugh supported the Million Man March.[9]

The Million Man March attracted black males from all income levels, ages, religious communities, lifestyles, ideological perspectives, and social status. It tapped into a sense of desperation and a real and deep condition pertaining to the status of black males as a population. This sense of desperation and concern was so deep that it gained the support of black males who were at odds, fundamentally, with Farrakhan's masculine vision.[10] At the time of the March, the leadership establishment within black America, including the most influential black intellectuals, was seemingly impotent toward addressing this ideal and indifferent to this pervasive masculine condition. At the level of ideas and action, the impotence of the black establishment produced an ethical vacuum that opened a door for traditional and anti-progressive leadership, especially where the conditions of black males were concerned. The Million Man March presented an option in the face of limited options that spoke to something deep and pervasive. Yet it exalted a masculine ideal that did more to demonize black males than offer a transcendent vision that would speak to the real and immoral conditions in which too many black males find themselves. What is more, the Million Man March distorted the diverse masculine identities and lifestyles that exist among black males, identities and lifestyles that are often unexamined and are hidden behind hurricanes and tsunamis of stereotypes that are associated with black males.

The Million Man March was unprecedented in its efforts to address the gender-specific condition of black males in America. However, it produced no visible and long-term project with the aim of transforming the lives of black males. Its greatest effect was the extent to which it communicated the need for black males to "man up." It echoed a masculine sentiment, rooted in Abrahamic masculinity, that has been around for thousands of years. The Million Man March symbolized the extent to which the Abrahamic ideal is institutionalized in the world, America, and black America. Since the Million Man March, no rival men's movement or rival form of masculinity has emerged to overcome or offset the Abrahamic ideal and its public and pervasive import. The Abrahamic ideal remains a virtue, practice, and hope that is communicated by religious institutions, families, and men and women, across black America.

## Engaging Abrahamic Masculinity

Given the institutionalized nature and ongoing popularity of the Abrahamic ideal and its distorting effects and its impact on the lives of black males and black females, there is a need for a thorough reexamination of its continuing popularity in the world, especially among African Americans. Because feminism and womanism have been limited in impacting gender relations among African Americans, there is a need for different angles of vision and different strategies for engaging and understanding gender among African Americans, especially black males. Because Abrahamic masculinity does not exist in a historical vacuum, there is a need to engage the religious, historical, and culturally specific ways in which this ideal has expressed itself and continues to express itself.

As I indicated at the outset of this paper, Abrahamic masculinity pervades Judaism, Christianity, and Islam. However, it expresses itself in culturally specific ways. The culturally specific manifestations of Abrahamic masculinity are historically conditioned. What is more, there are regions and contexts of history and culture where this deeply religious ideal is institutionalized and extolled. One region and context where Abrahamic masculinity is highly pronounced is the American South. Because of its deep association with Abrahamic religion, especially Christian fundamentalism and revivalistic evangelical Protestantism, the American South is an ideal site for such an investigation.[11] Also, because African American cultures have been deeply shaped by southern legacies such as slavery, Jim Crow, and the Great Migrations, an engagement with race, gender, and religion is illuminated by a southern reading. For the most part, the South is an underexamined region where race, gender, and sexuality are concerned. Consequently, most African Americans as well as most Americans are unaware of the extent to which notions surrounding masculinity, gender roles, and sexuality have been culturally conditioned by southern expressions of Abrahamic masculinity. Ironically, the most sophisticated religious thinkers and cultural and gender theorists have been women, black feminists, and womanists, with southern roots. Alice Walker, Angela Davis, Delores S. Williams, Jacquelyn Grant, bell hooks, Beverly Guy Sheftall, and Katie G. Cannon are among these black feminists and womanists with southern roots; understandably, the South has conditioned their critiques of masculinity and their visions of gender relations among African Americans. In one form or another, the South appears in their work.[12] However, with the exception of Alice Walker, bell hooks, Delores S. Williams, and Angela Davis, the South and its impact on gender identity among African Americans has been treated in very modest ways. Each of these thinkers has engaged the history of slavery and Jim Crow and their influence on gender identity and socialization. However, despite their significant efforts the South remains an open region as far as understanding and overcoming the legacy of Abrahamic masculinity. For the most part, the regional and historically conditioned legacy of Abrahamic masculinity demands greater scrutiny and theoretical understanding.

## Black Males, Masculinity, and the South

Although the South has played a role in the gender assessments of feminists and womanists, it has gone virtually unexamined in similar assessments among male scholars. More than black women scholars, black male scholars have made less than modest forays into, and assessments of, Abrahamic masculinity. This may be attributed to, in part, the influence of such masculinity on the work of black male scholars. The most visible and influential example of this neglect of masculine dominance is in the work of James H. Cone. His pioneering legacy as a black liberation theologian both embodies and engages the legacy of Abrahamic masculinity. Cone's work speaks volumes about the historical and regional significance of Abrahamic masculinity. As a black man who was born and raised in the South (Bearden, Arkansas), Cone pioneered and articulated a theological vision that was deeply rooted in Abrahamic masculinity.[13] This is particularly true with regard to its early stages of development. His first book, *Black Theology and Black Power*, is a masculine theological manifesto, a manifesto of a southern black man that challenges and protests the Abrahamic masculinity of white males. Abrahamic masculinity stood front and center when James H. Cone wrote *Black Theology and Black Power*, and it informed his other work, including *The Spirituals and the Blues*, which I quote at the outset of this paper. Overall, Cone has spent his entire career in a political and professional contest with Abrahamic masculinity, and his work is an important religious and theological resource for understanding and engaging it.

At the level of race, class, gender, sexuality, and religion, the exclusion or omission of the American South as a site of investigation has not been lost on a minority of gender and cultural theorists.[14] As one of the most influential and popular gender and cultural theorists in America, bell hooks has consistently engaged the American South and its relation to race, class, gender, and sexuality in America. Her prolific and ongoing body of work articulates the omissions, marginality, and criticism that are offered here. For at least twenty years, hooks has engaged in a critique of second wave feminism, white male and black male patriarchy, patriarchy among women, and American capitalism, which is connected in profound ways to the American South. By her own admission, her experience as a black woman born and raised in the South and as a child of working-class black people in Kentucky has informed her work as a feminist and cultural theorist. From her groundbreaking 1980 black feminist text, *Ain't I a Woman: Black Women and Feminism*, to her most recent work, *Belonging: A Culture of Place*, the American South has been an integral part of her engagement with race, class, gender, and sexuality.[15] At the level of the personal, political, and theoretical, the work and influence of hooks is instructive in examining the historical and regional construction of gender, especially masculinity.

Hooks's work on gender, especially her protests against patriarchy, has been a serious engagement with black men. Black men with southern roots have stood out in her work. Her experiences with black men, blood kin, and significant others have informed her outlook and work on gender. From her grandfather, to her father, brother, and significant male others, southern black men have conditioned how she views masculinity.[16] In many ways, hooks's experience with southern black men is symbolic of countless black women and men, across classes, generations, and regions, whose lives have been impacted by black males with southern roots. Given the weight of this influence, any engagement with masculinity and black males demands that such roots be attended to. Engaging Abrahamic masculinity means engaging the southern roots of black masculinity. This means linking the connections between Abrahamic religion, the South, masculinity, and black males. It also means attending to the migratory aspects of masculinity, the migration of black males from the South to spaces beyond the American South. These spaces include the American Northeast, the Midwest, and the West Coast. Making connections between Abrahamic masculinity and the southern roots of masculinity is instructive for the next generation and next wave of gender studies and gendered visions of transcendence. Such connections are also instructive for engaging hip hop.

## Hip Hop, the South, and Abrahamic Masculinity

Hip hop is a secular expression of Abrahamic masculinity. As a secular expression of Abrahamic masculinity, it embodies the fascination with power, status, and wealth inscribed by the Abrahamic ideal. In addition to power, status, and wealth, it embodies and extols those aspects of Abrahamic masculinity that are destructive and negative. The most destructive and negative forms of hip hop, especially those that are explicitly violent and misogynistic, can be understood and engaged through an examination of Abrahamic masculinity in the South. There are very real connections between the history of Abrahamic masculinity in the South and the violence and misogyny evident in a lot of hip hop. There is a southern history of militarism, terrorism, and gendered violence connected to Abrahamic masculinity that stands as a backdrop to the masculine violence and gang activity that now plagues America and is vocalized through rap songs.[17] In many parts of the United States, masculinity, as it is expressed through gang activity, is increasing as an ethical and public problem. From Compton, California to the Carolinas, there are disturbing connections between gang activity and the paramilitary violence of the Ku Klux Klan.

The Ku Klux Klan was born out of the bosom of Abrahamic masculinity. As a product of Abrahamic masculinity, it perpetuated an American and southern tradition of war, a tradition that is evident in much of the language of hip hop. From the end of Reconstruction to the end of Jim Crow, the Ku Klux Klan functioned as a military and terrorist organization. The founders of the Klan were the children of Confederate soldiers. These were men who believed that their fathers were emasculated by war and took it upon themselves to avenge their fathers and regain their lost masculine status and power. Black communities were the primary targets of their vengeance. Decades after the Civil War, black communities were held under siege due to Klan activity. Violence was the chief means by which these southern white males exerted their masculinity and control over black communities. The lawlessness of the Klan and its impact on the South negatively affected the gender identities of black males and black females. Gratuitous acts of southern violence, including misogynistic violence, emasculated black males and exploited the sexuality of black females. This genealogical link between the Abrahamic masculinity of Klansmen and the destructive masculinity associated with gang activity is illuminating when considering the negative effects such masculinity has on women, children, and other males. What separates the history of the Ku Klux Klan and the masculinity of gangs is that for most of its history, the Ku Klux Klan went unprosecuted and unpunished. Up until the civil rights era, the Ku Klux Klan lived above the law. By contrast, the overwhelming legal consequence of gang masculinity among blacks is incarceration and/or death.

The connections between Abrahamic masculinity, the South, and hip hop were made visible in a recent motion picture, a film that depicted the criminal exploits of a black man with southern roots. In 2007, Denzel Washington portrayed a mythical Harlem drug dealer in the motion picture, *American Gangster.*[18] *American Gangster* was a crime film that was loosely based on the life and criminal exploits of Frank Lucas, a Harlem drug lord who was born in 1930 in LaGrange, North Carolina.[19] Frank Lucas was a drug kingpin who controlled and operated a heroin organization during the Vietnam era. His organization consisted of young black males, new immigrants from the South. They were known as the Country Boys, a label given to them because of their thick and distinct southern accents. In the film, Lucas is portrayed as a southern patriarch who is both benevolent and violent. He is surrounded by loyal and devoted family members, including his mother, whom he imports from North Carolina to Harlem. As a benevolent patriarch, he ensures that everyone, especially his family, is provided for. He protects his empire and maintains order through ritual acts of violence. Overall, he exudes all of the qualities of Abrahamic masculinity. What is more, this Abrahamic masculinity is a powerful and seductive force that captures the imaginations of young males, especially his young family members. In the film, Atlanta rapper T.I. plays Steve, one of Lucas's impressionable young nephews. Steve is a talented baseball player. Steve's father is portrayed by Common, a Chicago rapper. His father makes Lucas aware of Steve's talents as a baseball player. Lucas is impressed, and he uses his many connections and arranges a tryout for his nephew with the New York Yankees. In a very telling scene where Steve is alone with Lucas, Lucas inquires about his tryout with the Yankees. Steve responds to Lucas by saying that he is not interested in playing baseball. "I don't want to play baseball," he says. "I want to be like you, Uncle Frank." This scene between Lucas and his nephew captures the seductive and powerful nature of the Abrahamic ideal.[20]

Frank Lucas became the first of at least two generations of black males whose lives would be permanently damaged or destroyed by narcotics traffic in America.[21] It was during the Vietnam era that then-president Richard M. Nixon launched an unprecedented war on drugs, a war whose punitive effects echo into the present, reaping devastation all over the United States. Frank Lucas was the first of two generations of black males who would be prosecuted and receive lengthy prison sentences for their participation in the drug trade. However, unlike many black males who have participated in narcotics traffic since the Vietnam era, Lucas escaped the fate of indefinite incarceration and death. Today, at eighty years of age, Frank Lucas is a sociological anomaly, a former drug kingpin who has survived the most destructive effects of the underground economy, the American criminal justice system, and Abrahamic ideal of masculinity. In interviews since the release of *American Gangster*, he has expressed no regret and no remorse for the role he played in the narcotics trade in Harlem and as an instigator of drug-related violent crime during the 1970s.[22] He justifies his actions by pointing to the poverty and racial violence that he experienced and witnessed as a young man in North Carolina. When talking about his forays into lawlessness and gangster life, he points to traumatizing life events such as witnessing a male relative being killed at close range by a white man with a shotgun. He further points to his limited education (Lucas is functionally illiterate) and the limited opportunities afforded to many black males from his generation. In his words, "Nobody gave me nothing. I had nothing. I came from nothing. I had no education. I did what I had to do." The kinds of sentiments that Lucas expresses can be heard on countless rap songs, by young black males who could very well be his sons and grandsons. Although Lucas was a member of the blues generation and not the hip hop generation, his sentiments are very hip hop. What is more, stories like that of Frank Lucas have driven, and continue to drive, much of the production of hip hop today.

## Reflection, Hope, and Transformation

In light of the masculine concerns outlined in this paper, concerns related to hip hop, masculinity, and religion, I wish to initiate a new philosophical, religious, and ethical enterprise. As I indicated at the outset of this paper, Abrahamic masculinity is an underexamined historical, cultural, and religious phenomenon. The way it expresses itself through hip hop is just one manifestation of this dominant form of masculinity. What I wish to do is engage in a reflective and analytical enterprise whose goal is to influence black males, how masculinity is perceived, and those who are affected by the masculine conditions in which black males are currently trapped. In light of the concerns of this paper—the masculine conditions of black males and the struggles of African Americans in America—a critical and constructive apparatus is necessary if new masculine possibilities are to emerge within and among the black male population. For this reason, it is necessary to treat masculinity and gender comprehensively and to attend to their specific contexts. To this end, I align this work with thinkers like bell hooks and with social and gender theorist Patricia Hill Collins, whose recent theoretical work is akin to work that I seek to do. In *Black Sexual Politics: African Americans and the New Racism*, Collins revisits and reconsiders the gendered impact and legacy of slavery, Jim Crow, and the Great Migrations.[23] It is a twenty-first-century reevaluation of gender that is informed by the Desegregation era, more than three decades of social change since the 1960s. In this work, Collins discloses the links between the past and the present. As a social and gender theorist, Collins takes seriously the role that history plays in influencing the constructions of race, class, gender, and sexuality in the United States. She treats the past as a necessary component for explicating and engaging the construction of race, class, gender, and sexuality today. Similar to bell hooks, her work is very important for understanding and engaging the historical and gender-specific conditions that affect black males and females in the United States. *Black Sexual Politics* is primarily an analytical work concerned with explicating and untangling the past and present complexities that attend the construction of gender in the United States, and a model for the kind of analytical work I'm proposing here. It is fundamentally a reconstructed analysis of American history and its relationship to race, class, gender, and sexuality. I wish to build upon this work by adding a religious and a philosophical dimension to it. In the end, what I hope to do with this work is open up new space for how masculinity and gender are understood and engaged. Overall, this enterprise seeks to instigate new possibilities for transformation at the level of masculinity and gender.

## Notes

1. James Cone, *The Spirituals and the Blues* (Maryknoll, NY: Orbis, 1991), 129.

2. Lawrence Chua, "bell hooks," *BOMB Magazine* 48 (Summer 1994): 8.

3. Rick Ross, *Deeper Than Rap*, executive producers Rick Ross, Ted Lucas, and Kali Khaled, released 2009, Def Jam, compact disc.

4. See, for example, Kimberle Crenshaw, "Beyond Racism and Misogyny: Black Feminism and the 2 Live Crew," *Boston Review* 16 (December 1991), http://bostonreview.net/BR16.6/crenshaw.html; T. Denean Sharpley Whiting's *Pimp's Up and Ho's Down: Hip Hop's Hold on Young Black Women* (New York: New York University Press, 2007); Juan Williams's *Enough* (New York: Three Rivers, 2006); and Johnnetta Betsch Cole's "What Hip Hop Has Done to Black Women," *Ebony Magazine* 62, no. 5 (March 2007): 90–96.

5. For accounts of the historical and moral connections between Judaism, Christianity, and Islam see Karen Armstrong, *A History of God: The 4,000 Year Quest of Judaism, Christianity, and Islam* (New York: Random House, 1993); J. Maxwell Miller and John H. Hayes, *A History of Ancient Israel and Judah* (Philadelphia: Westminster, 1986).

6. See Renita J. Weems, "Reading Her Way through the Struggle: African American Women and the Bible," in *Stony the Road We Trod: African American Biblical Interpretation* (Minneapolis: Fortress Press, 1991), 57–80; and Alice L. Laffey, *An Introduction to the Old Testament: A Feminist Perspective* (Philadelphia: Fortress Press, 1988).

7. For excellent accounts of media representations of popular religion, including its masculine dimensions, see Shayne Lee, *America's New Preacher: T. D. Jakes* (New York: New York University Press, 2005); Jonathan L. Walton, *Watch This: The Ethics and Aesthetics of Black Televangelism* (New York: New York University Press, 2009); and Milmon F. Harrison, *Righteous Riches: The Word of Faith Movement in Contemporary African American Religion* (New York: Oxford University Press, 2006).

8. See Garth Kasimu Fletcher, ed., *Black Religion after the Million Man March* (Maryknoll, NY: Orbis Books, 1998); Sara Diamond, *Not by Politics Alone: The Enduring Influence of the Christian Right* (New York: Guilford, 1998); Ron Stodghill II, "God of Our Fathers," *Time Magazine*, October 6, 1997, 34–40.

9. The extent to which Farrakhan's vision and leadership was consistent with the social and political views of Reaganite white males, see Manning Marable, "Louis Farrakhan and the Million Man March," in *Speaking Truth to Power: Essays on Race, Religion, and Radicalism* (Boulder, CO: Westview, 1998), 139–48.

10. See Michael Eric Dyson, *Race Rules: Navigating the Rule of the Color Line* (New York: Addison-Wesley, 1996), 150–95.

11. See H. Richard Niebuhr, *The Kingdom of God in America* (Middletown, CT: Wesleyan University Press, 1989); Mark A. Noll, *The Rise of Evangelicalism: The Age of Edwards, Whitefield, and the Wesleys* (Downers Grove, IL: InterVarsity, 2004); and James Davidson Hunter, *Evangelicalism: The Coming Generation* (Chicago: University of Chicago Press, 1987).

12. See Alice Walker, *In Search of Our Mothers' Gardens: Womanist Prose* (New York: Harper, 1983); bell hooks, *Ain't I a Woman: Black Women and Feminism* (Boston: South End, 1981); Jacquelyn Grant, *White Woman's Christ, Black Woman's Jesus: Feminist Christology and Womanist Response* (Atlanta: Scholars Press, 1989); Katie G. Cannon, *Black Womanist Ethics* (Atlanta: Scholars Press, 1988); Delores S. Williams, *Sisters in the Wilderness: The Challenge of Womanist God-Talk* (Maryknoll, NY: Orbis Books, 1993); and Angela Y. Davis, *Blues Legacies and Black Feminism* (New York: Vintage Books, 1998).

13. See James H. Cone, *My Soul Looks Back* (Maryknoll, NY: Orbis, 1986); James H. Cone, *Black Theology and Black Power* (1969; reprint, San Francisco: HarperCollins, 1989); James H. Cone, *The Spirituals and the Blues* (1972; reprint, Maryknoll, NY: Orbis Books, 1992).

14. There is now a new and growing body of literature, "New Southern Studies," which is now taking on the concerns expressed in this paper. Much of this new literature has been influenced by second wave feminism and cultural studies. The writings of black feminists and black male scholars with roots in the American South, along with scholars of various backgrounds who are sensitive to the southern context, are informing these new investigations. Much of this work is being done by historians and literary critics. See Houston A. Baker Jr., *Turning South Again: Re-thinking Modernism/Re-reading Booker T* (Durham, NC: Duke University Press, 2001); Craig Thompson Friend, ed., *Southern Masculinity: Perspectives on Manhood in the South Since Reconstruction* (Athens: University of Georgia Press, 2009); and Riche Richardson, *Black Masculinity and the U.S. South: From Uncle Tom to Gangsta* (Athens: University of Georgia Press, 2007).

15. Both bell hooks, *Ain't I a Woman: Black Women and Feminism* (Boston: South End, 1981) and bell hooks, *Belonging: A Culture of Place* (New York: Routledge, 2009) are texts that embody the enormous influence that the South holds in hooks's career-long engagement with gender and culture in the United States.

16. Hooks's outlook on masculinity and its connection to her personal relations with black males with southern roots are articulated in bell hooks, *We Real Cool: Black Men and Masculinity* (New York: Routledge, 2004).

17. For accounts of masculine violence in the history of the South see Stephen Kantrowitz, *Ben Tillman and the Reconstruction of White Supremacy* (Chapel Hill: University of North Carolina Press, 2000); David R. Goldfield, *Still Fighting the Civil War: The American South and Southern History* (Baton Rouge: Louisiana State University Press, 2002); and Craig Thompson Friend, ed., *Southern Masculinity*. Also see the autobiography of Richard Wright, *Black Boy* (1945; reprint, New York: Perennial Classics/HarperCollins, 1993).

18. Mark Jacobson and Steven Zaillian, "American Gangster," directed by Ridley Scott (2007; Universal City, Universal Studios).

19. The story of Frank Lucas was popularized by New York journalists. His story circulated for years before becoming the subject of a major motion picture. One of the influential journalistic stories written detailing the myth and exploits of Frank Lucas is Mark Jacobson, "The Return of the Superfly," *New York Magazine* 33, no. 13 (August 14, 2000): 36–45.

20. This story becomes lyrical fodder for rapper Jay-Z, who was commissioned to write one of the soundtracks that accompanied the movie, *American Gangster*. Jay-Z, *American Gangster*, produced by Shawn Carter, released 2007, ROC-A-FELLA Records/Island Def Jam Music Group, compact disc.

21. See Manning Marable, "Facing the Demon Head On: Race and the Prison Industrial Complex," *The Great Wells of Democracy: The Meaning of Race in American Life* (New York: Basic Civitas Books, 2002), 147–64; Ellis Cose, "The Prison Paradox," *Newsweek Magazine* 136, no. 20 (November 13, 2000): 40–49.

22. See "The Making of American Gangster," interviews and behind-the-scenes footage related to the film, *American Gangster* (Universal City, CA: Universal Studios, 2008). Also see Mark Jacobson, "Lords of Dopetown," *New York Magazine* 40, no. 39 (November 5, 2007): 66–68, 70.

23. Patricia Hill Collins, *Black Sexual Politics: African Americans, Gender, and the New Racism* (New York: Routledge, 2004).

# PART III

# Gender and Sexuality

# 7

# "I Am a Nappy-Headed Ho"

## *(Re)Signifying "Deviance" in the Haraam of Religious Respectability"*

**Monica R. Miller**

### Introduction

On June 9th, 2007, the NAACP, along with countless religious and political leaders in the black community, gathered together to symbolically "bury" the "N" word. This seemed to be a logical move, according to many, in the media-flurry and upset over the now-famous "nappy-headed ho" statement made by radio host Don Imus on April 4th, 2007.[1] I invoke this particular historical moment and these symbolic acts as moments that give shape to the manner in which, I believe, a "politics of respectability" has been endemic not only within black religious institutions, but also within the wider black publics in general. In *Righteous Discontent: The Women's Movement in the Black Baptist Church, 1880–1920*, Evelyn Brooks Higginbotham writes that many Baptist women put much emphasis on respectable behavior in their attempt to transgress pathological representations of black people. Higginbotham refers to this strategy as a "highly self-conscious concession to hegemonic values in their attempt to approve and reinforce their sense of moral superiority over whites."[2] While the politics of respectability was a social strategy to counter white supremacist constructions of black people, it invariably placed emphasis on "conservative Victorian values of temperance, sexual purity and cleanliness." These values are significant because they are the dominant constructs often employed by the black middle class to effectively police the behavior of their economically marginalized counterparts.

There is a precariousness by which this politics of respectability both emerges and constrains possibilities of embracing "difference" in general. I use the rubric *difference*[3] as explicated and deployed in and through the work of Jacques Derrida. Understood in this way, *difference* represents an alterity, a uniqueness, or in his words, a "distinction," "inequality," or "discernibility" and so on. And yet, according to Derrida, the rubric *difference* is also something that is postponed, or deferred. Taken from the verb "to differ"—*difference* represents what Derrida calls "the possible that is presently impossible." In this essay more specifically, I play with the domain of *difference* to connote both a problematic *and* a possibility. It is an idea that is used to constrain when deployed from within a normative stance, and yet, something that remains a possibility of our postmodern condition.[4]

The concept of "difference" can cause moral panic, or exaggerated fear and anxiety. Religious discourse is not let out or precluded from being a part of the fear and anxiety. Religious discourse adds to the anxiety through its single-mindedness and its emphasis on respectability. As a result, morality is held as sacred, and thus stands as a wall of conformity stifling expressions of *difference*.

## The Argument: Beginning with Difference

Using the trope *difference* as a point of departure into the *haraam* of respectability—this essay attempts to destabilize the discursively constructed positionality of "respectability" that inhabits the *haraam* of our religious musings. Methodologically, a "missionary-style" sexual position lodged between "this" and "that"—and "them" and "us"—has seemingly ignored expressions of *difference* and privileged "respectable" bodies of "sameness," ultimately suppressing "deviance" and rendering the plurality of lived lives among black women *monogamous* in meaning.

The argument of this essay unfolds by first turning to formative interdisciplinary literature on material culture of "difference." Then building off of this work, I turn toward the Don Imus controversy, as an empirical public case study. I then attempt to turn out the [discursive] *haraam* [of religious discourse] by reclaiming the "deviant" material existence of the "nappy-headed ho"—a "subaltern" that "cannot speak." I make use of this cultural typology as a textual story whose "deviance" acts as a sort of prophylaxis in "turning out" the *haraam*, making wet those dry crevices of thought that constrain im/possibilities of communal reclamation.

The use of "discursive *haraam*" is a play on the Arabic word *Haraam*—that which is "forbidden" not only within the actual spaces of normativity in general, but equally so within discourse itself. In Islam, the term is often used to describe that which may be prohibited by the religious text or Allah. This essay does not seek to take a particular stance on the religious inheritance of the word; rather, I simply use it as a way to provoke the connections between ideas of forbiddances and religiosity as such. In other words, the "*haraam*" is in and of itself an intellectual production that retains a particular kind of ideological positionality of respectability, therefore constraining *difference* through categorical marginalization and the use of "deviance management."

By privileging the materiality of "deviant" bodies, I want to resignify *difference* by lubricating the interstices of religious discourse—queering the flawed internal logic of identity policing by privileging the materiality of "deviant" bodies. I put respectable black religiosity to bed with the profane in a sexually unprotected and conceptually unrestricted way that embraces "*difference*."

## Material Culture of Difference

A turn toward the resignificatory power of material culture provides a moment to make wet the dry arid walls of discourse—accomplished by reclaiming the "risky" ontology of those that stand on the outside of dominant respectability. This reclaiming offers a materialist moment of embracing the alterity of *difference*; a moment to reposition the moral positionality often supported in and through and given purchase by, the rhetorics of religion and theology. As the late political philosopher Iris Marion-Young's work reminds us, "Only changing the cultural habits themselves will change the oppression they produce and reinforce, but change in cultural habits can occur only if individuals become aware of and change their individual habits. This is a cultural revolution."[5]

This process of "turning-out" or "making-wet" a dry, rigid discursive *haraam* necessitates a rethinking and redoing of normativity writ large by embracing what political scientist Cathy Cohen calls "oppositional practices." In her article "Deviance as Resistance: A New Research Agenda for the Study of Black Politics," Cohen challenges a black queer political agenda to highlight and privilege the experience of those "who through their acts of non-conformity choose outsider status . . . in considering the resistant potential of intentional (although limited) 'oppositional practices.'"[6] In a similar sense, in "Punks, Bulldaggers, and Welfare Queens: The Radical Potential of Queer Politics?" Cohen continues the push for a "de-centered identity" by incorporating queer theory as a framework in which heteronormativity is identified as a system of regulation and normalization, one that embraces a sexuality that can "reject the idea of static, monolithic, bounded categories, on the one hand, and political practices structured around binary conceptions of sexuality and power, on the other."[7]

Cohen's project of mapping queer lenses onto the political constructions of dominant sexuality makes room for expanding varieties of sexual expression. Thus sexual *difference* transgresses the stable categories of sexuality, allowing for a political project in which *difference*, broadly construed, incorporates *all* the bodies and practices that stand on the *margins* of "normative" sexuality; a normativity that polices the "nonconforming" sexual expressions of many. While Cohen provides a theoretical mode of envisioning embracing "deviance," let's consider a less-considered subject position, the ontological reality of the "nappy-headed ho."

## Don Imus and Nappy-Headed Ho's: A Public Lens

What's ethically "risky" about the nappy-headed ho? The infamous "nappy-headed ho" statement caused outrage and cries of racism within and among the black community—amidst the unrest and anger on behalf of blacks, there was a troubling way in which the black community missed a powerful moment of resignification. Rather than embracing the "nappy-headed ho," she became the deviant subjectivity denied over and against more respectable black bodies. In the historical lineage of mammies, jezebels, and welfare queens, there the nappy-headed ho narrowly served as a reminder of a racially unjust past—rather than an opportunity by which to embrace the polysemy of representations of womanhood in the black community—deviant or not.

The morning of April 4th, 2007 was just another day of pissing people off for Don Imus. However, what was done on this day would ignite a domino effect of interesting events within the black community. According to Don Imus, the women on the Rutgers [all-female] basketball team [mostly women of color] were "rough looking"—"hardcore ho's." Referring to the team, Imus said, "That's some rough girls from Rutgers. Man, they got tattoos and—That's some nappy-headed ho's there. I'm gonna tell you that now, man, that's some—woo. And the girls from Tennessee, they all look cute, you know, so, like—kinda like—I don't know."[8] An apparently "gender-troubled" Imus crossed the line, and his scapegoat for rationalizing his use of "ho" would ultimately become—rap music. Despite the powerful and real history of white supremacist representations of black women in general—here the "nappy-headed ho" in part only existed within the linguistic rhetoric of Imus's parody. In other words, while the black community "heard" the sound of racism right away, they did not ask, what "qualifies" as a linguistic injury, and for whom? Not only through the racialization of the signifier "nappy"—but equally so by the ballplayers' nonconforming gendered performance and wild-nappy hair—perhaps not the most "feminine" of girls Imus has seen in his day. We know, as scholars have shown, that the effectiveness of racism unduly relies upon and comes in through other "articulated" categories such as gender and sexuality. Feminist theologian Laurel C. Schneider reminds us that these seemingly natural categories are in fact "co-constitutive." In other words, they arise, emerge, and are constructed in and through other socially constructed categories such as gender and race. Schneider writes about the ways in which white supremacy and ideologies of colonialism have been fundamentally interdependent upon these social categories as "biological." Schneider writes that "correlating race and sex or gender brings into question the natural status of all three categories, implying that they could be otherwise."[9] While racism was the primary charge against Imus—the overreliance on the narrative of race denied critical analysis of other pressing concerns, such as gender. In this sense, Cohen argues that

> [w]hile he called the Rutgers women "ho's," he could have just as easily called them "nappy-headed-bulldaggers" or dykes since the conversation between Imus and his underlings was as much about calling into question the sexual nonconformity of the players as much as it was about their gender presentation.[10]

Cohen's point is well taken—there was much more operating under Imus's signifiers than what the black community actually responded to. And while this may have been an *unintended effect* of black communal commentary and discourse on this issue, the reaction of the black community signified something equally pernicious to Imus's linguistic deployment. A close analysis of these events makes one question whether the black community seemed more outraged that Imus called the "wrong" group of girls nappy-headed ho's—rather than his deployment of the word at all. The ontological reality of the "nappy-headed ho" was never denied by the black community—rather, what was made clear by the progression of events is that she exists as "them"—not "us." She is separated from the respectable members of the black community by an ideological gulf of respectability and acquired capital. This gulf separated by respectability is made even more evident when Al Sharpton publically confronted Imus on April 9th, 2007, by bringing his daughter, a graduate of Temple University, on air saying, "This young lady just graduated . . . , went to Temple. She is not a nappy-headed ho, she's my daughter." Again, the materiality of the "nappy-headed ho" was *not* denied; rather, she was left without a cultural home, as such.

Thus Imus's "nappy-headed ho" tirade led to interesting assumptions, conclusions, and mobilizations on behalf of the black community. Imus argued that if the black communities were to pressure him regarding his usage of the word "ho"—then they must likewise deal with rappers who similarly use the word. With pressure mounting on the hip hop community, Oprah Winfrey dedicated two shows to discussing the "nappy-headed ho" comment by bringing seven Spelman students on air in addition to various members of the hip hop community to discuss "personal responsibility." In speaking with the seven Spelman students about whether or not any of them had been called a ho in the past, one remark in particular caught my ear. A student by the name Leona remarked, "I've heard a lot of rappers say that they are speaking about the 'hos from the street' and the ho's from their experience," going on to mention, "but they have to understand that men don't make distinctions between those ho's and us. When we go to a club they don't say, 'Let me see your school ID' and distinguish whether they're going to call us a ho or not."[11] Again, there is a particular kind of logic of cultural *difference* at work here.

And, the strangeness continued. From Oprah's Town Hall Meeting, the precariousness by which the black community responded to a perceived linguistic injury took full effect in the burial of the "N" word by religious leaders. Does "*difference*" need to be buried—or resurrected? It was said that if "ho" was an unacceptable and inflammatory word to be spoken and rapped about, then the word "nigger" also had to be taken head on. On Monday July 9th, 2007, hundreds of "mourners" gathered together in downtown Detroit to bury the "N" word—the symbolic and longstanding expression of racism in American society. Two horses dragged a pine box with a bouquet of black roses, finally laying the coffin to rest at a historically black cemetery, with a headstone. Detroit Mayor Kwame Kilpatrick said, "Today we're not just burying the N word, we're taking it out of our spirit . . . we gather burying all the things that go with the N word. We have to bury the 'pimps' and the 'ho's' that go with that. . . . Die, N word, and we don't want to see you 'round here no more.'"

The materiality of the "nappy-headed ho" became the deviant signifier by which respectable black women's bodies were used in comparison. Ho's ontologically exist "out there" in the world, not within the corporeality of educated black college women. While it comes as no surprise that *religious* leaders would come together to bury the symbolic remnants and signifiers of the strange, deviant, and outcast—again, I question if a symbolic burial also signaled something of a politics of respectability, I argue that the media spectacle manufactured within the black community is representative of a more deeply engrained ideological positionality of denying "*difference*." This denial can also be evident within black religious scholarship when broadly conceived. While the actions of the black community within the larger publics are played out in a public *haraam* of moralizing and personal responsibility—here, I now turn to the *unintended* quelling of *difference* in the discursive *haraam* of religious respectability.

## The [Discursive] *Haraam* of Religious Respectability and "*Difference*"

What is *difference*? Is it not a particular kind of economy made alive by and manufactured through perceived "differences" between the construction of simple binary oppositions? Is it not represented as the difference between signifier and the signified? We are ensconced in a world of difference. However, this acknowledgment is only half the battle won. I am pushing for a queer transformational consciousness that respects *difference*, for it is the *perceived* "*differences*" of our lives that remain the problem. On this point, Cohen writes:

> *[D]ifference* in and of itself—even the *difference* designated through named categories—is not the problem. Instead it is the power invested in certain identity categories and the idea that bounded categories are not to be transgressed that serve as the basis of domination and control. The reconceptualization not only of the content of identity categories but of the intersectional nature of identities themselves, must become part of our political practice.[12]

Beyond a nod of acknowledgment, more difficult becomes *how* to think and theorize this *difference* within a sea of epistemological sameness where the dominant methodological posture is one of diversity management, rather than embracing the *alterity* of *difference* in more general terms. This positionality of respectability rears its head, often unconsciously, through cultural imperialism—and becomes ever more apparent in the ways in which *difference* is often explicated and described through religious rhetorics of morality. In other words, by *reading* how religion is [discursively] deployed when theorizing *difference*, we can better grasp and understand the ways in which our ideas, concepts, and taxonomies of religion become, in part, a way to authenticate and authorize a particular moral rendering of *difference*, as such. In other words, how are efforts to rethink *difference* constrained both theoretically and methodologically by various uses of religion and theology—oftentimes as a hegemonic signifier policing the boundaries and margins of "deviant" practices?

In *Genealogies of Religion: Discipline and Reasons of Power in Christianity and Islam*,[13] Talal Asad reminds us that ideations of religion come loaded with particular histories and political and social interests; in other words, renderings and realities that we must acknowledge *and* accept. While it has been intellectually efficacious and perhaps trendy to resignify religiosity within a model of liberation, this resignification does not eliminate particular codes and norms embedded within religion. Put in another way, these moral renderings do not become absent from our theological and religious grammar. In a Derridean sense, it is the *trace* of respectability [or what some have called cultural imperialism] that becomes lodged within and captive to our religious *habitus.* Social theorists such as Pierre Bourdieu and Antonio Gramsci, among others, remind us that the inscriptions and inculcations of the materiality of the bodily comportment and its practices often carries within them, unexamined and taken for granted, assumptions that become understood by the subjects as normative. Often, in our efforts to combat the "deviant" stereotypes that are understood to be the product of white racism upon black bodies, we end up defending the properness of black sexuality, womanhood, and so on, over and against the "riskier" typologies that are causally explicated as stereotypical culminations of the perversion of white supremacy.

In this sense, Kelly Brown Douglas in *Sexuality and the Black Church*[14] argues that, "Carnal, passionate, lustful, lewd, rapacious, bestial, sensual—these are just some of the many terms that come to mind when thinking of the ways in which White culture has depicted Black people's sexuality"[15]—going on to show the manner in which constructions of black women such as "The Jezebel" and "The Mammy" are depraved typologies of the white perception of, and attacks upon, black bodies. The strategies of respectability, while applauded in their intent, in form end up denying the exponential range of *difference* within expressions of sexuality, desire, and so on. Understanding this typology as "distorting" black women's sexuality, Douglas describes it thusly:

> ["The Jezebel" is] a person governed almost entirely by her libido. She has been described as having an insatiable sexual appetite, being extraordinarily passionate, and being sexually aggressive and cunning. Such stereotyping has produced the paramount image for

> Black womanhood in White culture—the Jezebel image. "Jezebel" has come to symbolize an evil, scheming and seductive woman.[16]

Although the historical renderings of white distortions of black sexuality are undeniable, the black community reacts to the ways in which the Jezebel image is described, as if, having a large sexual appetite and being sexually aggressive is *only* a product of the racist white gaze, rather than another possible way in which differences in erotic preferences and taste become expressed and achieved. That is to say, aside from the ways in which white culture has made use of these images as a way to authenticate and authorize a particular kind of racist gaze, is there anything inherently wrong with a Jezebel way of being in the world, if one so chooses? The Jezebel image is not necessarily deviant *per se*; rather, it heuristically represents a real way of being in the world by which constructions of desire, passion, sex, and so on, are performed.

And what's more, religion and concepts of the divine vis-à-vis an "authentic black faith" assist in reimaging *all* people as divine. Douglas writes, "A sexual discourse of resistance is necessary to call Black people back to their African religious heritage, which rightfully views human sexuality as divine."[17] Here the authenticity of faith under this rubric informs all humans in the image of the divine—such that, to deny another is to ultimately deny god. While religion and theology work here to construct an inclusive theology, this construction of black religious authenticity is used and employed strategically to make the act of homophobia both a "sin and betrayal" of black faith, or in Douglas's language, sin and betrayal of *authentic* black faith. While the construction of a theology of resistance works to challenge ideological perspectives on homophobia using a causal [religious] cost-benefit within the black community [to be truly religious is to *not* be homophobic], this rendering erroneously places religion as the hegemonic signifier of moralizing. In form, this redoubling of an authentic black faith offers religious capital to a stance of relationality by constructing and authenticating discourse of "proper" black religion such that all other, nonrelational, interpretations become antithetical to an authentic black faith. This positionality lets black faith off the hook of retaining any violent ideological sentiments since an authentic black faith is inherently relational. It also likewise offers a religious *reason* to be affirming of *difference*, since in this thought structure, all humans are cosmologically reduced to reflect an image of god—as if acceptance of relationality necessitates any kind of moral or religio-ethical rationale.

There is no denying, even in the efforts to construct an authentic black faith of liberation whereby all expressions of *difference* are embraced, that a problematic tendency still exists within the practice and theorizing of black religion as a "proper" ethic and norm of respectability. These problematic tendencies are sometimes written in discourse and at other times in invisible codes that dictate "proper" ways of being in the world. This "properness" exists beyond but also within politically correct moralized visions of affirmation and a sincere willingness to be open and affirming of forms of *difference*. In other words, a politics of respectability is often cloaked under more progressive constructions of the signifier "liberation." In *Loving the Body: Black Religious Studies and the Erotic*,[18] ethicist Katie G. Cannon writes that, "Living between the razor blade tensions of heteronormativity and hypersexuality, Evelyn Brooks Higginbotham contends that the politics of respectability caused some women to promote the ill-fitting Victorian cult of true womanhood as the proper way to eradicate distorted images of the sexually immoral Black woman"[19]—thus creating policing strategies of proper dress, talk, mannerisms, and so on. Whether or not an authentic "black faith" exposes the heresy of racism and whiteness in the world according to some,[20] what is more interesting beyond the rethinking of liberatory black faith outside of the white Platonized tradition is a consideration of the unexamined effects of respectability that are complicit with a particular kind of black religious *habitus*. In other words—a consideration of the kinds of bodies and practices that are reclaimed *in* the construction of a liberative practice of faith becomes a necessary reflection in order to examine the often taken-for-granted and unexamined choices whereby the *habitus* of respectability embedded in religion makes its appearance beyond politically correct rhetorical and discursive constructions of liberation.

Rather than using religiosity as a strategy to construct an economy of cost-benefits of embracing or *not* embracing *difference*—perhaps we consider the ethically risky bodies as a sort of anti-religion, as that which works against cultural imperialism, as that which creates a sort of anxiety to and for the solidity of our own moral renderings. Rather than denying the existence of the "nappy-headed ho," we instead, in a political sense, come out of our closets of respectability to reclaim a *politics of difference* and deviance as our starting point for religious, theological, or ethical reflection. We perhaps proclaim "I am a nappy-headed ho," and we thus queer the lines between "them" and "us." As one example among others, the work of the late Marcella Althaus-Reid seeks to reclaim perversions and things considered "indecent" as a materialist intervention of deconstructing the "moral order" embedded within religion and theology. With a focus on using poor urban women's experience as a starting point for reflection in *Indecent Theology: Theological Perversions in Sex,*

*Gender and Politics*, Althaus-Reid pays attention to the richness embedded in that which is traditionally understood as rebellious, noting that even theologians of liberation are not "immune to idealism and romantic visions of femininity in accordance with much contested, yet still normative theological views of gender and sexuality."[21] Throughout this text, Reid doesn't deny the deviant or the indecent; rather, she uses that which remains on the outside of the moral boundaries to challenge various constructions of authority and sexual subversions. She offers new ways to do a liberatory theology, beginning with the realm of the sexual.

What does it mean, for example, to embrace sexual *difference*? This question is poignantly answered by Gayle Rubin, when she writes that to embrace sexual *difference* is to "refer to what has otherwise been called perversion, sexual deviance, sexual variance, or sexual diversity." Here she offers a way to embrace the wide variety of *difference*, sexual or not.[22] Rethinking in this way expands our notions of "sexual *difference*" beyond gendered and biological attraction and beyond the binary oppositions of gay/straight. As Judith Butler argues:

> I think that for the most part people who work in a "sexual *difference*" framework actually believe in some kind of symbolic position of the masculine and the feminine, or believe there is something persistent about sexual *difference*understood in terms of the masculine and feminine.[23]

And yet, under what conditions and contexts does *difference* become embraced? In other words, what creates desire and a greater push to rethink *difference*, riskiness, and deviance? All too often—talk of "breaking silence" on *difference* becomes grounded in motifs of crisis and moral panics such as, for example, HIV/AIDS. Despite the achievements of liberating theology and the un/doing of ideological and metaphysical heresies such as Platonism—this leap does not resolve deep-seated cultural dispositions inherited from black religious norms toward *difference* and deviance, and more conspicuously, revealed in and through the larger publics of culture and society. Because of this complex history of internalized dominant ideologies, sexual *difference*, and "deviance" within the black community, it continues as the colonized within the colonized. In other words, it is the colony that includes *everything* outside of the "normative" black family; for example, those called the "welfare queens, punks, bulldaggers." As Cohen reminds us, this can also be extended to include folks such as the promiscuous teenager, the queer, the single black woman refusing to get married, multiple partnered relationships, and so on.

I search for, and am in favor of, a reframing of *difference* as embracing the fluid movement of expressions that are not locked and fixed within illusions of binary oppositions. Rather, they are moved by a *queer consciousness* that ruptures such binaries, and welcomes the "possibility of change, movement, redefinition and subversive performance—from year [to year], from partner to partner, from day to day, and even from act to act."[24] Similar to white supremacy, phobias more generally arise up out of the insidious ways in which the regulating systems of our lives are constructed. Embracing *difference* must move beyond an "assimilations model" that seeks to hide the at-risk, vulnerable, "nonconforming," stigmatized people of our communities under the rubrics of stable and fixed categories of identity and practices. On this point, Cohen argues that the "politics of respectability" that functions within black cultural life is a kind of politics that seeks to "police, sanitize, and hide the nonconformist members of the Black community." These "nonconforming members" are the ones who, according to Cohen, stand on the margins of stigmatized sexual *difference* and who are not recognized by dominant sexuality.

And so, while it is undeniable that the confluence of white cultural ideologies and understandings of black sexuality as "Carnal, passionate, lustful, lewd, rapacious, bestial, sensual . . ."[25] and so on have constrained images and representations of black women, we cannot, if we are to embrace *difference*, conceive of sexually charged stereotypes as solely the product of white supremacist logic appropriated in larger society. This logic not only fixes signifiers of *difference* within a frozen historical moment and a particular type of ideological inheritance, but also denies the plurality of our many-ness, and constructs a moralizing respectability that denies the multiplicative reality of our lives.

The "respectability" in the discursive *haraam* of religious respectability is evidenced in the gaps of silence—and that which is negated from discursive space. The "nappy-headed ho" was denied a cultural home in the broader publics of cultural criticism, just as the Jezebels are denied literary space in our theoretical and conceptual musings. The "nappy-headed ho" provides an anti-religion to our moral constructions—a dose of atheism for the religiously converted, a dose of sex for the sexually repulsed, a dose of polygamy for the monogamous, and a dose of *difference* to our constructions of sameness. Mary Douglas reminds us that what is perceived as "dirt" is in fact only "matter out of place." Thus dirt only becomes dirt when it transgresses social norms and values. Our theological and religious renderings of subjectivity have turned into a *haraam* of respectability. In our efforts to thwart the darts and prove white supremacist attacks on the black body to be wrong, we have created an internal colony among ourselves, whereby morality polices stigma and deviance. The discursive *haraam* of our theological constructions have become too safe. Becoming autoimmune and deconstructing itself, this *haraam* reflects something similar to the language of "indemnification" adopted by Derrida to describe the *globalatinization* of religions.[26] Making use of biological language, Derrida argues that religion can be seen as an immune system; a system that keeps the "body" of believers safe from "foreign attacks" and "threats." As such, dogmas, confessions, doctrines, and rituals are invariably constructed as strategies to work hard against any chance of contamination against the social body. In the end, the battle has a sad ending, according to Derrida. The body, the social body, becomes what he calls autoimmune. Autoimmunity is another way by which it deconstructs itself—a "rejection of religions rejection," a rejection of alterity and otherness. However, to truly embrace the *other*—is to embrace *difference*, deviance and "dirt." According to Levinas, relationality and the truly ethical are reliant upon looking at the face of the *other*—not burying them in tired symbolic funerals and played-out moratoriums.[27]

## Implications

In an era of "safe" this and "safe" that, we fear the worst. Everything is seemingly too safe these days. With threats of "dis/ease," foreign bodies, pesticides, and contagions of all sorts, we most certainly live in a world traumatized by and through a moralized political economy of fear and "safety." It is a place where we become skeptical of that which is different and deviant. On the margins of our moral renderings, which work to produce stability for ourselves, there are bodies, like the "nappy-headed ho's" and the jezebels, and welfare queens, dykes, and so on. These bodies stand as threats to our constructed realities of stability and coherence. The faces of the other stare back, offering an empirical moment in which to use the realities of their lived lives to make more "risky" the *haraam* of our own respectability.

Embracing constructions such as the "nappy-headed ho" threaten to destabilize the unwavering foundations upon which our ideas of morality are built, whether it be static meaning, ideas of purity, monogamy, or any other dominant moral order that upholds power and privilege. Expressions such as these are seemingly "contaminated" with vulgarity, promiscuity, polysemy, polygamy, and polyamory [in a metaphorical sense]; their realities are so fleeting sometimes that all we, the scholars, see are glimpses, whether it be the absence of its presence or the presence of its absence. Or maybe, as Zizek argues, we are *simply afraid of the real—perhaps we are more comfortable with that which shields and suppresses us from what is real—Tylenol, Diet-Coke, decaffeinated coffee, and so on.* The ontological reality of *difference* and "deviance" has the ability to act as a sort of anti-structure or a prophylaxis to the stability of our closets of respectability. What would it mean for our religious and theological constructions to embrace a politics of *difference* as a way by which to disrupt the permanence of respectability so seemingly lodged in our strategies of social protest? Young reminds us that respectability is very much about

> conforming to norms that repress sexuality, bodily functions, and emotional expression. It is linked to an idea of order: the respectable person is chaste, modest, does not express lustful desires, passion, spontaneity, or exuberance, is frugal, clean, gently spoken, and well mannered. The orderliness of respectability means things are under control, everything in its place, not crossing the borders.[28]

Crossing the borders of respectability means we must be willing to get wet. We must be intentional to immerse ourselves in the sea of *difference* by making a calculated move to make our constructions less safe. We must have a willingness to try a new sexual position beyond a missionary-style rendering of the same. At the edges of our flat, arid, moral, teleological, and theological *haraams* lies a moment of coming out of our closets of purity to embrace *difference*—the embodiment of presence, of the absence, or our suppression. And there she stands, in all her nappiness and ho'ish glory. It's often asked in religious circles, "What if god was one of us?"[29] What if? What if I am/we are/god is, some nappy-headed ho?

## Notes

1. "Don Imus and Nappy Headed Hos," April 7, 2007, video clip, accessed February 27, 2010, YouTube, http://www.youtube.com/watch?v=RF9BjB7Bzr0.

2. Evelyn Brooks Higginbotham, *Righteous Discontent: The Women's Movement in the Black Baptist Church, 1880–1920* (Cambridge, MA: Harvard University Press, 1994).

3. Throughout this essay, the concept "difference" is italicized to invoke Derrida's understanding of "*difference*" as both possibility and impossibility.

4. For more on "*difference*" see Jacques Derrida, *Writing and Difference*, trans. Alan Bass (New York: Routledge, 1978).

5. Iris Marion Young, *Justice and the Politics of Difference* (Princeton: Princeton University Press, 1990), 152.

6. Cathy J. Cohen, "Deviance as Resistance: A New Research Agenda for the Study of Black Politics," *Du Bois Review* 1, no. 1 (2004): 27.

7. Cathy J. Cohen, "Punks, Bulldaggers, and Welfare Queens: The Radical Potential of Queer Politics?" in *Black Queer Studies: A Critical Anthology* (Durham, NC: Duke University Press, 2005), 25.

8. "Imus Called Women's Basketball Team 'Nappy-Headed Hos,'" *Media Matters for America*, April 4, 2007, http://mediamatters.org/research/200704040011.

9. Laurel C. Schneider, "What Race Is Your Sex?" in *Disrupting White Supremacy from Within* (Cleveland: Pilgrim, 2004), 143.

10. Cathy J. Cohen, "Gangsta Rap Made Me Do It: Bill Cosby, Don Imus, and Black Moral Panics," in *Democracy Remixed: Black Youth and the Future of American Politics* (New York: Oxford University Press, 2010), 34.

11. The Oprah Winfrey Show, "A Hip-Hop Town Hall," *Oprah.com*, July 13, 2009, http://www.oprah.com/oprahshow/A-Hip-Hop-Town-Hall/6.

12. Cohen, "Punks, Bulldaggers, and Welfare Queens," 46.

13. Talal Asad, *Genealogies of Religion: Discipline and Reasons of Power in Christianity and Islam* (Baltimore: Johns Hopkins University Press, 1993).

14. Kelly Brown Douglas, *Sexuality and the Black Church: A Womanist Perspective* (Maryknoll, NY: Orbis Books, 1999).

15. Ibid., 31, 99.

16. Ibid., 36.

17. Ibid., 122.

18. Anthony B. Pinn and Dwight N. Hopkins, *Loving the Body: Black Religious Studies and the Erotic* (New York: Palgrave, 2004).

19. Ibid., 12.

20. Kelly Brown Douglas, *What's Faith Got to Do With It?: Black Bodies/Christian Souls* (Maryknoll, NY: Orbis Books, 2005).

21. Marcella Althaus-Reid, *Indecent Theology: Theological Perversions in Sex, Gender and Politics* (New York: Routledge, 2001), 6.

22. Gayle Rubin with Judith Butler, "Sexual Traffic: Interview," in *Feminism Meets Queer Theory*, ed. Elizabeth Weed and Naomi Schor (Indianapolis: Indiana University Press, 1997), 83.

23. Judith Butler, "Against Proper Objects," in *Feminism Meets Queer Theory,* ed. Elizabeth Weed and Naomi Schor (Indianapolis: Indiana University Press, 1997), 73.

24. Cohen, "Punks, Bulldaggers, and Welfare Queens," 23.

25. Douglas, *Sexuality and the Black Church*, 31.

26. "Globalatinization" is a term Derrida uses to talk about the ways in which religion has become universalized to a point of hegemony. See Jacques Derrida, *Acts of Religion* (New York: Routledge, 2002).

27. Emmanuel Levinas, *Totality and Infinity: An Essay on Exteriority* (Pittsburgh: Duquesne University Press, 1969).

28. Iris Marion Young, 137.

29. Joan Osborne, vocal performance of "One of Us" by Eric Bazilian, released September 1995, on *Relish* 1995, Island/Mercury, compact disc.

8

# Dark Matter

## *Liminality and Black Queer Bodies*

**Roger A. Sneed**

In the 1990s, Cleo Manago coined the term "Same Gender Loving," or, SGL, to denote sexual difference among African Americans.[1] Manago's argument was that the term "gay" was so associated with white, middle-class men that it held little value for African American men who loved or had sex with other men. Manago and the New York City–based group Black Men's Xchange articulate an argument for the term SGL that echoes and draws upon black women's turn to the term "womanist" instead of "feminist."[2] Both womanists and SGL-identified African American men argue that this process of naming is one of self-love and affirmation of one's belonging to a unique community. Further, Manago and the BMX argue that, given the entrenched racism and classism within the so-called "gay movement" and the ways in which the symbols and nomenclature of this gay movement had grown within exclusively white contexts, it would be incumbent upon black men who love men and black women who love women to begin speaking for themselves.

The argument advanced by Manago and echoed by Essex Hemphill, Marlon Riggs, and others is rooted in racial tension within queer communities. Keith Boykin and others report that black queers often encounter racial discrimination when going out to clubs, bars, and the like. Further, queer communities display racial discrimination in the form of leadership patterns, residential patterns, and, most visibly, dating/sexual patterns. Via the visibility and racial privilege of white gays and lesbians, the term "gay" evokes images of white persons. Such racial evocation is reinforced in the glossy covers of magazines oriented toward queer communities. Magazines like *Out*, *The Advocate*, and *Instinct* rarely feature queers of color on the covers. Other visual representations of queers rarely focus on queers of color. Queers of color appear in advertisements or on gay-themed shows like the U.S. version of "Queer as Folk," or "Will and Grace," but those appearances are merely that: appearances. These appearances of black bodies in predominantly white gay spaces are marginalized, trotted out only in service of a racial fetishizing of black identity.

Manago is quick to point out that black SGL persons are also marginalized within African American communities. Black churches vilify the sexualities of black men and women who love and have sex with members of the same gender. Conceptions of black masculinity and black femininity rooted in resistance to white assertions of black sexuality contribute to a communal disapprobation of same-gender affections. Manago's argument is that the term "SGL" reflects a critique of that communal disapprobation.

However, I want to begin with Manago's deployment of an alternative description of black sexual difference as a way of describing the liminality of black queer existences and experiences. The deployment of such a term—the search for a new way to describe our experiences, the search for a new way to describe ourselves beyond hegemonic terms imposed upon us by others, is reflective of the liminal spaces that black queer bodies occupy. Simply put, by liminality, I meant that black queers find themselves betwixt and between worlds. They find themselves within black communities that often do not understand or appreciate sexual difference; however, when among white queers, black queers find very little common ground, as many white queers operate firmly within white privilege.[3]

## Liminality of Black Queer Bodies/Identities

The betwixt and betweenness of black queer experience and existence calls into question the attempts to present stable and rigid categories for understanding African American religious experiences. I am not arguing that there is not or should not be a "normative" order within African American religious thought and studies. However, what I find useful and compelling about the betwixt and betweenness of black queer experiences is the challenge to the black theological academy's presentation of a personal, immanent God. It is the theological challenge presented by liminality that pushes black religious thought forward.

Victor Turner's articulation of the notion of liminality may appear to limit my appropriation of the concept in application to black queer bodies and expressive culture. Turner is clear that he considers those who are liminal (or liminars) should "be distinguished from 'marginals.'" He describes marginals as those whose memberships in "two or more groups" conflict with each other. Certainly, black gays and lesbians would not be considered liminal by this distinction. As Turner is concerned with ritual liminality, black homosexuals cannot, by his definition and description, be taken up into this concept.[4]

Although the task of this essay is not to refute Turner's distinction, I think it necessary to offer a brief articulation of liminality and applicability to black queers. While I find Turner's description of liminality provocative, it is limited to the context of ritual. Although marginality might be an attractive position from which to discuss black queers and creativity, I think it is necessary to say something different. Marginality as I understand its deployment in black religious and cultural thought is a description of a kind of social relationship. Marginality in the case of black religious and cultural thought refers to groups that occupy the margins of established social narratives and parameters. Black homosexuals, by dint of past and current interpretations of sexual difference, occupy marginal social status. That marginality, as Turner indicates, might occasion creative expression in direct response to imposed marginality.

However, what I seek here is to discuss liminality in a theological sense. Turner's anthropological assessment of ritual liminality is provocative and instructive; however, it is not final, nor is it closed to expansion or reformulation. Pragmatist William Hart advances the concept of Afro-Eccentricity in order to discuss African American autobiographical narratives that are not part of what he calls "the Standard Narrative of Black Religion."[5] This standard narrative positions the black Protestant church as "coterminous" with black religion. Further, this standard narrative fails to consider any other forms of black religious narrative.

Those who challenge this standard narrative do exist on the margins of a normative black Protestant religiosity.[6] However easy it may appear to simply categorize these people as marginal, I think that Hart's notion of Afro-Eccentricity bespeaks a liminal presence and experience. These persons, existing betwixt and between controlling narratives, begin to forge new identities and new ways of thinking about, approaching, and appreciating the world. Although these Afro-Eccentrics begin to forge new ways of looking at the world, their ambiguities are never fully or neatly resolved. This ambiguity, this "dissonance and improvisation . . . challenges our expectations of normality and propriety."[7] Hart calls such a challenge "bluing." While Hart uses the concept of "bluing" the standard narrative and characterizes this as an improvisation, my reading of Hart is that what he speaks of is liminal experience.

The betwixt and betweenness, this liminality of black bodies in general, is explicated in greater detail by Kevin Everod Quashie in his examination of the ways in which black women construct selfhood. For Quashie, the cultural idiom of the girlfriend "shapes and engages contemporary critical theory."

Black women's critical understandings of themselves lead Quashie to interpret the construction of "girlfriend subjectivity." This girlfriend subjectivity is an oscillation "between states of (dis)identification" as a liminal identity.[8]

This is a different reading of liminality than is presented by Turner, and is not tied to ritual practice. Quashie conceives of liminality as a state in which the body is extended "outside of the boundaries imposed by itself, boundaries that sometimes impede coalitions between self and other (self)."[9] For Quashie, it is the engagement with liminality that enables black women to find god in themselves. He argues that black women's literary productions reveal a black female subjectivity that is able to take the externally imposed marginality that renders black women liminal and move toward a self beyond "selves." Quashie seems to imply that the aforementioned oscillation in black women's understanding of self and selves enables black women to see beyond those rigid categories of "God" and "self." God and self are no longer balkanized, no longer rigidly demarcated so that God stands over and against black women while black women remain subject to a (male) God.

I argue that this ability that Quashie locates in black women's lives and experiences is also present in black queers' lives and experiences. What I find fascinating about Quashie's use of liminality in connection with black women's subjectivity and his idea of black women (un)becoming subjects is the potential it has for the reformulation of black subjectivity beyond theism. How I extend this reading of liminality to black queers is in and through readings of black queer expressive culture.

## Liminality for Butler and Ndegeocello

I highlight Octavia Butler's novel *Fledgling* (2007) and Meshell Ndegeocello's album *Peace Beyond Passion* (1996) as representative of liminal creativity. These cultural productions serve as examples of a liminal black queer body whose creativity is fostered by their liminality, and de-centers rigid constructions of black masculinity, femininity, and divinity. Using Butler and Ndegeocello, I show that black queer usage of liminality as a creative space offers new interpretive frameworks that move black queer subjectivity beyond theism and toward a humanist conception of self.

Works of science fiction, such as Butler's *Fledgling*, often rely upon liminality in order to tell stories. Science fiction is a discourse that takes futuristic settings and projects onto them current issues and problems. Science fiction enables us to discuss particular social issues using settings that do not directly confront the consumer. For example, Samuel Delaney's science fiction writings constantly challenge and push the boundaries of normative understandings of race, gender identity, and sexual orientation.[10]Science fiction queers social issues.

In her last book, *Fledgling*, Octavia Butler offers an example of the queering of race and sexuality in science fiction. Here, Butler uses the mythic figure of vampires to interrogate race and sexuality. The female protagonist, Shori, awakens in a cave, badly injured and suffering amnesia. She quickly comes to realize that she is not like other humans; rather she is from a race of people referred to as "Ina." Shori soon learns that her entire extended family has been murdered; thus she is alone in a world that she does not remember. As Shori realizes that she is what humans call "vampires," she forges symbiotic relationships with human beings that benefit humans by extending their lifespan. Shori also begins to understand that she is not fully Ina. Rather, she is the result of a genetic experiment that seeks to enable Ina to walk in the daylight—the key to which is in melanin. As such, Shori constitutes a dramatic leap forward for Ina, but her existence is a frightening prospect for some of the Ina.

As the mystery about the attack on Shori and the destruction of her Ina family unfolds, Shori's liminality is "called out" by older Ina. As one elder Ina delineates the differences between human and Ina, he describes humans as a violent, profligate species plagued by brief, brutish lives riddled with disease and violence. He exclaims that the Ina are not humans and that they should never try to be them.[11]

This is an argument against Shori's very existence. Shori is a hybrid, neither human nor Ina. However, she is both human and Ina. Shori's liminal existence as neither fully human nor fully Ina allows for the forging of a new identity. Here, it is instructive to note that, at the end of *Fledgling*, Butler does not take the easy path of allowing Shori to regain her memories and remember what her full-blooded Ina family was like. Shori must forge onward, without the stabilizing memories of her past.

Shori queers race, sexuality, and familial construction. Her black skin is an anomaly for the Ina. Still, she is not what we understand as "black"; she is not an African American. Nevertheless, the color of her skin is signified upon by the older Ina as being "inferior." This signification betrays how the Ina have been so thoroughly influenced by the allegedly inferior humans. When convicted of the assault upon Shori and destroying her family, the same elder Ina attacks Shori. He screams, "Murdering black mongrel bitch . . . what will she give us all? Fur? Tails?"[12] This is clearly a signification upon historical presentations of black skin as a marker of extreme otherness. Black skin is a dangerous harbinger of change. For whites, and in this case, for the Ina who have essentially identified themselves with whiteness, Shori's genetically engineered blackness signals a new identity that is frightening.

Butler also portrays a reconstructed concept of family. The Ina do not behave in the ways in which popularly constructed "vampires" behave. In *Fledgling*, the vampire's saliva creates a bond between the Ina and the person bitten. Further, an individual Ina requires several people from whom s/he can obtain blood. As such, the patriarchal, nuclear family so prized within American culture is subtly deconstructed and supplanted by an older, more egalitarian and less restrictive familial structure that is more matrilineal and matriarchal than patrilineal and patriarchal. Further, Shori and the Ina's method of constructing families is not rooted in a heteronormative understanding of family. Through the reconfiguring of the vampire figure into the liminal character of Shori, Butler is able to position the rediscovery of self as a critique of the homophobia inherent within the heteronormative construction of family.

Like Butler, Meshell Ndegeocello queers race and sexuality. However, she accomplishes this through her music. Ndegeocello's music is evocative of the liminality of black queer existence. Outside of her music, Ndegeocello is a bisexual woman who had, at one point, been in a long-term relationship with feminist author and daughter of Alice Walker, Rebecca Walker. Ndegeocello draws on funk, jazz, hip hop, soul, and rock and roll to create music that cannot be easily classified. As such, while she has had modest commercial success with a few singles, her albums rarely make it onto the Billboard Top 100 charts. Nevertheless, I find her works provocative. Her songs plumb the depths of the various experiences that frame human existence.

From her meditation on black belief in Christianity to her stripped-down lament for her mother's life under misogyny, Ndegeocello's songs are sonic examples of womanist critiques of American society.

While she has released eight studio albums altogether, I wish to focus on her sophomore release, the 1996 album *Peace Beyond Passion*. An exploration of liminality in black life, *Peace Beyond Passion* is an intensely political and passionate album that flies in the face of the conventional rhythm and blues (R&B) albums of the time. The first half of the album is dominated by songs that contain overtly religious (one might even say sacrilegious) themes. These songs are also rife with social, political, and cultural criticism. After an instrumental piece titled "The Womb," Ndegeocello hits the listener in the face with the first verse of "The Way": "Jesus cured the blind man so that he could see the evils of the world / Perchance blindness is but a dark thought overcome by the light."[13] The song is a complaint and a critique of the way in which

Christianity positions itself as a force for good but often becomes a destructive force in people's lives.

The next verse is virtual heresy: "Maybe Judas was the better man, and Mary made a virgin just to save face." Ndegeocello is calling Christian protestations of salvation into question. Instead of being a force for good, Christian interpretations of "the way" lead to death and misery. If "The Way" is the complaint, then a subsequent song, "Leviticus: Faggot" is an unvarnished example of Ndegeocello's indictment of Christianity. This song chronicles the life, and implied death, of a young gay man who is disowned by his family. The end of the song sees Ndegeocello/Michael asking to be saved from this life. The power of this song is in its frank indictment of homophobia, and its use of Christian imagery against the perpetrators of homophobia.

Ndegeocello wrestles first with divinity and then with humanity. The end of *Peace Beyond Passion* is a riff on Marvin Gaye's "Inner City Blues (Make Me Wanna Holler)." Instead of a song that reflects on larger social concerns, Ndegeocello's "Make Me Wanna Holler" takes the listener through the travails of Ndegeocello's mother's life. What makes Ndegeocello want to holler is her mother's unfulfilled life and her father's closed heart. It might seem odd to end an album titled *Peace Beyond Passion* with such a discordant and melancholy song. However, I think it is in keeping with Ndegeocello's artistic temperament and critical framework.

The album itself is a journey through liminality. While this album could also be read as an argument about marginality, I think that this album is an example of a creative response to, and borne out of, a liminal experience and existence. The experience of being betwixt and between racial, sexual, gendered, and religious identities fosters creative responses that attempt to make sense of this liminality; this threshold experience often gets mistaken for "eccentricity." The creative response birthed out of this tension reflects the state of not being what you were (or were presumed to have been), but not quite being something or someone else.

In separate interviews, Ndegeocello contends that her work reflects her understandings of ambiguity in human life. In an interview for the website afterellen.com, Ndegeocello articulates why she titled her 2009 album "Devil's Halo":

> Regarding the new album title, Ndegeocello says it refers to the "good and evil to be found in all things." She adds, "Nothing is perfectly good or bad, and the album is about finding beauty in

> imperfection, in contrast, in being, seeing, knowing, struggling with the humanity of imperfection and the imperfection of humanity."[14]

For Ndegeocello, the joy of being human is found not only in recognizing but also in celebrating the often-contentious nature of existence. As such, the production of the album is a creative response to moving beyond rigid descriptions and constructions of black identity and toward an identity not delimited by racialized and sexualized constraints.

As I read Octavia Butler and listen to Meshell Ndegeocello, I am drawn to the possibilities toward which they point us. In "God Siva," Ndegeocello sings, "I realize we are, in truth the truth we seek. God, perfect this very moment."[15] For both of these artists, the human becomes a powerful symbol. It is the human—usually in the form of the marginalized, queered body of the black woman—who points us toward new possibilities of being. However, they do not shy away from or limit descriptions of the state of being from which we move away. Neither artist is interested in a sanitized, mythic past in which a stable black identity heroically struggled against the titanic forces of white supremacy.

Butler and Ndegeocello's cultural productions attempt a move toward a black identity that is not framed by "blackness." They move toward a both-gendered identity liberated from rigid constructions of "woman" and "man," sexual selves unfettered by inflexible sexual roles, and religious commitments not constructed and construed via a singular, all-powerful, yet invisible deity. This is not to say that either artist is explicitly (or implicitly) atheist. Rather, they do not preoccupy themselves or impose upon their characters and songs the kinds of theistic assumptions that undergird the majority of black religious and theological discourse. For example, Butler describes herself as a pessimist, but I find in her writing a deep hope for humanity, however humanity is construed. *Fledgling* is both a critique of humanity and a desire to prod humankind along. In a 1999 interview, Butler said that she goes wherever her imagination leads.[16] That is what is powerful about her use of science fiction, and Meshell Ndegeocello's use of music.

The Afro-Eccentricity of these two figures points toward a deep appreciation of difference in black life. These forms of difference may indeed be science fictional, as they involve projecting into the future and imparting future hopes onto present situations. The process of becoming, of evolving into something or someone else, is a standard trope within science fiction writing, and I think that it is what lies at the root of black religious scholarship. The worlds we envision are not unlike the worlds that Butler and Ndegeocello envision, and the means by which we and they articulate those visions are not dissimilar. Butler and Ndegeocello use their imagination in order to offer critiques of the world and offer possibilities of what we might become. The black queer body, in the final analysis, is not a problem, not a marginalized figure that will always point back to the heteronormative body at the center of discourse. Nor is the black queer the heroic yet still marginal body that will deliver us from our wayward ways.

## Conclusion

What I have attempted to do through this brief look at Octavia Butler and Meshell Ndegeocello is follow in the womanist/black liberationist trajectory of utilizing black cultural productions in order to offer religious scholarship new ways of interpreting African American experiences. Their respective cultural productions in the form of literature and music do not merely repeat lamentations about black identities as marginal. Instead, what they do is delve into the oppositional sensibilities that lurk in the background of our rigid sexual and racial dichotomies. However, they do so not in order to reproduce heroic narratives. In other words, the black subject in their respective works does not function in order to condemn whiteness or white supremacy. Indeed, their works play with oppositional sensibilities and do not lead us to neat resolutions. In other words, the queerness of black bodies or blackness of queer bodies is not resolved so that a new black identity advances to the foreground and becomes a controlling narrative. What neither Butler nor Ndegeocello seek is the reproduction of a hegemonic discourse with the ascension of the black queer body as that which will define an authentic sexual or racial identity.

This essay is designed to be a modest intervention in what William Hart calls the standard narrative that governs black religious discourse. While black theologians rely upon a weak humanism by which they can produce and promote their projects, I favor a robust or strong humanism, a nontheism that promotes human powers to respond to human problems. What I find especially compelling in the alternative cultural productions highlighted in this paper is the thought that they are meditations on moving from one state of being to another. Further, I am intrigued by the ambiguities with which they leave the reader/listener. I read these productions as promoting a healthy approach toward liminality. In other words, as I read Butler and listen to Ndegeocello's albums, I find in these productions an approach toward human existence in general and black life in particular that seeks to find comfort in the "betwixt and betweenness." Being on the threshold of a new identity, a new way of being that has not yet been defined or described, is a joy, not a burden.

## Notes

1. "Communities of African Descent Media Resource Kit," *GLAAD*, http://web.archive.org/web/20061002013523/http://www.glaad.org/poc/coad/coad_media_kit.php.

2. Cleo Manago, "About BMX," *Black Men's Exchange*, http://www.bmxny.org/bmxaboutus.htm.

3. Keith Boykin, *One More River to Cross: Black and Gay in America* (New York: Anchor Books, 1996), 212–35; Dwight A. McBride, *Why I Hate Abercrombie and Fitch: Essays on Race and Sexuality* (New York: New York University Press, 2005), 105–31.

4. Victor Turner, *Dramas, Fields, and Metaphors: Symbolic Action in Human Society* (Ithaca, NY: Cornell University Press, 1974), 232–33.

5. William David Hart, *Black Religion: Malcolm X, Julius Lester, and Jan Willis* (New York: Palgrave Macmillan, 2008), 8.

6. Ibid., 11–12.

7. Ibid.

8. Kevin Everod Quashie, *Black Women, Identity, and Cultural Theory: (Un)becoming the Subject* (New Brunswick, NJ: Rutgers University Press, 2004), 78.

9. Ibid., 83.

10. I have made an extensive argument for how Delaney's work, along with other literary productions by black gay men, can serve as a hermeneutical lens through which black theology can participate in understanding black queer experiences. See Roger Sneed, *Representations of Homosexuality: Black Liberation Theology and Cultural Criticism* (New York: Palgrave, 2010), 116–20.

11. Octavia E. Butler, *Fledgling* (New York: Seven Stories, 2005), 298.

12. Ibid., 306.

13. Meshell Ndegeocello, vocal performance of "My Way," by Meshell Ndegeocello, released June 2006, on *Peace Beyond Passion*, Maverick, compact disc.

14. Jamie Murnane, "Interview with Meshell Ndegeocello," *AfterEllen,* November 30, 2009, http://www.afterellen.com/people/2009/11/meshell-ndegeocello?page=0%2C0.

15. Meshell Ndegeocello, vocal performance of "God Shiva," by Meshell Ndegeocello and Wendy Melvoin, released June 2006, on *Peace Beyond Passion*, Maverick, compact disc.

16. "Possible Futures and the Reading of History: A Conversation with the Incomparable Storyteller Octavia Butler," by Cecilia Tan, *CeciliaTan* (blog), May 3, 2007, http://ceciliatan.livejournal.com/15404.html.

# 9

# Invisible Hands

## *An Epistemology of Black Religious Thought and Black Lesbian Sexual Desire That Disrupts "Crystallized Culture"*

**Nessette Falu**

### Introduction

Womanist is coined and defined in Alice Walker's *In Search of Our Mothers' Gardens* as an encompassing identity that represents a number of dimensions describing black feminists or feminists of color who, among other things, are also "women who love other women, sexually and/or nonsexually."[1] In spite of Walker's framing of womanist, recent scholarship drawn from Walker's conceptual framework has given little public attention to the lives and experiences of black lesbians. Correcting this is important, in part because the experiences and lives of black lesbians expose a wealth of unique ideas about struggle, transformation, and community with diverse religiosities and spiritualities that could help African American religious studies in general, and womanist scholarship in particular, provide a more nuanced and encompassing understanding and embracing of black queer life.

In this paper, I argue that a critical examination of the religious diversity within black lesbian communities calls attention to epistemological ways of deconstructing ideas of queer/gay desire as "illegitimate and abnormal."[2] The purpose of this paper is to show a relationship between forms of knowledge production about queer/gay desire and religious or spiritual practices.[3] My goal is to envision how black religious thought can be understood as shaping mechanisms for survival and transformation through diverse religious and spiritual identities. I will focus on an analysis of the film *Black Womyn Conversations* by Tiona McClodden and of some stories from the text *Spirited:*

*Affirming the Soul and Black Gay/Lesbian Identity* edited by G. Winston James and Lisa C. Moore,[4] I will explore the manner in which religious and spiritual black lesbian experience in the U.S. is driven by knowledge production, and I will tie this to Anthony Pinn's theory of a quest for complex subjectivity as a marker of religious and spiritual sensibilities that marks the push against societal constraints on humanity. I will also engage Lorde's feminist analysis of interdependence to reinterpret some of the ways that contemporary black lesbians continually search for meaning through sexual difference.

Furthermore, turning to Michel Foucault's *History of Sexuality I,* I will argue that religion and medicine deployed "sexuality" to advance systems of rules and norms to control desire-pleasure. The work of Foucault in this volume examines deployment of sexuality in ways that frame power dynamics to behave as negative and pathological discursive cultural streams impinging upon the sexual desires of black lesbians. Finally, I will offer an epistemic perspective on black lesbian experience by reading Susan Bordo's feminist work on the body as "crystallized culture" through a conceptual framework I name "black queer entrapment." Bordo's arguments set the stage for understanding how power dynamics might be hosted by or filtered through the body as "black queer entrapment."

## Push for Desire: Interdependence and the Quest for Complex Subjectivity

In her 1979 essay, "The Master's Tools Will Never Dismantle the Master's House," Audre Lorde called for an "interdependency across women to interconnect differences of race, sexuality, class, and age" as a push for the inclusion and "consideration of lesbian consciousness, specifically that of the black lesbian" in feminist dialogue.[5] For Lorde, women's practices driven by needing and desiring to nurture each other produce a particular knowledge of interdependency forging a discovery of human agency.[6] I interpret this interdependence as a major source of the empowerment that shapes and produces the black lesbian human agency Lorde espouses in this essay. Interdependency can be critically useful if all women authentically unite and draw upon their differences of race, sexuality, class, age, etc., to ultimately become empowered as a group that exercises collective human agency. To this end, Lorde is pushing for unifying all women in community that can press against patriarchy and other forms of oppression that specifically affect black lesbians. However, the tensions across race, sexuality, and class relations among lesbians were, and still are, significant layers of constraint specifically affecting black lesbians. These constraints treat many black lesbian communities as invisible and illegitimize them in many spaces.

*Black Womyn Conversations* (*BWC*) and the *Spirited* anthology are significant indicators of an increased push by black lesbians, via sharing their personal stories and perspectives, to seek conversation and community with other black lesbians. This push is highly suggestive of Lorde's idea of "interdependence" among black lesbians. The idea "interdependence" among black lesbians reflects the increased recognition of their agency regarding both their sexual desires and their relationships to religiosities and spiritualities.

Likewise *BWC* and *Spirited* exemplify Anthony Pinn's theory of the religious quest for complex subjectivity. The religious quest for complex subjectivity is defined as "a desired movement from life as corporeal object, controlled by oppressive forces to a complex conveyer of cultural meaning, with a detailed and creative identity."[7] Pinn regards subjectivity as complex in that various identities are held together in multiple, tangled ways, giving broader meaning to the self.[8] In other words, a black body can recognize its connection to, or place within, a black community that is actively grappling with, wrestling against, and resisting the dehumanizing historical and social circumstances. Pinn describes this idea of the black body's struggle as "the key (autonomous existence) for individual subjectivity in creative tension with the demand for quality of relationship (community)."[9] Such identification by black queer bodies in communal relationship can forge greater desire and focus for understanding and creating positive life meaning within individual life. Pinn's ideas are illuminated by *BWC* and the *Spirited* stories because these black lesbian voices are drawing upon each other's shared struggles on sexual desires, expressions, and identities in order to form better individual quality of life. In this sense, the quest for complex subjectivity seems to be a pathway by which the black lesbian experience, as a process of belonging and even becoming legitimate citizens, culminates in and yields a longing for community. In other words, it culminates in Lorde's notion of interdependence.

*Black Womyn Conversations* can be interpreted as a calling for, and display of, interdependence across black lesbians seeking to interconnect diverse experiences at the grassroots level. The *BWC* film is a grassroots project because it brings black lesbians with diverse thoughts and profiles in dialogue together, and stages Lorde's idea that "within the interdependence of mutual differences lies the security which enables them to descend into the chaos of knowledge and return with true visions of [their] future."[10] These grassroots efforts target women from different walks of life who would otherwise not be made visible to tell their stories and perspectives.

In the film, some women speak about renouncing the homophobia of diverse religious settings. Others speak about their comfort level of how they are treated because of their masculinities. Still others speak regarding their willingness to take risks to be visible in the world as a black lesbian and how their presence positively impacts other black lesbians. In the film, I recognize a search or quest for new knowledge and for sharing old knowledge about connections across the women's religiosities and spiritualities and their sexual identities, sexual desires, and sexuality. For example, one woman, referred to as "Q" in the film, says she was Christian, but subsequently embraced Buddhism because of homophobia within churches. She is very confident in conveying that her religious experience as a black lesbian Buddhist is a better one than her Christian experience. She recognizes that her past religious space is what contributed to her self-denial and unhappiness. As a result, she embarked on a quest for a more liberating religious experience that would affirm her. For these women, religious or spiritual experience is tied to improving their lives as a whole, including their social conditions.

## Deployment of Homosexuality and Its Meaning for Black Religious or Spiritual Thought

Religion as an institution of power is not in isolation but works in tandem with other institutions of power in treating the black queer body as material and as a site of construction.[11] In recognition of this, I will examine medicine and religious institutions together under critical scrutiny for the ways in which they both regulate the freedom of bodily desire and pleasure. The effects of medical and religious power are major factors reinforcing the pathological constructions internalized and embodied by many sexualized black queer bodies. These pathological constructions lead to distorted, oppressed, and repressed homosexual desires and pleasures.

According to Foucault, "Medicine made a forceful entry into the pleasures of the couple: it created an entire organic, functional, or mental pathology and carefully classified all forms of related pleasures.[12]" For example, Foucault refers to normalizing medical surveillance of sexual practices to manage and expose sexually transmitted diseases (STDs). While treatment and prevention of STDs are important, medicine's regulatory power indeed shaped sexual pathological stigma, especially HIV. As a result, psychiatric evolution of "homosexuality" as abnormal and HIV/AIDS as a former gay disease developed. This stigmatizing medical history cannot be ignored because it has served as a medical-cultural means of constraining "homosexual" desire and pleasure by invoking public fear and targeting gay subjects.

For example, the American Psychiatry Association's (APA) history of medically stigmatizing homosexuality during the mid-twentieth century as abnormal had significant impact not just on repressing and oppressing homosexuality but reinforcing a "confessional science" that was also modeled by religion as described by Foucault.[1] Catholicism, the tradition of primary concern for Foucault, was invested in this subjugating practice leading to homosexual embodiment. The deployment of homosexuality as abnormal and deviant resulted in the embodiment of social pathologies by homosexual bodies. Moreover, Foucault's ideas of "confessional science and religious rituals" targeting homosexual bodies mark, in dehumanizing and subjugating ways, black queer bodies as abnormal.[13] Institutional violence against vulnerable bodies by medicine and religion has been used to torture, dehumanize, and subjugate gay *black* bodies.

Pinn's work challenges one to think about historical and sociological pathways to study the religious and spiritual body as material, as a carrier of social ills via the ways that the body moves against dehumanization for transformation. The threaded message throughout the *Spirited* anthology and *BWC* stories suggests that diverse religious and spiritual black lesbians shape and use their community to access a quest for complex subjectivity by wrestling with and producing knowledge that negates same-sex desire and practices as abnormal. In turn, I recognize that the voices of diverse religious and spiritual black lesbians from the *Spirited* text suggest that religiosities and spiritualities are rooted in particular sexual epistemological production. This is a reason to identify violent materialities afflicting black queer/gay folks, and their affective responses contesting dehumanization that entraps many black queer/gay bodies within a dreadful experience via homophobia, hate crimes, and even medical/religious rituals.

## Invisible Hands: Black Spiritual/Religious Lesbians Resisting Culture Crystallization

The hands of black lesbians represent sexual struggle and the unity in community in embracing this struggle to experience the legitimacy of queer/gay desires. Metaphorically, the bodies that these sexual hands belong to are rendered invisible because the epistemological or knowledge that informs their religious and spiritual personal approaches as conveyed in the *Spirited* anthology and *BWC* stories are unrecognized in the academy and public sphere. They deconstruct ideas of homosexual desire as "abnormal" by opening their bodies as material that hosts struggles and pleasure. In *Unbearable Weight*, Susan Bordo asserts that the body is a carrier of culture, and through the body's manifestations, it is also the carrier of cultural origins of power, consciousness, and complexity. She regards the body as a site of struggle because it internalizes images, symbols, and ideologies that ultimately become "cultural currents or streams." Bordo studies the ways in which female bodies in particular manifest these cultural streams through cultural symptoms that become physical, because it appears as "remarkably overdetermined symptoms of some of the multifaceted and heterogeneous distresses of our age."[14]

Bordo's notion of bodies that materialize as sites of struggle can be appreciated in Monique Meadow's story. Her story, like the others, exposes embodiment and knowledge production of sexual desires and pleasures that press against social ills. Monique, in her *Spirited* essay, "And Then I Met the Goddess," yearned for an "earth-loving, body-honoring path that would liberate her from guilt, shame, and confusion."[15] Although Monique was born and raised Baptist, she could not free herself of the "shackles" upon her bodily and sexual desires as a lesbian. It wasn't until she discovered and learned about Wicca and engaged once in sexual rituals with her Wicca community that she "unleashed her desire for a destiny that was as a healthy, self-loving lesbian woman." She says that her spirituality "as a witch helped her to not be resigned to sexual expression warped by shame." Monique identified through shame and guilt that her sexuality and sexual desires were pathologized and constrained, driving her to find a spiritual space that would fully engage her sexual being.

Monique Meadow's story suggests the capacity to bear cultural streams of power and symbols as sinful, abnormal, and deviant that both medicine and religion have reproduced over time as an invisible, yet medically, socially, and religiously pathological body. The *Spirited* anthology narratives about navigating and contesting religiosities and spiritualities show that their bodies are sites of struggle that cannot fully escape becoming targets of pathologizing cultural streams. Thus those bodies must perpetually negate the physical manifestations of these pathological cultural streams such as shame, guilt, and deprivation-like depression.

How do such cultural streams filter through a black queer body in general and the black lesbian's body in particular? Bordo's analysis of crystallization of culture is useful here. It is a conceptual framework that couches a process by which bodily manifestations and expressions take place as a result of the body converging with cultural streams or currents. Bordo uses anorexia as a cultural manifestation of the body to recognize that "psychopathologies develop within culture to be characteristic expressions of that culture, to be indeed the crystallization of much that is wrong with it."[16] Similarly, the process by which sexual epistemologies develop for the *Spirited* women point to a cultural manifestation of the body unraveling and shedding layers of oppressed states of mind. This appears as a convergence of ideas about shame, deviance, and abnormality within the queer/gay desiring body. Here lies the wrestling against such convergence permanently crystallizing in forms like the social construction of being "closeted," depression, self-hate/fear, and denial of sexual, social, and even tugs of war with religious/spiritual pain and pleasure.

As for Q, she says she learned to self-deny her same-gender sexual desiring sensibilities, and consequently, it took time to learn to affirm her sexuality after removing herself from Christianity in Dallas. By recognizing that her religious space contributed to her self-denial and unhappiness, Q shows her intentionality in questing for a more affirming religious experience. Q says, "Nichiren Daishonin Buddhism gave me the spirituality to tap into a power with my inner self and begin to heal from low esteem about my sexuality that interfered with even having healthy sexual relationships." For her, Buddhism filled a void of inner peace, which was tied to her sexual affirmation.

For Q, Monique, and others, awareness and making sense of how the cultural social ills are internalized and manifested through their bodies as self-hate or depression is the crux of their epistemological struggle and transformation. The streaming and intermingling of such perceptual and bodily ills become very complex and difficult to untangle via academic and social discourse. As a result, they should be centralized conceptually to help carefully identify the myriad of manifestations of culture oppression against the black queer/gay body. I call this myriad of manifestations of cultural oppression "black queer entrapment," and I define it as a socioculturally entangled subjectivity that contests the social, medical, and religious pathologies internalized and materialized as negative images and experiences about their queer/gay desires and practices.

Modeling Bordo, I situate black queer entrapment that helps legitimize the self by subverting representations of the ideological and cultural oppressive images, meanings, and signifiers that subjugate queer/gay desires. Black queer entrapment can be studied as body materiality that *Spirited* women like Monique internalize and deconstruct to be the entrapped array of mental, physical, and perceptual manifestations of behaviors such as shame, guilt, and denial of homosexual pleasure. Black queer entrapment reproduces a myriad of epistemological relationships with old and new religiosities and spiritualities because of the tension between embodied struggle and pleasure. Therefore, the relationship between religiosities/spiritualities and sexual pleasure can be interpreted through the ways in which the *Spirited* and *BWC* women call upon their bodily longings for intimacy as a dimension that reshapes their ways of knowing life-meaning religiosity or spirituality.

## A Spirituality of Resistance

Kelly Brown Douglas provides some interpretive tools for studying an epistemology of black lesbian religious and spiritual thought and sexual desire as a domain of black religious thought/queer studies. By visualizing forms that participate in constructing black bodies, Douglas suggests a spirituality of resistance. Douglas's book, *What's Faith Got to Do with It?*, explores how the black church inherits the mechanisms and structures of power that attempt to control bodies through sexism or heterosexism. These mechanisms and structures are also cultural streams that touch upon a Foucauldian regulatory power analysis. She attributes such power mechanisms to "Platonized Christianity." For Douglas, Platonized Christianity is a system of beliefs and ideas with origins in Plato and Socrates that infiltrate and shape Christian theology. By affirming hierarchical dualisms, Platonized Christianity gives rise to sexual ethics that denies the body and inhibits sexual activity. For Douglas, both "closed monotheism and Platonized sexuality" interact with each other to create a power within Christianity strong enough to lynch and crucify disregarded bodies, such as black bodies, in ways that desexualize or hypersexualize them.

Douglas's examination of Platonized Christianity is an attempt to identify how religious power has historically, ideologically, and theologically shaped and influenced inhibitions against the sexuality, especially homosexuality, inherited by the black religious community. However, her theological and historical work as womanist discourse only glosses over black homosexuality, and thus it needs expansion. Identifying major historical and theological origins of power and control is extremely important but insufficient to fully understand the present-day queer/gay embodiment of institutional religious power, racism, and negations of difference.[17] The major limitation with her work is that it ignores the "how and why" of sexual constructions as abnormal, marking a difference between homosexuality and heterosexuality by the dualistic mechanisms of Platonized Christianity. The *Spirited* women, like in Elisa's story below, compels us to take this difference seriously by speaking of women's wrestling with sexuality and sexual desires in poignant yet celebratory ways that suggest a disruptive difference between heterosexuality and homosexuality across black women's experience. The function of "spiritual resistance" must be diagnosed through the praxis and experiences of communities of black queer women. To this end, Douglas's analytical project of Christian black bodies, including homosexual bodies, gives little room to further engage and affirm the religious and spiritual diverse plurality of black queer religious thought and its particular relationship to sexual desire among black lesbians today.

Elisa Durrette was raised Christian and on a path to know a Jesus figure who embodied her sexuality in order for her to "become a witness of God's love and her own sexual ecstasy and identity."[18] She had been taught that homosexual thoughts were sinful and her sexual desires should be handed over to God. Elisa's religious teachings and experience subjugated her sexual thoughts and yearnings and became an inadequate form of religious ecstasy that fell short of being encompassed by "real ecstasy." Although her struggle to come to terms with relinquishing this oppressive and repressive religious knowledge was an enduring process of self-discovery for inner peace and acceptance, she ultimately says that it wasn't until she fell in love with Cynthia that she was face to face with the love of Jesus. Her first kiss with Cynthia unleashed a real ecstasy that affirmed all her forms of pleasure both religious and sexual. She says, "Yes, it's true that Jesus had loved me, but Cynthia let me know." Elisa's sexual and love expressions and sensations through a kiss with Cynthia were liberating, spiritual experiences. She sought a way to affirm her religious desires for feeling close to God and Jesus, and this could only take place by allowing herself to find affirmation in her queer/gay desires.

Elisa and Monique forge sexual knowledge through practices that signify a way to fully affirm and shape their religiosity and/or spirituality. This is a kind of "quest for complex subjectivity" because they seek to access a higher life meaning rooted in the ways they perceive in order to know and express their sexual desires. Studying embodiment through black queer entrapment can expose the ways that the material body is constructed by the institutional and ideological power of religions, and even medicine. Black queer entrapment is neither an LGBT nor queer identity nor a sexuality category fixed upon the body, though this possibility deserves some additional analysis. Like Bordo, I situate it as representative of how signifiers impact and create the material body as "carriers of social ills crystallizing culture."[19] Black queer entrapment can be a tool of analysis because it suggests that the black queer body is material as it wrestles with an array of mental, physical, and perceptual manifestations and behaviors such as shame, guilt, and the self-denial of homosexual pleasure.

Elisa also mirrors a key intervention that Kelly Brown Douglas terms spirituality of resistance. Douglas defines spirituality of resistance as "a sense of connection for black folks to maintain their own heritage as well to the divine in spite of the ways that society demeans their black humanity."[20] Douglas says that a spirituality of resistance "acts as a buffer of defense against white cultural characterizations of them as being unworthy of freedom, dignity, and even life."[21] On one hand, Elisa, Q, and Monique suggest that their spiritualities are the resistance against marginalizing their sexual desire from their own bodies, and in this way their spiritualities act as a buffer against the effects of heterosexual normativity. A black lesbian spirituality of resistance can identify the engaging ways that black queer bodies might maneuver black queer entrapment in community. However, the particularities of self-prohibition via body control as defined by Bordo must be carefully accounted for if there is potential to interpret black lesbian knowledge production and experience vis-à-vis a spirituality of resistance. If Douglas's idea of a spirituality of resistance can be gleaned from the *BWC* and *Spirited* stories, the diverse specificity of Elisa, Q, and Monique's religiosity and spirituality points to larger, but more profound, research questions about what it means to be a black lesbian body and still religious or spiritual. In other words, what's black and queer about the expression of diverse religious or spiritual thought?

Demonstrating the ways a celebratory resistance against societal and religious control over their sexual desires might reveal a nuanced sexual ethics that is no longer about controlling the sexuality of bodies and their sexual identities in private and public spheres. More importantly, the influential relationship between community and the individual black lesbian body is best appreciated by religious/spiritual sexual ethics or practices that seeks to own, affirm, and unleash body control and inhibitions that are internalized by the individual body and even the community through entrapment. The subverting of power and control disrupts the entrapments of social control.

In conclusion, I have sought to show a nascent relationship between diverse black religious thought formation across a diverse group of black lesbians, while also demonstrating that their knowledge formation about sexual desire comes through understanding queer subjectivities and deconstructing the materiality of black queer entrapment. Speaking out and sharing of black lesbian experiences should not simply point to "coming out," for that would reinforce the idea of being closeted and reproduce black queer entrapment. Instead, a release of a sense of freedom comes in publicly acknowledging that difference is not ultimately what immobilizes, but rather, the stigma-related silence that attempts to trample and inhibit free-flowing body expressions. The invisible hands of the *BWC* and *Spirited* black lesbians give rise to the unrecognized politics of struggle and pleasure, and yet still participating, in fully visible and visceral ways, across the bodies that encounter each other. Indeed, I hear these courageous voices through the words of James Baldwin:

"The questions which one asks oneself begin, at last, to illuminate the world, and become one's key to the experience of others. One can only face in others what one can face in oneself. On this confrontation depends the measure of our wisdom and compassion."[22]

To this end, in shaping womanist religious discourse, Alice Walker's multidimensional definition of womanism is more fully actualized via exposing black lesbian visibility as a particular sexual resistance and entitlement undergirded with diverse and fluid religious or spiritual dimensions empowered by greater human agency. In the final analysis, black lesbian sexual expression is a means by which new dimensions of black religious thought may help rupture fixities upon black queer bodies. Thus black queer entrapment as a sexual epistemological tool of analysis for black religious thought and womanist religious thought can help trace the legitimizing ways by which a quest for complex subjectivity might be embodied and navigated by black queer religious and spiritual bodies.

## Notes

1. Alice Walker, *In Search of Our Mothers' Gardens: Womanist Prose* (San Franciso: HarperCollins, 1983), xi.

2. I will also often refer to "abnormal" in the traditionally conceived view of deviating from the normal in ways that signify states of being as undesirable and worrisome by the normative.

3. I define religiosity as the religious practices by these women that are solely and directly connected to institutional, traditional, and doctrinal religion. Spirituality, which some women clearly differentiate from religiosity or religious practice, is referenced as the experience and practices that speak to inner awareness and an experience that is not religious (as I just defined) but tied to mystic, social, and even religious forces and energies. In this essay, I am limited in making fuller theoretical and practical distinctions between religiosities and spiritualities. However, the women's stories I present give either a blend of both or one or the other. For this study and beyond, I am choosing to be inclusive of both religiosities and spiritualities since they provide me with a wider circle of black lesbians who are publically articulating their struggles and transformations regarding their sexualities.

4. As source materials, I use parts of the nationally and internationally recognized and awarded 2008 independent film by Tiona McClodden, *Black Womyn Conversations*, of forty-nine black lesbian monologues on race, gender, and sexuality ranging from eighteen to sixty years old. I will also examine several essays from *SPIRITED* to support my claims. It is through these stories that trends of knowledge production about sexual desire unveil the deeper spaces of struggle and pleasure deconstructing embodied cultural pathologies. They identify as and represent a variety of religious and/or spiritual experiences and identities such as Wicca, Buddhism, Christianity, Yoruba, Candomblé, Sekhmet, and the nonreligious as spiritual. Many have switched from the Christianity of their childhood practice.

5. Audre Lorde, "The Master's Tools Will Never Dismantle the Master's House," in *Sister Outsider* (Berkeley: Crossing, 1984), 110.

6. Ibid., 111.

7. Anthony B. Pinn, *African American Humanist Principles* (New York: Palgrave Macmillan, 2004), 66.

8. Ibid.

9. Ibid., 105.

10. Lorde, 111.

11. Michel Foucault, *The History of Sexuality, Volume I* (New York: Vintage Books, 1978), 152.

12. Ibid., 41.

13. Ibid., 64.

14. Susan Bordo, *Unbearable Weight: Feminism, Western Culture, and the Body* (Berkeley: University of California Press, 1993), 141.

15. Monique Meadows, "And Then I Met the Goddess," in *Spirited: Affirming the Soul and Black Gay/Lesbian Identity,* ed. G. Winston James and Lisa C. Moore (Washington, DC: Redbone, 2006), 241–47

16. Ibid.

17. Kelly Brown Douglas, *What's Faith Got to Do with It? Black Bodies/Christian Souls* (Maryknoll, NY: Orbis Books, 2005), 75.

18. Elisa Durrette, "Love Lessons," in *Spirited*, ed. James and Moore, 81–93

19. Bordo, xxi.

20. Douglas, 172.

21. Ibid.

22. James Baldwin, *Nobody Knows My Name* (New York: Vintage International, 1954), xiii-xiv.

# 10

# "Beyond Heterosexuality"

## *Toward a Prolegomenon of Re-Presenting Black Masculinity at the Beginning of the Post–Civil Rights, Post-Liberation Era*

**EL Kornegay Jr.**

> *The great problem is how to be—in the best sense of that kaleidoscopic word—a man.*
>
> –James Baldwin

My older sister made a statement shortly after the death of our mother I will never forget: She felt our mother "was a lesbian." My sister laid out a historical accounting of the evidence she felt supported her claim. There was a certain discomfort that came along with the statement: one that I always felt rested with my sister, but came home to roost with me. I understand now that source may have been what she saw as a contradiction between our mother's somewhat pious Christian faith claim and the possibility of her being a lesbian. Whether or not my mother was a lesbian remains a mystery. However, what remains is the great problem of how to reconcile my own reality of who I am with the mythic truth of who my mother is to me. My sister's point of view caused me not only to reflect on what it meant to entertain the idea that the woman I cherished and loved as my mother was possibly a lesbian, but how her approach to sexuality and gender translates into the problem of raising a boy to face masculinity and my ability to endure it.

I see my mother's sexual orientation as such, and had not, until now, ever searched my mother's garden for answers to the possibility my sister raised concerning who our mother was as a sexual creature and who I might be as the living fruit of her sexual allowances.[1] And yet, if I am to go forward, I cannot, as Baldwin notes, lean heavily on the examples of dead great men [or women], of vanished cultures, natural history, or scientific or religious theories: I must expose something private about my mother and about myself that was nurtured in her fertile womb. Such is the case, if I must go in search of something that helps to explain who my mother was and is to me. This might help my sister to "get over" the messiness of our mother's life so she can accept her own, and it might help me to have a "stiffening of the will" that enables me to move beyond the limits of the prison of masculinity that she raised me to resist.

Using my mother's story, the essays and novels of James Baldwin require a different kind of approach and a different way of reading, which I call *narrǣontology*.[2] This term signifies a shift in how we tell the story of Being. It is a neon theology or a "graphic" theology that is a hermeneutical and exegetical disruption of the dialectic between the sacred and the profane used to produce the politics of respectability informing black religion and policing black life. If the difference between womanist to feminist is like "purple is to lavender," the difference between womanist to narrǣontology is what Alice Walker might be to James Baldwin. It is a womanist-like approach inasmuch as I find that the life of my mother and the literature of Baldwin have helped me outwit oblivion in a world that continues to tell me the answer to who I am naturally can never be "yes."[3] It is a way to talk about how the ascension of a black male to the pinnacle of American hegemonic masculinity does not change that sentiment. It is a way to talk about how the things I have used to identify myself—blackness and heterosexuality—have not as yet improved my condition when I consider the low yield relative to my lifelong investment in both. Navigating this new epoch requires a side-by-side womanist/narrǣontology reassessment of the race, sex, and gender rubric used to define myself and others like me. This prolegomenon serves as a model for possibly doing something other methodologies have yet to do—try a different way get beyond heterosexuality.

When it comes to religion and sexuality it seems that we prefer to talk about it at arm's length. In other words, through theory and theology we distance ourselves from the very things we are subject to be living out. It is easier to talk about other bodies' penises and vaginas than it is to talk about, touch, taste, and smell our own dicks and pussies, especially in relation to religion and theology. James Baldwin, on the other hand, requires us to think about how black bodies and black sexuality inform the black religious experience. Baldwin makes us think about those moments whereby the divine and black bodies connect via dicks, pussies, fingers, toes, tongues, and plastic attachments to produce a glorious moment accented by cries of "Oh Jesus fuck me!" or "Oh my fucking God!" as a testimony of our "entering into communion" with another sexually.[4]

My mother never spoke directly to me about sex, yet her library had its share of sexually charged literature. Maybe it was religious conviction coupled with a sexual restraint fashioned as it was for southern black Christian women of her time. Whatever the case, she was able to convey an idea of who she was *and maybe who she wanted me to become* through the novel. She knew the Bible could only give me so much, and where it could not or where she would not allow the gospel to venture was left up to my personal exploration of those novels. It is quite fascinating to go back now into my mother's literary garden and search my memories of the bounteous offering she planted there for her children. She never said anything about the books being gone or how long they remained absent from her shelves. She balanced their absence with healthy doses of church, scriptural references on the importance of prayer, worship, and service to God.

Among the portraits, photo albums, and books ranging from *Falconhurst Fancy* and the *King James Bible* was James Baldwin's *Another Country.* I first read *Another Country* when I was about fourteen. It was the first time in my life I encountered such a vivid mosaic of race, religion, and sex that included homosexuality. This is not to say that the other novels did not offer inferences of human sexuality, love, same-sex desire, or same-sex acts, but it was Baldwin's unpretentious narrative that swung the door open wide to the messiness of human life and love. Baldwin brought all of the disparate parts together, assembling under one roof the racial, sexual, and religious issues that frame America. In doing so, Baldwin had done something that "had been virtually ignored in American literature."[5]

By allowing me to be exposed to those novels and to Baldwin, my mother was able to convey to me the complexity of her world, while helping me to discover my own complexity in preparation for the world I was soon to enter. The post–civil rights, post-liberation world would be *another country*, and she knew that the gospel, black masculinity, and heterosexuality could carry me only so far. She understood that I would be "virtually ignored" because of my race and endangered because of my gender. My mother used literature and her kitchen table—the *welcome table*—as a place to prepare me for the world I was soon to enter.

There were many people who visited my mother's home, yet only a handful of special folk sat around the kitchen table. I saw them as being different from guests, for guests were relegated to the living room. The kitchen table was the place where my mother's gracious hosting relented in favor of her sociopolitical fire, her gifted radical mind, and the conviction of her Christian beliefs. My mother acted out her belief of love and justice in front of *all* children and I think *because of her children.* She enacted for us the rubric of the gospel to love one another as you love yourself. Her kitchen table was a space where I learned the love ethic espoused and interpreted as the bedrock of the gospel of justice. This justice played itself out through the love shared with the "uncles" and "aunts" who lived their lives beyond what their religion and tradition told them about themselves and love. It was there that I learned that to deny love was to deny justice and that to deny justice or love is to deny God's own self.

In a great way, James Baldwin is like the bachelor/bachelorette friends so loved by my mother that they were designated as "uncle." The designation of uncle carried with it something a bit more important in terms of how my mother viewed these men and women and how I was to view them. They acted as the Oedipal avuncular whereby the mother-brother bond is in some cases dramatically stronger than the marital bond.[6] Yet, my "uncles" did not represent a punitive figure in the way of Oedipus, but a figure "free to be more loving" to my mother and us, her children, *and even my father.*[7]

These uncles were family, and family always found their way to the kitchen. This is where the raucous humor and unbridled laughs filled the house. This is where my "uncles" and "aunts" came to sit and be themselves *out in the open.* My mother's kitchen table was a welcoming space, and if the novels introduced me to the issues of race, religion, and sexuality, then my mother's kitchen table introduced me to the antidote of the justice found in loving openly. Baldwin says:

> Love takes off the masks that we fear we cannot live without and know we cannot live within. I use the word "love" here not merely in the personal sense but as a state of being, or state of grace—not in the infantile American sense of being made happy but in the tough and universal sense of quest and daring and growth.[8]

My mother's kitchen table was a *welcome table* in that it was a space where I learned that breaking bread with addicts, persons living with disabilities, the less-educated, same-sex/gender-loving folk, people of modest means, and with *radicals*, was the norm. It is where I learned grace is a gift that comes with a price paid in the unsafe quest to dare love others. It was with her in a small black homestead community, in eastern North Carolina and the segregated South, that I first made the connection between love and justice, as well as a connection between the sacrament of breaking bread with those who lived and loved differently as its manifestation. She taught me that the only difference that mattered was whether or not a person loved others openly. The religious and theological bedrock of love and justice found at my mother's kitchen table extended to the church and beyond. There was always an open invitation to difference. That perpetual possibility for justice to be practiced at home reflected the call for justice to be practiced everywhere.

Such justice required daring, growth, and the love of many people. My mother taught me how to embrace difference as an integral part of a lifelong quest to engage in loving and being loved by human beings. When I was younger, I learned how to be welcoming in doing the "unmasculine" things associated with masculinity: cooking, cleaning, washing—caring.As with Baldwin, my mother's welcome table was where I learned how important it is that "men express the feminine within themselves, that they adopt the kind of tender nurturing usually associated with women."[9] I was her son, her disciple, and unbeknownst to me Baldwin's too. I became a "gentle" man and in the process an unmasculine man.[10]

Baldwin wrote to his nephew—and to me through him—"You were born where you were born and faced the future that you faced because you were black and *for no other* reason."[11] Like Baldwin, my mother understood the limitations of the power of black masculinity and heterosexuality for little colored boys. She understood it would not be enough to fight against what Baldwin calls a "powerful masculinity" that is quite inescapable.[12] This powerful hegemonic masculinity creates homophobia, which is not simply defined as a fear of homosexuals, but the deeper fear of being "unmasculine."

For Baldwin, being homosexual is not synonymous with being unmasculine and being heterosexual is not synonymous with being masculine. Therefore homophobia is not a fear/suspicion of homosexuals by heterosexuals, but a fear—in either case—of unmasculine behavior. Many men and some women fear and dislike an unmasculine male. In part, such behavior is based on the denial of loving oneself, loving others of both the same sex and the heterosexed openly. The "great problem" of how to be a man, for Baldwin, is the ability to love openly without fear. This dilemma and the oblivion of living unable to love is the "male prison" with which all men—heterosexual and homosexual—must contend. So then, the great problem for a man is not heterosexuality or homosexuality, but being identified as unmasculine: a social-political-economic-religious impotence rendering black males unable to engage fully in (hegemonic) masculinity and enabled to resist the need to be homophobic. I am contrasting the impotence associated with being unmasculine with the idea that black masculinity was "equated with heterosexual virility" because it complicates the prevailing idea of homophobia.[13]

There are two primary forms of homophobia: phallic homophobia and black homophobia. Phallic homophobia is concerned with sexual performance and sexual desire. Phallic homophobia is circumcised onto the bodies (through the penises of most black males) and circumscribed into the minds of black males. It is a phallic-oriented consciousness, which is something black males are often accused of possessing as a preoccupation or for some an occupation. First, phallic consciousness can be understood in the context of covenant making and covenant breaking. The choice of whether or not to be circumcised is a reminder of the divine covenant between God and man. Sexual desire invokes (in me) all of the divine maxims associated with when or when not to have sex, how to or how not to have sex, how many to have sex with, or whom to have sex with or not. Phallic homophobia is the fear of being caught placing our dicks in situations (e.g., bars, clubs, events, streets, people, alliances) where our sexual desires and sexual orientation go against the socio-religious covenant (heterosexual contract) we inherited. Phallic homophobia is a fear of being seen as unmasculine based on how we use our dicks. Black homophobia is a fear associated with not being able to live up to the societal demands or phallic prodigiousness of American democracy, and to not be able to uphold the phallic prodigiousness of black patriarchal *and* matriarchal demands of race, heteronormativity, the black family, the black church, and black Christianity. This form of homophobia is a psychological circumscription co-constituted by race, sex, gender, culture, and religion. Our dicks represent the conundrum of our social-political-economic-religious virility and impotence: our *black power*. In this instance, being born with a big dick matters most if you have wealth, fame, and power to match. Social virility, so coveted by men and the women who judge black males according to socio-economic success, signifies masculine righteousness, and that the covenant between our dicks and God is being fulfilled heterosexually and heteroeconomically. Yes, size does matter, but the only way to know is if you have experienced the difference sexually and economically. In this form of homophobia, the black homosexual becomes the scapegoat for the sexual-religious issues, such as the problem of circumcision, faced by black males, versus that energy being directed in an all-out assault on the inequalities fueling the social-political-economic-religious ineptitude suffered by many black males. This form of homophobia represents the fear of being deemed or made unmasculine by hegemonic masculinity, which is "broadly supported by social institutions, as not only the ideal way to be a boy or man, but ultimately the only way."[14] We end up chasing or being made to chase the "icons of religion, sports, historical figures, economic and political leaders and the entertainment industry."[15] These icons make up the walls of the male prison that supports hegemonic masculinity. These iconic representations of "true" masculinity are locked away in the male prison. Though unavailable to almost all black males to achieve, many still try to mimic what they represent often with devastating results. Reified by the exploits of black male sports, religious, economic, and political icons, black males either get locked into the myth of the male prison or locked up because of it![16] Either way, black males chasing the status and riches associated with hegemonic masculinity follow paths of self-destruction for themselves and others. Hegemonic masculinity is addictive and seductive to the point that it becomes a cult-like phenomenon that many men and women alike become complicit in maintaining. This is because of what hegemonic masculinity means with regard to socio-political-economic-religious opportunities and the perception of safety it offers from unmasculine behavior and unmasculine males. This is why homophobia is so pervasive and so deadly to black males, black women, the black church, black faith, the black community, and our capacity to love.

Black homophobia, then, is synonymous with black genocide. Black males are caught in the conundrum of hegemonic masculinity, whereby they are called to be a paternal-provider figure without the power to act on their love in a socio-political-economic-religious sense. They are faced with a seemingly unattainable and unacceptable standard of patriarchy. Hegemonic masculinity is often manifest as a sexualized physical bravado that leads to loveless acts toward themselves, and toward other black males, black women, black children, and the black communities in which they live. Many black males are perpetually attempting to create life and to love without the social-economic-political virility and courage needed to sustain it. As such, many black males are forced into repeating the sins of the past and being remanded to a sexually dependent identity that is easily controlled by homophobia.

As I understand it now, my mother taught me to fear neither difference, nor homosexuality, nor being unmasculine. In other words, being a *punk*, *sissy*, or *faggot* were not bad or sinful or both. I was given the opportunity to understand my own sexual thresholds and the messiness that would come with it. My mother showed me that what was good and right was to never be afraid of my desires, but to be cautious of the ramifications associated with acting on them. Baldwin teaches me not to allow the world to make me think with my dick, not to fear how I use it or to care how others use theirs. Baldwin says, "It does not take long, after all, to discover that sex is only sex, that there are few things on earth more futile or more deadening than a meaningless round of conquests."[17]

In looking back, I understand now that sex was something to be enjoyed, but it was not something that defined me as a man. Baldwin says that such definitional terms of "homosexual, bisexual, heterosexual . . . have very little meaning."[18] What mattered most was the fact that "if one's to live at all, one's certainly got to get rid of the labels."[19] Again, what I think my mother understood for her boy to become a man, he had to be able to live beyond the labels and to know how to love justly. Sometimes a good dick would not be enough, a big dick would not be enough, nor would *being a dick be enough.* I would need to know this if I was to conquer the many obstacles faced by many black males in America. My mother exposed me both literally and figuratively to examples of the possibilities of manhood, and through her understanding of womanhood, fought to create in me a social and religious virility that would save me from or break me free of the male prison.

What I realize now is that I have spent many years in the male prison and can attest to the possibility of only being on parole and not completely free. I am sure that with a mother's certainty, she realized I was born into the male prison. *You were born where you were born and faced the future that you faced because you were black and for no other reason.*My mother attempted to protect me from the devastation that threatened me the moment I declared myself a man, which is something she knew when she first saw my infant face.[20] As soon as I stepped onto the road of black manhood I ran headlong into a normative definition of masculinity that is established and defined by the larger white male culture. The majority of black males are destined to encounter this definition of masculinity.[21] This situation has made it difficult for black males (myself included) to reimagine themselves in ways beyond the *powerfully reiterative and self-reinforcing* hegemonic form of masculinity and its homophobias. I eschewed the lessons of my mother and abandoned her garden. I, like so many other black males raised by black mothers who have prayed long and hard against their sons never growing up, suffer deeply when I fall prey to the drugs, jail, and violent deaths experienced in the Republic.[22] We become accomplices to our own undoing and imprisonment by supporting homophobia and reinforcing hegemonic masculine behavior, which is devoid of the capacity to love openly. Like many black males, I too fell prey to the pressure to define myself through black heterosexuality and let my intractable socio-economic ineptitude make me homophobic. Dwight Hopkins says, "When black men adopt and implement the patriarchy of the larger white male culture [hegemonic masculinity], they can act out a very sinful and potentially deadly force on those around them."[23] So then, the "potentially deadly force" of hegemonic masculinity is not heterosexuality: it is homophobia.

To be denied the opportunity to love or to be loved is the greatest injustice to impose on anyone. As I stated earlier, I learned through her example of womanhood how to act out a social and religious virility that could save me from the male prison. My mother was *virile*: she defied the conventions of her time and she gave me that understanding of virility so that I could fight against the conventions of this post–civil rights, post-liberation era. She fought against the paternal forces of hegemonic masculinity with the power of her maternal soul: Audre Lorde says:

> For women, the need and desire to nurture each other is not pathological but redemptive, and it is within that knowledge that our real power is rediscovered. It is this real connection which is so feared by a patriarchal world. Only within a patriarchal structure is maternity the only social power open to women.[24]

I say that the real power available to both women and men to fight against hegemonic masculinity and homophobia *is* maternity. My mother understood that only the power of maternity would help me to fight against the hegemonic masculine pathologies of homophobia that are so pervasive among many black males, black women, black churches and communities. She gave me the knowledge to be nurturing and to be "gentle." She showed me how to protect the genius of my virility from those who would try to force me to use it according to the labels manufactured and enforced by hegemonic masculinity and homophobia. I was taught to rely on the maternal to understand who I am paternally and that I am both; she taught me to be spiritually androgynous and to respect the queerness of that. Baldwin says that to be androgynous

> . . . is to have both male and female characteristics. This means that there is man in every woman and a woman in every man. Sometimes this is recognized only when the chips are, brutally, down—when there is no longer any way to avoid this recognition. But love between a man and a woman, or love between any two human beings, would not be possible did we not have available to us the spiritual resources of both.[25]

Androgyny and maternity comprise the power of the unmasculine. I am learning spiritual androgyny requires me to be both mother and father. When the chips have been *brutally down*, the only way I avoided oblivion was to recognize and implement the spiritual resources of both to free myself from the danger of the male prison, hegemonic masculinity and homophobia. I have been on both sides of my mother's kitchen table—not only as her son the witness, but as a sinner, an addict, homeless, broke, broken, brokenhearted, and homophobic. Like so many that had gone before, at that welcome table I was healed by my mother's love—*as these go may others come.* Maternity is not only nurturing: it is redemptive. Baldwin says, "when men can no longer love women [and children] they also cease to love or respect or trust each other" and that nothing is more dangerous.[26]

I know I was not raised to be dangerous, at least not in the physical sense to myself or to others, but I know I have been both. I have felt the power of hegemonic masculinity and homophobia as I allowed myself to be imprisoned by expectations of men not to act like a sissy, a punk, or a faggot. I have allowed myself to be imprisoned by the expectations of women not to be unmasculine and in the process make them feel unsafe. The brutality of hegemonic masculinity and homophobia requires the anarchy of a radicalized maternal love to overcome the fear of male "sorriness"; sorriness (homophobia) associated with not living up to a standard of masculinity, which keeps us from our human beingness. Such is the absurdity of America. My mother knew this, and what she taught me is the reason that I have managed to survive being unmasculine this long. Baldwin says:

> My mother was the only human being in the world. The *only* human being: everyone else existed by her permission. Yet, what the memory repudiates controls the human being. What one does not remember dictates who one loves or fails to love. . . . [O]nly love can help you recognize what you do not remember. And memory makes its only real appearance in this life as this life is ending—appearing, at last, as a kind of guide into a condition which is as far beyond memory as it is beyond imagination.[27]

Was my mother a lesbian? Am I a man? In a post–civil rights, post-liberation era should or will it matter? Whatever the serpent(s) may be in my mother's garden, she exists first and foremost as a human being. That leads me to think that what matters is this question: In a world that imprisons our human beingness—punks us and makes sissies and pussies of us all—do you remember how to love? I enter into a condition far beyond the memories of my mother's garden and beyond the wildest dreams of how she might have imagined me or how I might have imagined myself. I do so with a stiffened will, beyond heterosexuality and ready to re-present black masculinity in the post–civil rights, post-liberation era. *Thank you Uncle Jimmy, Thank you Momma.*

# Notes

1. I am picking up on Renee Hill's admonition against limiting womanist approaches by being selective in the appropriation of parts of Alice Walker's definition of womanism regarding "the issue of sexuality and sexual orientation." The garden metaphor is an effective way for me to enter into a conversation with womanist thought the experience of being reared by a mother whose sexuality and maternal capacity have been put in flux by her daughter. Renee Hill, "Who Are We for Each Other? Sexism, Sexuality, and Womanist Theology," in *Black Theology: A Documentary History, 1980-1992, vol. 2*, ed. James Cone and Gayraud Wilmore (Maryknoll, NY: Orbis, 1993), 346–46.

2. This neologism is a combination of *narratology* and *ontology*. The two are connected by the combination of two diacritical marks—diphthong plus a trema (which I call a shifthong)—to represent the complexity of speech and how multiple meanings and new meanings glide back and forth within, and emerge from, the same words and sounds. This represents for me what James Baldwin does with language, in that he takes old ideas and hidden meanings—taboo if you will—redistributes and re-poses them in a socio-religious-political matrix to signify something new (beyond socially respectability), something absurd (race, sex, gender designations), and something human and divine about our existence (a profane reality that is immanently divine). It signifies new meaning that points away from what was meant (historically) toward what it should mean (presently).

3. James Baldwin, "The Male Prison," from *Nobody Knows My Name* (1954) in *James Baldwin: Collected Essays*, ed. Toni Morrison (New York: Literary Classics of the United States, 1998), 232.

4. Ibid., 235.

5. David Leeming, *James Baldwin: A Biography* (New York: Henry Holt, 1994), 206.

6. I am using a portion of Kress and Hodge's interpretation of the social meaning of Oedipus to highlight how the avuncular relationships were a means of destabilizing the prime directives of patriarchy, which promotes a singular paternal inheritance of heteronormative behaviors that prove detrimental to black males. It is also an important motif in most of Baldwin's novels, e.g., *Just Above My Head.* Robert Hodge and Gunther Kress, *Social Semiotics* (Ithaca, NY: Cornell University Press, 1988), 213.

7. Ibid., 215.

8. James Baldwin, *The Fire Next Time* (New York: Vintage, 1962), 95.

9. Leeming, *James Baldwin: A Biography*, 382.

10. Ibid., 382.

11. Baldwin, *The Fire Next Time*, 7.

12. Baldwin, "The Male Prison," 231.

13. I use *faggot*, *punk*, and *sissy* because "gay" or "homosexual" do not account for (in my own estimation) the difference between the sexual lives of poor black people (transvestites trying to survive or poor unmasculine males trying to prove their virility hustling, living, and dying on the streets) and that of the gay political subject. This is much the same as Audre Lorde's assertion that "poor women and women of color know there is a difference between the daily manifestations of marital slavery and prostitution since it is our daughters who line 42nd street: it is

black men who suffer a similar fateful disparity. Audre Lorde, "The Master's Tools Will Never Dismantle the Master's House," in *Sister Outsider* (Berkeley, CA: Crossing, 1984), 113.

14. Robert Heasley, "Crossing the Borders of Gendered Sexuality: Queer Masculinities of Straight Men," in *Thinking Straight: The Power, the Promise, and the Paradox of Heterosexuality,* ed. Chrys Ingraham (London: Routledge, 2005), 114.

15. Ibid., 110.

16. Ibid., 29. Dwight Hopkins talks about the myth of black masculinity, which can be seen, if you will, as a subordinate/syntagm with the paradigm of white male culture characterized as hegemonic masculinity. See note 21 below.

17. Baldwin, "The Male Prison," 234.

18. James Baldwin, "Race, Hate, Sex, and Colour: A Conversation with James Baldwin and Colin MacInnes," interview by James Mossman, *Encounter* (July 1965): 55–60.

19. Ibid., 55–60.

20. James Baldwin, *The Evidence of the Things Not Seen* (New York: Holt, Rinehart & Winston, 1985), 19.

21. Dwight Hopkins, "A New Heterosexual Male," in *Global Voices for Gender Justice* (Cleveland: Pilgrim, 2001), 28.

22. Baldwin, *The Evidence of the Things Not Seen*, 19.

23. Ibid., 28.

24. Audre Lorde, "The Master's Tools," 114.

25. James Baldwin, "Freaks and the American Ideal of Manhood," in *James Baldwin: Collected* Essays, ed. Toni Morrison (New York: Literary Classics of the United States, 1998), 814.

26. Baldwin, "The Male Prison," 231–35.

27. Baldwin, *The Evidence of the Things Not Seen*, xii.

# PART IV

# Politics

11

# Aesthetic Pragmatism and a Third Wave of Radical Politics

Sharon D. Welch

In 1998, the sociologist Patricia Hill Collins sounded a clarion call for the revitalization of visionary pragmatism, a tradition deeply rooted in the African American tradition, but largely absent in many urban African American communities and sorely needed in progressive politics and in our common life. Collins advocates moving from the reactive stance of critique to the creative task of shaping policies and practices. She claims that "visionary pragmatism" cannot be reduced to a "predetermined destination," but signifies participation in a larger, ongoing collective struggle: "Black women's visionary pragmatism points to a vision, it doesn't prescribe a fixed end point of a universal truth. One never arrives but one constantly strives." Collins extols a pragmatism grounded in "deep love, intense connectedness and a recognition that those in the future will face struggles and challenges that we can neither imagine nor forestall."[1]

The visionary pragmatism described by Collins is essential for our work in this time of third wave political engagement, an era of activism that builds on the first two waves of radical politics and yet has its own energy, dynamics, and challenges.

The first wave of revolutionary politics was the forceful denunciation of the manifold forms of social injustice—slavery, the oppression of workers, and the secondary status of women—all forms of oppression defended for millennia as divinely ordained or part of the natural order of things.[2]

These struggles for social justice have been augmented by a second wave of activism, the work of identity politics, the resolute claim for the complex identities and full humanity of all groups marginalized and exploited by systemic oppression and silenced through cultural imperialism, such as people with disabilities, those who are gay, lesbian, bisexual and transgender, ethnic, racial, and religious minorities, and all deprived of cultural respect and full political participation.

Within these two waves of political activism, people have exposed and denounced with power and courage the five forms of social injustice identified by the political philosopher Iris Marion Young: exploitation, marginalization, powerlessness, cultural imperialism, and violence.[3]

While the critical work for social justice and for the full recognition and human rights for all peoples goes on, these tasks now occur within a third paradigm. Third wave radical politics is a response to the first two waves—to powerful declarations of defiance, rage, and joyous self-affirmation. Once we recognize that a situation is unjust, once we grant the imperative of including the voices and experiences of all peoples, how then do we work together to build just and creative institutions?

As we take up this creative task, we have much to learn from the visionary pragmatism analyzed by Patricia Hill Collins and manifest in the leadership of those who have led significant social change in the past (Nelson Mandela and Ronald Dellums, former Congressman and current mayor of Oakland) and in the leadership of one who may bring about significant social change in the present and future, President Barack Obama.

The leadership of Dellums, Mandela, and Obama is fueled by the intense connections highlighted by Collins, and by a lifelong commitment to human flourishing. What is remarkable, however, about the trajectory of the work of Dellums and Mandela is not only the depth of commitment but the duration of that commitment. When Mandela became one of the leaders of the African National Congress, the struggle for freedom in South Africa had been taking place for fifty years. His own work, from his first political involvement in the 1940s to his election as President in 1994, also spanned more than fifty years, including almost three decades spent in prison. In his autobiography, Mandela recounts the amount of creativity and time it took for even the most basic changes within the prison system, fifteen years to obtain the right to food that was equal in quality to that given white prisoners, twenty-six years to obtain access to newspapers.[4]

In his work for social justice within the United States and internationally, Congressman Dellums was a stalwart supporter of the freedom struggle in South Africa, and worked for sixteen years before he was able to lead the U.S. in participating in the international pressure of sanctions that played a key role in the collapse of apartheid.[5] In the case of President Obama, his leadership has just begun.

On an unseasonably warm fall evening in November 2008, I joined thousands of people in Grant Park, cheering the win in each state, and relishing the grand collective jubilation of shouts, dancing, cries, laughter, and hugs when the polls closed at 11:00 p.m. and we knew that we had done it.[6] Three years after that momentous election, however, there is a complicated mix of determination, frustration, and confusion. How have the joyous cries of "Yes, we can!" become the painful realities of lowered expectations and blocked and only partial changes in political processes and policies?

Before the vote on healthcare reform, some analysts went so far as to pronounce the failure of the Obama presidency, and more than a few progressives agreed, many even expressing profound disillusionment with electoral politics and the existing democratic process as a venue for significant social change. What is it that made the struggle for even modest changes in healthcare policy so difficult and so deeply contentious? What has made it so difficult to reach a national consensus on governmental responses to the shared recognition of economic crisis?

What has occurred since President Obama was elected is indeed unsettling and sobering, but it is also predictable and unsurprising to those who know the complexities of institutional change.

It is a painful fact that to care passionately about justice—to understand thoroughly the contours and dynamics of oppression—does not mean that we are equally skilled in the task of coordinating and managing human and natural resources justly, creatively, and in a way that lasts for the future. As an activist, I have seen the impact of speaking truth to power: the inspiration and sense of identity evoked by clarion denunciations of injustice and faithful witness to ideals of justice and peace. As we take up the task of using power truthfully, however, we recognize that the work is not done when the protests are heard. Rather it is here, it is now, that another type of work begins.

The move from knowing what *should* be done to actually getting it done is as great a shift ethically and philosophically as is the move from *is* to *ought*. For here, as we move from *ought* to *how*, we encounter a paradox. Not only does work for constructive social change take significant amounts of time, but there are also intrinsic differences between prophetic critique/vision and democratic leadership. We may critique alone and we may even envision alone, but to implement that vision, to build on that critique, requires the cooperation of other people—other people to actually carry out the work on a daily basis, other people to judge, refine, and critique new systems and processes. And, as you may have noticed, other people tend to have different ideas—not only different ideas of how to meet shared goals, but possibly better ideas about the most fitting, concrete ways to administer healthcare, or to support ecologically sustainable forms of energy production.

Furthermore, as we implement new forms of social organization, there is one type of response that can be reasonably expected and anticipated, the ubiquitous Western resistance to social change. Professors at Booth, the University of Chicago Graduate School of Business, teach courses in which leaders in corporations, nonprofit organizations, and educational institutions grapple with the complexities of social change. We often expect that a successful innovation will follow a steady trajectory, gradually and inexorably moving from little knowledge and little acceptance to being taken for granted as the way things are done. The researchers at Booth, however, found just the opposite in their study of successful business practices. While lasting innovations had an initial rush of success, this was followed by a dramatic decrease in support and a long period of intense resistance and uneven movement toward acceptance. Their conclusion: resistance cannot be prevented, but it can be overcome, possibly even taken as a catalyst for greater insight and creativity.[7]

There are indications that this may well be a longstanding pattern in Western culture. The words of Machiavelli, in *The Prince*, are instructive:

> And it ought to be remembered that there is nothing more difficult to take in hand, more perilous to conduct, or more uncertain in its success, than to take the lead in the introduction of a new order of things. Because the innovator has for enemies all those who have done well under the old conditions, and lukewarm defenders in those who may do well under the new. . . . Thus it happens that whenever those who are hostile have the opportunity to attack they do it like partisans, whilst the others defend lukewarmly.[8]

Machiavelli certainly helps us understand why the supporters of President Obama's healthcare reform and other policy initiatives have been relatively silent in contrast to those who fiercely resist any reform. And yet, it could be that the relative lack of passionate support for change is grounded as much in reason as in incredulity. In addition to known limits, any course of action may have devastating unintended consequences. It is in light of this reality that ecologists such as Anna Peterson (in *Being Human*) and Wes Jackson call us to a fallibility-based worldview: an acknowledgment that all that we know—whether through the resources of reason, imagination, intuition, or compassion—is partial, always vastly exceeded by that which we do not know.[9] For example, we can only ever have partial knowledge of the long-term impact of our agricultural and industrial practices, the ripple effects of changes in social and economic policies, and the unpredictable consequences of our attempts to nurture and sustain the generations that depend upon us.

Let us return to the question of the Obama presidency. Has the Obama administration failed? Are there any other strategies that could have ensured greater success? If Machiavelli and the researchers at Booth are right, it is unlikely that any other strategy would have gone more smoothly, or that any tactic would have ensured success. In fact, what many see as a particular failure of one administration is giving us essential lessons in the very nature of Western political practice. As we acknowledge the complexity of institutional change, we encounter a paradox, *a fundamental lack of parity between the moral certainty of our denunciation of existing forms of injustice and our ethically reasonable uncertainty about the justice and feasibility of our cherished alternatives.*

In short, these are the challenges of leadership, for which we need resilience and practical curiosity:

1. While we can reasonably expect significant challenges to any innovation, we can neither predict the reasons for the resistance, nor the identity of the bearers of resistance;
2. We cannot know in advance which visions will spark the imaginations of others, or which plans will prove to be plausible and energizing;
3. We can neither predict nor control the actual impact of our efforts.

Here, then, is our challenge as activists, as religious leaders, philosophers, and theologians. It is easy to mobilize political will against a common enemy and for certain goals. As Nelson Mandela stated, "It is a relatively simple proposition to keep a movement together when you are fighting against a common enemy. But creating a policy when that enemy is across the negotiating table is another matter altogether."[10]

We have yet to learn how to mobilize political energy when we acknowledge that even we, the "righteous vanguard," are flawed. While our goals of common flourishing are unambiguously clear, the means of attaining those same goals are intrinsically ambiguous and fluid.

In spite of these obstacles, there is change in corporate life. And in spite of these obstacles, there can be change in political life. These changes only happen, however, when we succeed in learning what the educator Lisa Delpit calls the "codes of power," which enable us to move from solitary or minority critique and vision to vital collective action.[11] In this process of mastering change, some analysts urge us to forego truth in the interest of success. Rosabeth

Moss Kanter, for example, states that there is often a clear disjunction between the institutional memory of change and the process of change itself. While the memory of successful changes in the past focuses on clarity, certainty, and consensus, the process of change as it occurs is characterized by conflict, risk, errors, and confusion.[12] Kanter writes:

> Where there is apparent consensus, there was often controversy, dissent, and bargaining. . . . Where the ultimate choice seems the only logical one . . . there were often a number of equally plausible alternatives that might have fitted too. . . . Where clear-sighted strategies are formulated, there was often a period of uncertainty and confusion, of experiment . . . and there may have been some unplanned events or "accidents" that helped the strategy to emerge.[13]

According to Kanter, those who master change must know and understand the conflictual, ambiguous process of change, and, they must create and utilize dualistic myths that deny that very ambiguity. She argues that "change masters" create myths in which "conflicts disappear into consensus," "accidents, uncertainties and muddle-headed confusion disappear into clear-sighted strategies." "The champions of an idea have to look unwaveringly convinced of the rightness of their choice to get people to accept the change."[14] Kanter assumes an inevitable hierarchy—those who engineer change, and those affected by it. As Kanter states, "those who master change know that they can never tell the 'truth,' but they also know what the 'truth' is."[15]

Many of us are committed, however, to another path, one grounded in womanist thought, in Buddhist practice, and in the political leadership of Ronald Dellums and Nelson Mandela. In the work of Monica A. Coleman, Barbara Holmes, and Victor Anderson, we have a ringing affirmation of the creative possibilities for human and nonhuman flourishing that grace our lives. And yet, Coleman, Holmes, and Anderson also point to the ambiguities and complexities of this gift. Holmes claims that "freedom takes on a different guise in each generation" and acknowledges that "I'm not certain that I know much more than my family members did about building a peaceful, interconnected society." She maintains, however, a resolute and joyous commitment to the journey of "liberation for all."[16] Coleman reminds us that there are multiple bests in any given situation.[17] Victor Anderson invites us to remain open to "a world that shows itself as processive, open and relational." He celebrates the power and promise of "creative exchange," those moments "when the self and community transcend isolated self-interests and seek human fulfillment and flourishing in relation to larger wholes." Anderson also explicitly calls us to face the reality of ambiguity even within the process of "creative exchange," what he calls the "grotesque":

> [T]he grotesque recovers and leaves unresolved prior and basic sensibilities such as attraction/repulsion and pleasure pain differentials . . . unresolved ambiguities may leave possibilities open for creative ways of taking an object or subject; for in the grotesque, an object is, at the same time, other than how it appears when one contour or another is accented.[18]

Holmes reminds us of a simple, yet easily forgotten fact: "We thought that we had it all figured out, but how could we have presumed that liberation would be easy?"[19]

The problem is that when moving from critique to the creation of policies and institutions, even when we share the same goals, hear the same cries of suffering, the particular responses to that suffering, the specific strategies for making healthcare accessible, education transformative, and economic systems equitable are often radically, and incommensurately, different. Furthermore, we cannot know in advance which policies, which institutional frameworks will fulfill our goals.[20] Even our most rigorous thinking will be partial, and, as Coleman so clearly states, even the "best new things involve some kind of loss." She also reminds us that, in our experience, and in the response of God to the world, there often are conflicting goals:

> God does not always offer five possibilities, ranking them in order of preference. There may be several equally "good" options. They simply lead in different directions. What we actually do is conditioned by our freedom. There is, however, no cause to assume that there is only one option that will embrace God's calling.[21]

Given the unfolding novelty that may characterize our common life, it is our challenge to honor a relationality that offers possibilities, while keeping in mind the ambiguity at the heart of these possibilities—the honest recognition that there are multiple bests, unforeseen consequences, and ongoing challenges. We are indeed blessed to have the stories of those who have lived in such deep and honest relationality. Nelson Mandela, for one, recounts the power, and yet the costs of relationally based, creative social change. In the electoral campaigns of the African National Congress in 1994, he spoke of both the need for a resolute commitment to freedom and a realistic perspective on the time required for institutional change:

> I told our supporters: Life will not change dramatically, except that you will have increased your self-esteem and become a citizen in your own land. You must have patience. You might have to wait five years for results to show.[22]

Although the African National Congress won 62.5 percent of the national vote, Mandela was aware that substantial work was yet to come:

> We have not taken the final step of our journey, but the first step on a longer and even more difficult road. For to be free is not merely to cast off one's chains, but to live in a way that respects and enhances the freedom of others. The true test of our devotion to freedom is just beginning.[23]

We have much to learn from the longstanding political leadership of former Congressman Ronald Dellums. Dellums warned against compromising too soon, and taught what was required to make transformative compromise possible.

In *Lying Down with the Lions*, Dellums recounts the history of his work in politics and the commitments and strategies that have shaped his work, a career grounded in two factors: an ongoing openness to listening to the stories of injustice and hope of those who were marginalized and exploited, and an astute understanding of the nature of the democratic process.[24]

Although affirming the "moral certitude" and "righteous rage" of those who are oppressed, Dellums's own political engagement led him away from denunciations of other people and social structures. In responding to those voices of suffering and rage, Dellums recounts that he had early on to make a choice: Was he going to be a "rhetorical activist" or "an effective legislator committed to securing social change through the process of governance"?[25]

Dellums learned the importance of these principles early in his political career. In a speech in Milwaukee in 1971, he referred to colleagues in the House of Representatives as "mediocre prima donnas," "with no real understanding of the pain and human misery being visited upon our people." Back on the floor of the House, Representative Wayne Hayes verified that the statement was accurate, and then asked Dellums, "I just wonder if you then want a bunch of mediocre prima donnas to pay more serious attention to your amendment?"[26]

The lessons here were clear:

> I had not come to Congress to attack and alienate my colleagues; I had come to challenge their ideas. I needed to step back from the personal. . . . I had to return to the educative role that Dr. King had laid out in his challenge to leadership. I needed to become better informed, to understand my opponents and be able to best them in open debate. I had to bring them along with me, not demand that they reject themselves. . . . I could not be content with a role as the radical outsider if I wanted people to pay heed to our radical ideas. I needed to develop arguments that my fellow legislators could take home to *their* constituents and imagine articulating at *their* constituents' day meetings.[27]

This is a lesson that many progressives have yet to learn. As we have moved from the stance of critical outsiders to empowered insiders, we may have thought that the mandate of the Obama presidency was greater, and the task less onerous, than it actually was, and is. The oft-repeated statement that the Democrats have a majority in both Houses is both factually true and practically irrelevant. Given the great divides within the Democratic Party on every issue of importance, from healthcare reform to military policy to reproductive choice and marriage equality, it has been as difficult to garner consensus among Democrats as it was in the past to gain accord between Democrats and Republicans.

This is as much a challenge for progressive activists as it is for members of the Obama administration: How can we find arguments that are persuasive to independents, to conservatives, to those fearful whites who are drawn to the polarizing and violent rhetoric of the Tea Party movement? We know how to create forms of public witness that denounce what is wrong—demonstrations, boycotts, sit-ins. What is harder, however, is finding the means of providing energizing and compelling public support for what *may* be right. How do we show support for the messy and ambiguous process of change? How do we symbolically and collectively express a fallibility-based worldview and delight in imperfect, impermanent creativity?

While certainty may at times be a creative delusion, uncertainty is the inescapable matrix of all our problem-solving efforts. In fact, the illusion that there could be strategies that guarantee ultimate victory is itself the product of injustice. My work as an activist, administrator, and ethicist has been profoundly shaped by the womanist critique of dominant ethics. The problem is that what counts as "responsible action" for the Euro-American middle and upper-middle class is predicated on an intrinsically immoral balance of power. We assume that to be responsible means that one can ensure that the aims of one's actions will be carried out. We are challenged by African American women and men—such as Katie G. Cannon, Karen Baker-Fletcher, Toni Cade Bambara, Dwight Hopkins, Paule Marshall, Stephanie Y. Mitchem, Toni Morrison, Anthony B. Pinn, Mildred Taylor, and Emilie Townes—to find the resources to see clearly both the imperative of action and the limits of our political insight and strategic power.[28]

Has, then, the Obama presidency failed? Has it succeeded? It is too early to tell, for its work, our work, has just begun. Our role is not only to support policies that we cherish, but also to find ways to bring others along. As we do this work, conflict and resistance may be experienced not as obstacles to be bemoaned, but as realities to be accepted, even played as the ingredients of greater creativity.

To seek the fitting response, not the definitive response, places us in the good company of those who, to use the words of Patrick Chamoiseau, "know through which vices to rifle in order to stumble upon virtue."[29] In our work as leaders, stumble we will, yet create we may, evoking the beauty and justice to be found in a group, a situation, a moment in time. This is our great challenge, our rich legacy, and our sustaining and empowering hope.

## Notes

1. Patricia Hill Collins, *Fighting Words: Black Women and the Search for Justice* (Minneapolis: University of Minnesota Press, 1998), 187–91.

2. Adam Hochschild recounts the audacity of the abolitionist movement. Within a century, an institution that had endured since the beginning of recorded human history had lost moral and political legitimacy. That the struggle was against "natural" hierarchies would neither be easy nor inevitable, was signaled in the resistance of William Wilberforce, one of the leaders of the British abolitionist movement, to any economic, political, or educational rights for either women, or for the British working class. Adam Hochschild, *Bury the Chains: Prophets and Rebels in the Fight to Free an Empire's Slaves* (Boston: Houghton Mifflin, 2005).

3. Iris Marion Young, *Justice and the Politics of Difference* (Princeton: Princeton University Press, 1990), 48–63.

4. Nelson Mandela, *Long Walk to Freedom* (Boston: Little, Brown & Company, 1994), 364–65, 381, 502, 505.

5. Ronald V. Dellums and H. Lee Halterman, *Lying Down with the Lions: A Public Life from the Streets of Oakland to the Halls of Power* (Boston: Beacon Press, 2000), 129.

6. For an analysis of governance and the Obama presidency, see Sharon D. Welch, "The Machiavellian Dilemma: Paradoxes and Perils of Democratic Governance," *Tikkun Magazine* 25, no. 3 (May/June 2010): 19, http://www.tikkun.org/nextgen/the-machiavellian-dilemma.

7. "Strategic Business Leadership: Creating and Delivering Value," taught by Holly Raider, Ronald Burt, Harry Davis. The University of Chicago Booth School of Business, Executive Education. July 13–17, 2009.

8. Niccolò Machiavelli, *The Prince*, trans. W. K. Marriott (1513; reprint, St. Petersburg, FL: Red and Black Publications, 2008), 11.

9. Anna Peterson, *Being Human: Ethics, Environment, and Our Place in the World* (Berkeley: University of California Press, 2001).

10. Mandela, 593.

11. Lisa Delpit, *Other People's Children: Cultural Conflict in the Classroom* (New York: The New Press, 2006).

12. Rosabeth Moss Kanter, *The Change Masters: Innovation and Entrepreneurship in the American Corporation* (New York: Simon & Schuster, 1983), 288–89

13. Ibid., 285–86.

14. Ibid., 288.

15. Ibid.

16. Barbara A. Holmes, *Liberation and the Cosmos: Conversations with the Elders* (Minneapolis: Fortress Press, 2008), 187, 190–91.

17. Monica A. Coleman, *Making a Way Out of No Way: A Womanist Theology* (Minneapolis: Fortress Press, 2008), 76.

18. Victor Anderson, *Creative Exchange: A Constructive Theology of African American Religious Experience* (Minneapolis: Fortress Press, 2008), 132, 11.

19. Holmes, 188.

20. As we move from prophetic denunciation to strategic implementation, there is much to gain from the resources of what my mentor, professor, and colleague Peter Hodgson calls "radical liberalism." Hodgson challenges us to follow the promise of liberalism's "openness to criticism, self-examination, and change." Hodgson's understanding of liberalism resonates with that of Paul Starr, who reminds us that at the core of liberalism is a willingness "to be judged by its real effects. . . . Mere gestures toward a good society are of no interest beyond a seminar room. Liberalism stands not only for the principle that we all have an equal right to freedom but also for the hypothesis that this is a workable ideal. . . ." In the current situation, Starr claims that the challenge is not that of winning elections, but whether or not liberals "can achieve the organizational strength and intellectual coherence to . . . lead." Peter C. Hodgson, *Liberal Theology: A Radical Vision* (Minneapolis: Fortress Press, 2007), 8. Paul Starr, *Freedom's Power: The True Force of Liberalism* (New York: Basic, 2007), 2, 220.

21. Coleman, 8, 76.

22. Mandela, 614.

23. Mandela, 624–25.

24. Dellums, 2–3.

25. Ibid., 76.

26. Ibid., 74.

27. Ibid., 76.

28. See, for example, the works of Katie G. Cannon, *Black Womanist Ethics* (Atlanta: Scholars Press, 1988); Katie G. Cannon, *Womanism and the Soul of the Black Community* (New York: Continuum, 1997); Karen Baker-Fletcher, *Sisters of Dust, Sisters of Spirit* (Minneapolis: Fortress Press, 1998); Karen Baker-Fletcher and Garth Kasimu Baker-Fletcher, *My Sister, My Brother: Womanist and Exodus God-Talk* (Maryknoll, NY: Orbis, 1997); Toni Cade Bambara, *The Salt Eaters* (New York: Vintage, 1981); Dwight L. Hopkins, *Introducing Black Theology of Liberation* (Maryknoll, NY: Orbis, 1999); Paule Marshall, *The Chosen Place, The Timeless People* (New York: Random House, 1984); Stephanie Y. Mitchem, *Introducing Womanist*

*Theology* (Maryknoll, NY: Orbis, 2002); Toni Morrison, *The Bluest Eye* (New York: Holt, Rinehart & Winston, 1970); Anthony B. Pinn, *Terror and Triumph: The Nature of Black Religion* (Minneapolis: Fortress Press, 2003); Mildred Taylor, *Let the Circle Be Unbroken* (New York: Bantam, 1973); Mildred Taylor, *Roll of Thunder, Hear My Cry* (New York: Bantam, 1984); Emilie Townes, *In a Blaze of Glory: Womanist Spirituality as Social Witness* (Nashville: Abingdon, 1995); Emilie Townes, *Breaking the Fine Rain of Death: African American Health Issues and a Womanist Ethic of Care* (New York: Continuum, 1998); Emilie Townes, *A Troubling in My Soul* (Maryknoll, NY: Orbis, 1993); Emilie Townes, *Embracing the Spirit: Womanist Perspectives on Hope, Salvation and Transformation* (Maryknoll, NY: Orbis, 1997).

29. Patrick Chamoiseau, *Texaco*, trans. Rose-Myriam Rejouis and Val Vinokurov (New York: Pantheon, 1997), 119.

# 12

# "We'll Make Us a World"

## *A Post-Obama Politics of Embodied Creativity*

**Barbara A. Holmes**

*And God stepped out on space and s/he looked around and said*
*I'm lonely—I'll make me a world . . .*

–James Weldon Johnson, "The Creation"[1]

*When do we accept and assume the responsibility of creating new worlds, new methods, and new understandings, in which to express both our otherness and our sameness to one another? . . . Is it not time for a truly contextual theology, even perhaps discordantly polyvocal and polycentric, which lifts up the absent and unheard voices, contexts and experiences that bring new languages, new understandings, new analyses to new and challengingly different questions?*

–Diana L. Hayes[2]

## Introduction

We are in a place we never expected to be in our lifetimes. Many of us who came of age on the cusp of the civil rights movement have witnessed the inauguration of the first bi-racial president of the United States. We have come from the denigration of Representative Barbara Jordan in the press: "She looks like a mammy and sounds like God" to Michelle Obama's creative renegotiation of her role as First Lady.[3] Her pointed but playful use of performative acts points toward new options for engaging racism in a purportedly postracial society.

Although we could not have imagined an Obama administration, we are now required to imagine its aftermath. We must also consider how we will make new worlds for another generation using embodied creativity, reflexive memory, and trickster resourcefulness. People of color don't need star leaders but they do need a plan that will not shatter when a bullet finds its mark or the march of time blunts the relevance of individual sacrifices. Martin Luther King Jr., Rosa Parks, Fannie Lou Hamer, and El-Hajj Malik el Shabazz represent iconic figures whose engagement with "the powers that be" of their era gave clues to the way forward. The Obamas offer a new model of empowerment for a new century: being that supersedes doing; angst-free justice seeking; and modifications of ironclad allegiances to that old Ship of Zion.

## World-Making 101

A politics of creativity is an orientation that negotiates intransigent issues and public policy through the lens of incongruity and art. Alice Walker's poetic inspiration for womanist thought invites a look at other literary offerings, one of which is James Weldon Johnson and his lyrical poem "The Creation." Weldon's poem begins with God stepping out to announce her surprising intention, "I'll make me a world."

There is a certain audacity and inevitability in this declaration, as well as the sense that the materials for such a project are already at hand. Despite her divine and presumed birthing prowess, She-God will not have to push, He-God will not have to impregnate. Instead, the spirit of creativity will capture quantum particles, assemble the poetry of spacetime, and mix the no-nonsense mortar of clay and breath into life abundant.

Whether or not we use a Christian/Genesis framework, world-making requires as its initial step, the quelling of chaos. Race is the most chaotic category of all because its existence requires a grotesque mix of deeply sedimented social aversions and mythology. Disorder reigns until divine/human action creates space for the new possibilities to emerge. World-making is the labor-intensive and justice-oriented work of the community; expressed through collective action, as well as through risk-taking charismatic leadership.

Yet social action alone is never enough to create new realities. It will make spaces for temporary changes, but those changes will ultimately collapse unless the unseen scaffolding of spiritual and psychic health provides support. As people of color, we persist in the efforts toward building reconciled societies, but neither activism nor politics will get us to our worthy but elusive goals. More is needed.

World-making 101 requires that we relinquish the narrative assertions that sass, bootstrap pulling, or heroism is any match for the global corporate manipulations that affect the quality of our lives. Instead, I am suggesting that an embodied politics of creativity changes us, so that we can walk away from the victim/victimizer stalemates and disrupt the patterns of polarizing political action.

Even the unexpected election of President Barack Obama does not lessen the urgency to make new worlds and to empower a just political order. Diane L. Hayes reminds us of this responsibility and offers a pathway toward the future. She urges us to create new worlds by fully inhabiting our multivalent differences and by envisioning a politics of creativity that gleans as much from First People, shamans, poets, and seers as it does from eurocentric values, vision, and political constructs.[4] Michelle Obama depicts the power of being "as an interactive event and space where people perform assigned roles and construct a social reality" that reclaims the past and projects new realities.[5]

## Did You See Her Arms?: Embodied Creativity as a Catalyst for Change

> As much as a black male president changes the way black people are involved in the narrative of American history, the idea of a black first lady . . . is a far more discomfiting and radical challenge that goes straight to the root of the historical structures of racism in America.[6]

Everything changed when President Barack Obama became the first recognized person of color to occupy the presidency of the United States, but even more changed when First Lady Michelle bared her arms. While candidate Barack Obama's unique cultural identifications confounded some, Michelle's did not. We knew her as the progeny of slaves, a worthy representative of embattled black womanhood, married to the quintessential twenty-first-century man.

> Unlike her husband, whose bi-racial background and international upbringing made fitting him into the Black male trope trickier, Mrs. Obama was an authentically and stereotypically Black woman: angry, sassy, unpatriotic and uppity. Painting Mrs. Obama in this light, her critics essentially asked: How can Michelle Obama be First Lady when she's no lady at all?[7]

Did you see her arms? Eluned Jones of the University of Kings College, Canada notes "the designation of Michelle Obama as 'First Lady' enshrines a black woman within the privileged domestic space which is seen as the moral and spiritual center of the nation."[8]

This space may be privileged as a symbol of romanticized femininity in the White House, but domesticity is disdained and delegated to women of color in every other house in America. Women of color generally, and African American women specifically, have occupied domestic spaces as "other mothers" to the progeny of the dominant culture for longer than anyone can remember. Underpaid and often misused, they transformed the spaces where they toiled into centers of surrogate love and nurture. Yet, they were deemed unworthy to assume the role of First Lady.

Michelle enters this scenario as an educated woman who is able to invert expectations of a first black First Lady without wordy challenges. And what are the expectations of a first black First Lady? The pundits imply that she should be grateful and compliant, "make her people proud," be glad that she married well, and play Clair Huxtable,[9] while exhibiting her membership card as one of the "talented tenth."

Instead, she dares to bare her arms and back, and in so doing, directs the gaze of a racially ambivalent society toward the history and legacy of her black female body.[10]

> For centuries, black female bodies have been defiled, used, and discarded, quite literally as refuse—simply because they are female and black, black and female.[11]

M. Shawn Copeland's discussion of the political dynamics of dark skin is telling. It turns out that embodiment is a crucial element in humanity's efforts to distinguish "us" from "them." Recent scientific research conducted by Birgitte Vittrup, at the Children's Research Lab at the University of Texas, in Austin, indicates that babies see color and learn to reject racial differences at a very early age.[12] Yet liberal parents in the study refused to continue to participate because they didn't want to talk to their children about race. Michelle Obama steps into the controversial maelstrom of color, gender, and the subconscious with an image that won't be forgotten. In her official picture, she stands with dark brown skin and with bare arms not on a slave block, but in an expensive black sheath as the First Lady of the nation.

So, who is this bare-armed woman? No one goes unlabeled in this news-driven society; so when the presidential quest began, the media stood ready to identify her. Clearly, she was not cut from the cloth of other first ladies. She was too tall, too strong, too much woman for a country obsessed with the insipid image of the woman-child as cohort of American presidents. It didn't take long for the opposition to imply and sometimes use the words "angry," "black," and "bitch." Jones quotes Burt Prelutsky, who wrote the following: "The burning question in my circle is if the First Family gets a female dog will she be the First Bitch or will she have to settle for second place."[13]

In response to the bashing and the fear of the black woman in any public space, Michelle Obama offers the world-making artistry of personal style and the creativity of her kitchen garden. She is unafraid of highly racialized images associated with past abuses, i.e., kitchens and bare skin. Instead she imaginatively neutralizes and creatively edits old stereotypes in the following ways:

> 1. She complexifies the physical image of black women. She does not hide her hips, but is not a booty-shaking video vixen. Her full embodiment, without apology or chagrin, dares the prevailing standards of beauty to destroy the hope of "thick" black women bound for greatness.
> 2. She is from Chicago, but avoids the "diva" fashion example set by Aretha Franklin.
> 3. She has a garden and tries to grow. In a Monsanto, genetically modified nongenerative seed prosecuting world, her garden is not only world-making, but it is downright dangerous.
> 4. She knows that her children are the next world-makers and that they are more important than the political hype, but attends to both.
> 5. She not only loves her mother, she has made peace with the generational "curses" that sometimes overwhelm us and rejects the radical individualism that supports the demise of extended families.[14]

World-making doesn't require the lifting of center-stage curtains, it only requires the artistry of humanness, deeply understood and enacted through commitments to one another.

Being, as a necessary counterpoint to doing, is inherent as Michelle Obama allows her personhood to testify. Her commitments to the community were formed early as a foundation for her twenty-first-century leadership role. This quote from her Bachelor's thesis is telling,

> Earlier in my college career, there was no doubt in my mind that as a member of the black community, I was somehow obligated to this community and would utilize all of my present and future resources to benefit this community first and foremost.[15]

Her thesis explored the ebb and flow of communal commitment after an Ivy League education. The study that she used was too small to lead to significant conclusions, but a trend did emerge. She found that the talented tenth could not sustain "the ties that bind" to their communities of origin at levels that would change the future of those communities. Their education at Princeton had neutralized them as activist justice-seekers. This is not a surprising conclusion. For many scholars trained in eurocentric institutions, there is always the temptation to "tend to our own garden" and to trade commitments for degrees.

Michelle Obama offers a model of engagement that does not require debates about this matter or any other. Instead, she presents her body, no longer a living cultural sacrifice, but a symbol of embodied integration of spirit, strength, and resolve. I can imagine the advisors flushed and nervously fluttering around Michelle as she shows them the dress she will wear in her official portrait: "But Mrs. Obama, First Ladies don't show bare skin, let us find an appropriate outfit."

Michelle knows what we know: appropriateness is a historically grounded concept. When black female bodies are inscribed with the lust of dominators, the decay of self-hatred, and the historical memory of being used as brood sows, all bets regarding appropriateness are off. In response to the urgent request for decorum, Michelle Obama offers a performative act of symbolic re-creation. She stages the scene as a silent witness. Arms bare, she places herself in front of the portrait of Thomas Jefferson.

Jones offers this insightful analysis of the symbolism:

> Placing herself in the sightline of that particular painting, we are reminded of the last black woman to sleep in the White House, one who could not be there in a recognized and official role, but as one of history's dirty little secrets. By locating herself in the foreground, in front of Thomas Jefferson, where she and not he is the dominant subject of the photograph, the one in focus and his

> eyes gaze upon her as well, Michelle Obama is rearranging historical space, reminding us of the ways narratives of power can and must be disrupted, forcing us to see her in the light of alternate history, one that includes Sally Hemmings and what her place in the White House might have meant.[16]

The struggles of the ancestors for freedom and for recognition of personhood are etched on our souls, yet the striving for post-Obama generations will not look like the resistance movements of the 1960s. The first black First Lady is pointing the way toward transformation through symbolic depictions of plight and power. Future generations will embody their possibilities, rearrange historical and contemporary spaces to make room for their gifts, and disrupt narratives of power with presence and bare-armed innovations. With no need for attitude, and no need for dialogue, First Lady Michelle Obama stands before us as a powerful black woman connected to history with her bare arms summoning the future. Gaze upon her strength and beauty and either weep or shout with joy.

## Young, Gifted, and Bi-Racial: The Angst-Free Obama Phenomenon

Before Obama, those of us engaged since the sixties to create new worlds were prepared like Thurgood Marshall to battle for justice until the end of our lives. And just before our last breath, we would pass the torch to another generation and hope for the best. When Barack Hussein Obama was elected President of the United States, his victory took place in a nation that previously had abandoned its citizens to the floodwaters of Katrina and still struggled with its seething racial discomforts.

As a presidential candidate, he was too good to be true. He was black by self-identification, with a neutral skin color, that was not too dark to scare white constituents, but also not too light to distance himself from an association with the "hood." He was bi-racial by genetic reality, raised by an Anglo grandmother, and married to a descendant of slaves. He was Christian by choice, and connected to Islam on his father's side. At the same time, he presented an amalgam of best hopes. He pimps a little when he walks in a swagger that people of color recognize, while evoking none of the red flags, such as hair texture or street rhetoric, that would trigger the powerful voter aversion of Anglo constituents.

Obama was elected because he fully embodied and articulated a double consciousness in tone and swagger, in background and look. Not the angst-laden double consciousness that W. E. B. Du Bois evokes that speaks to being torn and conflicted; instead, this is a political savvy that allows him to carefully bond with people who cannot bond with one another. Only the Creator or a computer program could have designed such a person. And yet he appears in the flesh and wins!

Do not misunderstand my intention. I wanted the impossible dream to become a reality; I wanted to believe that the myths and mantras of equality and grassroots accomplishment could manifest. I wanted it even more intensely when the politics of gender and race collided during Hillary Clinton's veiled appeals to the fears of the white majority. I wanted to see a person of color lead this improbable national social experiment, and when he won, I wanted to high-five and say, "Mr. President . . . Dude . . . where have you been all of our lives?"

At the same time, I wondered what on earth he would be able to do to "change" a nation so deluded about its "goodness" and so committed to a rapacious economic system. Whether we like it or not, we live in a nation where micro-insults and macro-abandonment of the poor and people of color is the norm. In the years that preceded the 2008 election, our nation had turned toward collective and systematized "meanness."

Examples of "meanness" as public policy abound. During the years that preceded Obama's election, Mexican workers were being lured to the United States by corporate interests to work for low wages in a crumbling economic system, while a wall was being built to keep them out. Citizens had no healthcare, and local and national authorities had systematically abandoned the poor.

Adding to this mix are the 2.3 million people incarcerated in an increasingly privatized prison industrial system, as well as the residual racial and xenophobic resentments in the general population. With these factors, the odds of a national shift toward change and transformation seemed slim at best.[17] However, like others, I held my peace, voted for him, and hoped for the best. As ethereal as hope is, it lifted the candidate above the waves of impossibility and handed him a mandate for change.

Fresh new candidates emerge in every generation but little changes on the political scene. I am part of the politically jaded boomer generation still singing the tunes of an aging Bob Dylan, yet, I was intellectually seduced by the idea of change. But the change that was most apparent to me occurred before the ascension of Obama. I watched the silence of several generations as unspeakable attacks on basic liberties were met with a profound and pervasive public passivity. One President after another promised utopia and delivered war.

As it turns out, Obama has his own dreams of "shock and awe" in Afghanistan; we are embroiled in yet another unwinnable war; and this president is beginning to sound as if he is the victim of the past administration's body snatchers. Accordingly, the game plan must change. To every generation comes the opportunity to transcend all options within reach in favor of the great leap toward transcendence. People of color can no longer depend on star politicians or public personalities to lead us out of this morass of public contentiousness.

President Barack Obama's implausible election invites us to rethink pathways toward imaginative reconstructions of the world as we know it. This invitation holds whether or not Obama's presidency is deemed successful. Once change comes, it forever alters the warp and weft of the life space. I am suggesting that in place of shopping, complacency, or career focus we make new worlds. We've done it before; we can do it again. New worlds emerge from constructive imagination and creativity. That's a great theoretical description of the process, but when you get down to the nitty-gritty, how does world-making happen?

World-making requires commitment, focus, and spiritual incongruity. It's that last element that creates the alchemy for the work that must be done There are no blueprints for world-making, no discernible pre-paved road from oppression to freedom. We can't even rely on the roads paved by others from the past to take us where we must go. Bernice Johnson Reagon, founder of the singing group "Sweet Honey in the Rock," says this: "Why would you take a road constructed by someone else? / it will take you where they want you to go; / instead go to an edge and leap."[18] She is not suggesting that we end it all; rather, she is inviting us into the risky business of world-making. We leap from despair to hope by subjecting our yearning and vision to processes of formation with the expectation of transcendence.

What we know for certain is that mainstream politics will never get us where we want to go. The party system is corrupt and bereft, and now, the Supreme Court has allowed the fiction of corporate personhood to compromise elections with their unlimited funds. As a result, we are without healthcare, high-speed trains, or solar energy. Our children eat ammonia-infused hamburgers at school and at the fast-food restaurants. We must hunt for natural foods that will not kill us and then pay a premium. If you wish to move toward a simpler and more holistic life, there are only a few options.

If we intend to make new worlds for our children to inhabit, we must push past what we already know toward newness and the unimaginable. African Americans have flourished in the practices of public demonstration; now we must reclaim our lives through art and creativity. World-making requires the preliminary practice of self-definition writ large in communal contexts. Political victories are delightful, particularly when they are unexpected, but they do not ensure that the gains of one generation will provide a foothold for generations yet to come. History has taught us that oppressions know how to morph, hide, and reappear in a different guise. If we are to embody "change we can believe in"[19] and "make new worlds," it will require as much artistic expression as political rhetoric. The poets should lead the way.

How else can we imagine beyond what we can see toward something more? Creativity in the church and in the public square will allow us to weave tapestries of possibility, and to veer from a familiar malaise toward wholeness. But it isn't easy to follow the call to particularity when it is more comfortable to follow crowds who don't seem to know where they are going or why. Making worlds requires a willingness to transform and to be transformed. As professor Monica A. Coleman notes, "As creative transformation leads us into the future, it necessarily challenges the world as we currently experience it."[20] I am hopeful that it will also challenge the church.

## World-Making Theology and the Politics of the Black Church

A post-Obama analysis requires a look at the black church and its role in the political future of African American communities. Black church politics and black theology are important to this conversation because both were evident during the critical race for the presidency. President Barack Obama's candidacy was almost impaled on the rocky shoals of the liberationist preaching of the Rev. Jeremiah Wright. The rhetoric, the press, the distancing, the pain on all sides, the looping metaphors, and the incredible lack of knowledge in the dominant culture of the art and performance of black preaching makes me wonder whether the continued "invisibility" of the black church is of benefit.

The shock of the dominant culture everywhere was worsened not by Rev. Wright's oratory, but because they thought that they knew everything there was to know about black people. Historically, people of color wanted the dominant culture to think that their lives were open books, because it served a purpose that advanced the preservation of the community. If they think that they know everything about you, then you are no longer a threat. Moreover, it is impossible to cook meals in white homes, mop their floors, have their children, and raise their other children without developing a sense of intimacy.

The result of that intimacy was that black people were dismissed as servants, athletes, and singers and the creators of religious and cultural treasures that could be borrowed by all.

The black church has served simultaneously as an interpreter of black life for the dominant culture and a crucible for the formation of liberation theologies. However, it now resists the change that it once sought. Women have been added to support roles, and yes, some lead, but statistics show that true institutional shifts are few and far between. The church is nostalgic and familiar and the object of great loyalty and historical importance, but the task in future generations is to either address the issues that plague this great Ship of Zion, or bless it and lay it to rest.

A new generation knocks on the doors of tradition. They are singing their own songs and rapping their own tunes. Their prophets come rhyming. Our task is to open the door, invite innovation, and suggest that change is a godly idea from the pulpit to the statehouse. The invitation is to challenge the politics of the status quo in the public and on the pews. I want another generation to lead us out of our zones of comfort and complacency. I want to see black women reject the leadership models they inherited, for a model all their own. I want them to leave mimetic preaching behind and abandon church order on the shores of Babylon. We are in need of new spiritual leadership and unlikely spaces for gathering and consolation.

This sense of being betwixt and between the glory days of the Old Ship of Zion and the uncertain future is reflected in the Obama family's decision to delay the choice of a church home in Washington D.C. They attended Trinity United Church of Christ in Chicago for many years, and have visited several local congregations. During each visit, they endured the posturing and the cell-phone picture-taking of worshippers. *Time* magazine reports that "President Obama has told his aides that his primary place of worship will be Evergreen Chapel, the nondenominational church at Camp David.[21] The chaplain there as of this writing is the Rev. Carey Cash.

> If the White House had custom-ordered a pastor to be the polar opposite of Jeremiah Wright, they could not have come as close as Cash. (As it is, the White House had no hand in selecting Cash.) The Navy rotates chaplains through Camp David every three years. Cash . . . the 38-year-old Memphis native is a graduate of the Citadel and the great-nephew of Johnny Cash . . . and yes that means Obama's new pastor is a Southern Baptist.[22]

The Obamas are creating their own spaces for worship without reference to preaching style or cultural heritage, but with attention to nature, and the "getting away" that Jesus did regularly to escape the groupies and the politicians.

I see the black church caught like a bird in a snare. In love with its past and unable to see the future, it still drags its traditions, myopia, and phobias with it. I wonder what would have happened if Noah had dragged the ark with him after landing safely. The homophobic rage and egoic rejection of difference in the wider society is amplified in a church whose lifelong affair with familiarity threatens its relevance. But all is not lost! If the women will reject the mold and embody the newness of spirit-led congregational leadership, there may be hope. If the rejected and marginalized will claim their leadership in the body politic and in spiritual communities, there is great hope.

## Summary

While we cannot predict the future, we do know that it does not leap into being out of a void but is launched by the creativity and steadfastness of preceding generations. Now, with Michelle Obama as our example, we bare our arms and square our shoulders in preparation for the tasks ahead. It is our turn to engage in incongruous world-making activities that will impact the future politics of both church and state. The clarion call is to create, survive, connect, and declare a new reality. We will not sacrifice new generations to the tasks of explanation or entreaty, nor will we require that they expend their energy attempting to nullify "the powers that be" in the church and in the public sphere. We will not rely on politicians to lead the way. We will not narrow the discourse to insider Christian themes, but embrace all who move toward an egalitarian future. Hear the words of veteran civil rights activist and peacemaker Vincent Harding:

> Not only is something trying to be born in America, but some of us are called to be the midwives in this magnificent desperately needed and so painfully creative process. . . . Perhaps we are the ones who will walk through the great danger into the marvelous opportunity for helping our nation begin in a new way to realize its best possibilities—to be born again. Perhaps we are not only the ones we've been waiting for, but we are the ones who have already begun to do the work of creating a more perfect union. And we are not alone.[23]

Harding is calling for the end of century-long battles fought for equality in favor of a politics that is more artistry than skirmish. This world-creating birthing process is not women's work alone. All of us, who teeter on the precipice of several identifications, must declare without reservation that more than a vote is needed. More than affinity through faith, culture, color, gender, sexual orientation, is needed. Together, we must make new worlds.

## Notes

1. James Weldon Johnson, *God's Trombones: Seven Negro Sermons in Verse* (New York: Viking, 1927), 16.

2. Diana Hayes, "Response to David Power, O.M.I.," in *The Multicultural Church: A New Landscape in U.S. Theologies*, ed. William Cenkner (New York: Paulist, 1996), 107.

3. Molly Divins, "She Sounded Like God," *New York Times Magazine*, 29 December 1996, 17.

4. Hayes, 107.

5. Barbara A. Holmes and Susan Holmes Winfield, "King and the Constitution and the Courts: Remaining Awake through a Great Revolution," in *The Legacy of Martin Luther King Jr.: The Boundaries of Law, Politics, and Religion* (Notre Dame: University of Notre Dame Press), 173–211, 176.

6. Eluned Jones, "'Obama's Baby Mama': How Michelle Obama Uses Self-Narrative in the Media to Negotiate Racism," unpublished conference paper, *The Obama Phenomenon: Race and Political Discourse in the United States Today,* Hooks Institute's Scholarly Dialogue, April 4, 2009, University of Memphis, Memphis, TN, 7.

7. Verna Williams, "The First (Black) Lady," 86 *Denv. U. L.* Rev. 833. 834 (2009).

8. Jones, 8–9.

9. Clair Huxtable was a character on the Bill Cosby Show played by Phylicia Rashad. The show depicted a stable and affluent African American family.

10. Jones, 1–2.

11. M. Shawn Copeland, *Enfleshing Freedom: Body, Race, and Being* (Minneapolis: Fortress Press, 2009), 1.

12. Po Bronson and Ashley Merryman, "See Baby Discriminate," *Newsweek*, September 5, 2009.

13. Jones, 1–2.

14. Michelle Obama's mother moved into the White House with the Obama nuclear family after inauguration.

15. Michelle LaVaughn Robinson, "Princeton-Educated Blacks and the Black Community," a B.A. thesis presented to the Department of Sociology, Princeton University (1985).

16. Jones, 3.

17. Peter Monaghan, "Prison Studies," *The Chronicle Review*, section B, November 6, 2009, B6.

18. Bernice Johnson Reagon, Lecture, the Return Beat Theology and Arts program of Memphis Theological Seminary, Rhodes College, Memphis, TN, July 2008.

19. The slogan from Barack Obama's presidential campaign.

20. Monica A. Coleman, *Making a Way Out of No Way: A Womanist Theology* (Minneapolis: Fortress Press, 2008), 89.

21. Sarah Pulliam Bailey, "Has Obama Chosen a Church?" *Christianity Today Politics Blog*, June 29, 2009, 1–74, http://blog.christianitytoday.com/ctpolitics/2009/06/Obama_choose.

22. Ibid., 1.

23. Vincent Harding, "Midwifing a New America," *OneLife Institute News* 3, no. 4 (Autumn 2008).

13

# Scholarly Aesthetics and the Religious Critic

## *Black Experience as Manifolds of Manifestations and Powers of Presentations*

**Victor Anderson**

This short essay is about the black cultural politics of scholarship within Black Studies and Black Religion. Much of the impetus for this essay is derived from my graduate seminars in "Black Religion and Culture Studies I and II" at Vanderbilt University. In 2008, I initiated a graduate program in Black Religion and Culture Studies. While teaching my seminars, I began to note that among students was a certain scholarly aesthetics operating in their readings and questioning of texts. They were asking some very old questions, which I thought we, who have been dealing with deconstructing race and race theory in religion for some time, had put to rest. Their questions were not very different from those on black experience and black culture that informed and circulated throughout my generation of black scholars. Our questions about blackness were derivative of three powerful movements in the 1960s and early 70s: Black Power, the New Black Aesthetics, and the Black Studies movements.

I noticed the manner and urgency in which my students were struggling with old questions such as: What makes one black? Must black scholarship be political? Are black films, literature, and arts anything produced by a black person? To what extent may black scholars embrace multiculturalism as a mode of difference and remain distinctively black? Isn't there something about being black that is shared with no other race? I heard them evoking W. E. B. Du Bois's double consciousness in new ways, within a new moment, as they both affirmed and condemned representations of blackness in music videos, gangsta rap, and hip hop in contemporary black popular culture. They had old questions in young minds. This led me to think about black experience as manifolds of manifestations and powers of presentations, which seemed missing in the scholarly aesthetics of my students. This short essay is based on this experience.

When I talk about a scholarly aesthetics, I have a number of things in mind. I regard reading to be an act of gathering. It is literally taking up into one's head the working out of people's ideas, their own thinking about something, and laying those ideas or thoughts out on paper or screen. In this regard, film and visual media are also reading material. As I think about it, the screen best captures the "feelings" involved in reading the thoughts of another. I get involved emotionally, albeit in a slight and faint manner. Still, I get involved in what I am reading. The words strike my attention. I get pulled into the words that make up sentences, and the sentences convey and complete thoughts. Together, the flow of sentences provides for me a paragraph that offers complex relations of ideas, support for conclusions, evidences for accepting a thought, qualifying thoughts with examples and instances, and enhancing ideas qualitatively with adjectives and adverbs. Other words intimate actions: a question (a question mark, ?), stop (as in a period, .), partial stop (a semicolon, ;) emphasis (an exclamation point, !), hold in question (indexical marks, " "), or hide (ellipses, . . .).

What I read conveys pictures to be grasped as I consciously take up the ideas represented in reading. In reading, I don't just passively receive word pictures. I consciously attend to the words, sentences, paragraphs, the ideas and thoughts, which strike me in "such and such" a way. I take interest in them. I find myself sometimes bored and sometimes not; sometimes the word order of sentences, their complexity and constructions, strike me as perplexing and sometimes not; sometimes I am slowed down in my reading by a word that I have not encountered and sometimes not; and sometimes the picture of what is written strikes me as alarming, daunting, tragic, ironic, tearful; and sometimes I find myself empowered, enabled, and edified by what I have read. Sometimes what I read stirs in me acts of questioning things and ideas that I once took for granted. So, I keep on reading with questioning intent, as if to settle a problem raised by my reading or to complicate even more associated ideas taken for granted. In such moments, I want to offer different ways of seeing the problem or complicate ideas taken for granted. In all such acts, I am operating with and performing what I call a "scholarly aesthetics."

Scholarship proceeds by way of imitation. Originality is fiction, although fiction is not to be devalued. It too has its proper place in experience. We learn to write by imitating standards and deploying rules governing word order in sentence constructions. We copy alphabets until they become "natural." We become experts in pronunciation or articulation by imitating a standard. From first compositions through to dissertations, we measure good scholars by how well they have mastered styles of arguments, vocabulary, sophistication in detailing their written work, and producing bounded or digital copies that pass the quality control officer's stamp of approval. Such scholarly practices as these are also part of the profile of a scholarly aesthetics. For some, good scholarship is marked by a disinterested attitude. Here, ideas and thoughts are imagined as having a life of their own and valued within their solitary meanings. Other scholars mark good scholarship by "research." The scholar imagines himself-herself as an archivist, ever moving backward to discover the beginnings of our ideas. The backward gaze is also a profile of a scholarly aesthetics. Still for others, scholarship, at its best, is in service of political, social, economic, or cultural aims, purposes, or directives. Here, the scholarly aesthetics is that of the *avant-garde* critic. No doubt, such acts of imitation operate in my scholarly aesthetics and in that of my students too.

All of the many ways in which we read, write, and perform our scholarly aesthetics are determined by the flow of human experiences that make up the course of our lives. But human experience is always given in manifolds of manifestations and powers of presentations. Black scholarly discourse, for instance, has rarely confined itself to aesthetic forms, which have been most characteristic of the Germanic research models. For the black scholar, there has always been a surplus of aims—apologetic, polemical, moral, spiritual, and political—that marks our scholarship. Our scholarship has always lived uneasily with the standard of good scholarship measured by a preponderance of footnotes, block quotes, lexicons, and massive indexes. Now, this is not to say that black scholars are somehow less scholarly than this scholarly aesthetics suggests. Rather, our history, struggles, and historical specificities make our scholarship more than purely descriptive, explicative, exegetical, scientific, disinterested, singular, and characterized by boundary conditions that mark off uncrossable specializations, each exhibiting a totality of its own with little conversation or exchange between expert-based fields. Such is the hegemonic scholarly aesthetics that survives by imitation, repetition, and apprenticeship within scholarly guilds.

For the Black Intellectual Tradition, black experience is not singular but is best understood and performed in manifolds of manifestations and powers of presentations. As such, black experience remains the starting point of our scholarly work. But this fact is often eclipsed when "culture" comes to stand in for "experience," overdetermining the signifier "black" by rendering it an abstract noun, as in "blackness," and not the modifier of "experience" in manifolds. Historically, our talk of experience is co-joined with culture as the clue to black scholarship. Here, "black culture" signifies "black experience." When this happens, black experience is nearly equated with stylized blackness. And style stands in for experience.

The problem with style is that, while pointing to individuation, it tends to travel and circulate to create totalizing forms, which then play into a politics of authenticity that scripts what black scholars look like, how they speak, what their tone of voice must be if they are to be taken seriously, or how they articulate the black experience. All too often, cultural stylizations of black experience render (as in a stew) blackness a near monolithism, if not a near monotheism, says black feminist critic Barbara Christian. Rather than black experience as manifolds of manifestations and powers of presentations determining the significance of our cultural forms or stylizations of blackness, black culture overdetermines black experience, sometimes at the expense of immanent, reflexive criticism.

With W. E. B. Du Bois, black culture signifies a "black folk life" that was passing, as it were, into a mature modernism of form, style, and representation that would manifest itself singularly in a cultural renaissance comparable to Florence in the fourteenth and fifteenth centuries. Here was a cultural move individuated in form through strategic imitations in writing, artistic expressions, and innovations in musical performance. Such cultural moves are displays of what the Harlem Renaissance's cultural czar, Alain Locke, called the "New Negro," which was given legitimacy by white cultural patrons, the "Negro's Friends." One friend was Nancy Cunard. Her classic *Negro: An Antho*logy solidified the centrality of black cultural struggles, that is, experience and achievements in a Negro aesthetics. Originally titled *COLOR* by Cunard, the book was finally published as *Negro* in 1933. Here is Cunard:

> It was necessary to make this book—and I think in this manner, an anthology of some 150 voices of both races—for the recording of the struggles and achievements, the persecutions and revolts against them, of the Negro peoples. . . . Amongst many other subjects are writings on literature, education, social conditions and personal contact. Zora Neale Hurston has contributed some studies which portray the background of Negro folk-imagination, the poetic and rhythmic intensity of their religious expression, the sole emotional outlet that was permitted in slavery days. But the Negro is no longer preoccupied solely by religion.[1]

In this passage, Cunard highlights the centrality that black expressive culture plays in the aesthetic performance of black identity, hope, progress, and social change. She continues:

> What shall I say of the miraculous Theatrical and Musical Negro firmament? . . . that it is high time a separate book were made to do justice to a people so utterly rich in natural grace and beauty, a people who have produced the diverse genius of the spirituals and blues, the superb Negro choirs of America, the syncopation and tap-dancing, the dramatic and musical excellence of several first-rate actors and singers, the as yet in our white hemisphere almost unknown and unrecorded splendor of African rhythms.[2]

In Cunard's dedication and patronage, black expressive culture answers the problem made of ultimate concern by Kant's and Hegel's ideas of history, which is the exclusion of Africa from world universal history. Here, Culture doubly stakes out the basic dialectic between the "determinacy" of nature over all physical, historical-material drives of basic human life predicated on necessity and the "indeterminacy" of human self-transcendence and self-making against the containment of black bodies by white supremacy. This indeterminacy, I call "analogous nature." Du Bois eloquently described this dialectic between determinacy of nature (let's call this primary nature) and the indeterminacy of transcendence in black expressive culture, which is analogous nature, a "twoness," "a double consciousness" that exists in perpetuity as a panopticon over the *Souls of Black Folk*.[3]

So nontranscending and nontransgressive is this cultural aesthetics that it functioned as a cultural boundary marker controlling and policing the scholarly aesthetics in political and social studies of black religion and culture studies well into the early 1990s. Black expressive culture informs our very internal grasping of the meaning and significance of black experience, not only in the production of philosophy but in literature, arts, music, and even theology. Elsewhere, I described this cultural aesthetics as a cult, a cult of black masculinity, whose operations of power were so coercive as to blur any real distinctions that mark even gender and sexual notations on black bodies.[4]

Within its cultic formations, the whole race was to bear the burden of representing blackness in stylizations of life oriented toward racial uplift. Even Zora Neale Hurston found herself ostracized by the black cultural border police of the Harlem Renaissance in their power to contain difference. The opening poem of Cunard's *Negro* represents well this cultic performance. "I, Too" by

Langston Hughes is a poem of strength and voice—suggesting that African Americans, too, are a vital part of what it means to be American. "I, too, am America," says Hughes. For many of my generation within the black church, who performed this poem in district- and state-sponsored oratorical contests, this poem along with others, particularly those of Paul Lawrence Dunbar, formed for us a moral fabric of racial consciousness. They became symbolic flags of the cultural cult of black masculinity, a moral genius circulating and determining the black public sphere by virtues of strength, struggle, survival, and resistance, however covert or changing the styles.

Although black cultural stylizations shift, black experience, as manifolds of manifestations and powers of presentations, remained repressed by a black form, derived from the classical black scholarly aesthetics. In literary genres and in multiple recalibrations or fusions of the spirituals, blues, and jazz into emerging contemporary sounds, the new sounds or cultural moves would signify for some the achievements of the classical black scholarly aesthetics' self-transcendence in analogous nature from the determinacy of whiteness, white supremacy, and its relentless containment of black bodies. Even in black popular culture from the 1950s to the present, this genius or form expresses itself in powerfully voiced articulations from bebop, rock and roll, R and B, soul, and funk, to rap, gangster rap, hip hop, and neo-soul forms. However, while some see such innovations or improvisations on style as a black cultural achievement over white supremacy, others see these cultural moves, not as innovations on classical style but denigrations. For some, these cultural moves are displays of a degenerative transgressing of what could not be transgressed, namely, the sanctity of a black cultural politics of difference signified by an African American Form and policed by the dogma of black cultural essentialism. Black experience as manifolds of manifestations and powers of presentations fade from view. Black experience, as I think of it, is disciplined by a cultural logic of expressive essentialism.

It means little whether this essentialism is predicated on germ theory as was Du Bois's or is strategic and manipulative. The effects are the same when all black cultural forms are weighed by questions like: Mama, "What makes Lena Horne black? Is Mariah Carey black too? I know Halle Berry ain't black, Mama! Mama: Why does everybody keep saying Condoleezza Rice ain't black? and President Barack Obama ain't black enough? And Mama: What the hell is Tiger Woods? Child, you better watch your mouth!" Black culture operates in such instances as already an articulation of black experience, without manifolds. Within this scholarly aesthetics, to be black is to take ownership of a black cultural genius, determining the internal logic of a black cultural politics of difference and respectability circulating throughout the black public sphere. It is driven to canon formation.

Well over twenty years ago, before even his own blackness was called into question in the Cambridge incident, Henry Lewis Gates recognized that black literature or African American literature is the fruit of racial apologetics in the making of black cultural politics that might distort an expansive account of black experience. He also recognized the ambiguities entailed in the notion of a black cultural aesthetics at a moment when the black power and the new black aesthetics froze black experience under stylized cultural forms. Gates posed this ambiguity in these terms: whether "black poetry is racial in theme or [whether] black poetry [is] any sort of poetry written by black people."[5] Gates realized then that if answering in the traditional voice, the accent falls on the first pole. And quoting James Weldon Johnson, Gates writes:

> No people that have produced great literature and art have ever been looked upon by the world as distinctly inferior. The status of the Negro in the United States is more a question of national mental attitude toward the race than of actual conditions. And nothing will do more to change that mental attitude and raise his status than a demonstration of intellectual parity by the Negro through the production of literature and art.[6]

Commenting on Calverton's African American canon at the end of the Harlem Renaissance, Gates argues that it was "a canon that was unified thematically by self-defense against racist literary conventions, and by the expression of what the editors called 'strokes of freedom.'"[7]We see here that in this scholarly aesthetics, culture, as an expressive force, moves beyond the ambiguities of experience to stand in for experience. It represents black subjectivity, but not as complex subjectivities or manifolds. Black experience is bound by the formation of a black canon.

Jumping a generation from Harlem Renaissance theorists, when Gates examines the black cultural aesthetics of Amiri Baraka and Larry Neal's *Black Fire*, which introduced such notables as Sonia Sanchez and Nikki Giovanni, among others, he criticized it as signaling no significant movement from the classical black scholarly aesthetics, which was grounded in the cultural politics of difference circulating throughout the black intellectual tradition.[8] He saw one essentialist model replaced by another. Gates called *Black Fire* "the blackest canon of all."[9] He writes:

> The hero, the valorized presence in this volume is the black vernacular: no longer summoned or invoked through familiar and comfortable rubrics such as "The Spirituals" and "The Blues," but *embodied, assumed, presupposed* in a marvelous act of formal bonding often obscured by the stridency of the political message the anthology meant to announce. Absent completely was a desire to "prove" our common humanity with white people, by demonstrating our power of intellect. One mode of essentialism—"African" essentialism—was used to critique the essentialism implicit in notions of a common or universal American heritage. NO, in *Black Fire*, art and act were one.[10]

For Gates, if the classical black aesthetics disclosed black expressive genius in terms of racial consciousness, it did so only by negating the complex manifold of black subjectivity and constructing an essentialist litmus test. The multifaceted aspects of black experience, captured so well in Houston Baker's vernacular theory, collapsed under the totality of black power and black consciousness. The black subject, as subject, remained alienated from his/her cultural products, which black experience endowed with multiplicity and manifolds, all within the simultaneity of a collective social life, called the black experience. This phenomenon was well expressed by Albert Murray's assurance of the classical black aesthetics in black expressive culture. Murray writes:

> Art is by definition a process of stylization; and what it stylizes is experience. What it objectifies, embodies, abstracts, expresses, and symbolizes is a sense of life. Accordingly, what is represented in the music, dance, painting, sculpture, literature, and architecture, of a given group of people in a particular time, place, and circumstance is a conception of the essential nature and purpose of human existence itself. More specifically, an art style is the assimilation in terms of which a given community, folk, or communion of faith embodies its basic attitudes toward experience.[11]

Murray's cultural logic renders black cultural productions and their "essential meanings" just-so-many "survival techniques" and "the need to live in style."[12] It is a stylization of "the struggles for political and social liberty" and "a quest for freedom to choose one's own way or style of life."[13] But expressing one's style of life is not derived solely from the subjectivity of the artist. As Murray suggests, "it should be equally as obvious that there can be no such thing as human dignity and nobility without a consummate definitive style, pattern, or archetypal image":[14] an African American Form.

What I have said thus far ought not to be taken as suggesting that Black Culture Studies is anything but dynamic. Each discipline displays an impressive range of critical options for not only the critique of black experience but also of black cultural moves that represent black experience. Such a dynamism is shown in the many forms of criticism that are brought to bear on black experience from literary criticism, critical historiography, critical theory, ideology criticism, critical race theory, ethnography, and poststructuralism. While having a multiplicity of critical tools to engage in the critique of black cultural moves, the tools themselves unfortunately have been overdeployed not only in producing within analogous nature counter-discourses on hegemonic epistemologies that define and subjugate black experience under white supremacy and deprecating market forces. They also inscribe on black experience the burden of genius. For my students, this burden of genius is referred to as "strategic essentialism," which is represented by cultural expressive forms in the arts, entertainment, intellectual culture, and the black public sphere, including Black Religion.

The burden of genius is articulated well in the preface to the 1991 edition of James H. Cone's *A Black Theology of Liberation*, first published in 1970. Cone insists that the theological problem of American culture is white racism, and the task of Black Theology is to engage it by way of a new, revolutionary black collective consciousness in light of the black experience. This scholarly aesthetics produced a tradition of black theologies reduced to the survivalist culture of "the black community, the pain and joy it derives from reacting to whiteness and affirming blackness" and "the mythic power inherent in [its historical] symbols for the present revolution against white racism."[15]

With black culture, arts, music, and literature, Black Theology too became the symbolic expressive vehicle of a black spirituality corralled and policed by a scholarly aesthetics predicated on narrative returns, as Edward Said calls it in *Culture and Imperialism*.[16] This scholarly aesthetics returns to distinctively black sources. It returns to African traditional religions, slave narratives, autobiography, and folklore in order to accent the vital endurance and significance of black religion and forms of cultural solidarities that transcend the individualism that drives so much of our market culture and morality and robs the black community of moral vitality so needed today. The hermeneutics of return projects a grand narrative that evokes a great cloud of witnesses, whose heroic legacy of survival, resistance, and hope mediates the fragility of black experience today and binds contemporaries in need of a heroic black faith.

While not herself a self-identified black or womanist theologian, philosopher, and religionist, Barbara A. Holmes captures something of this scholarly aesthetics well when she says:

> The conversations in this book take seriously the unfinished state of the liberation project and the need for imaginative solutions that will provide the fertile soil for new initiatives. My grandmother used to say, "If you don't see a way out, stand still." After a century of activism, the desire to do something, to advance the cause of freedom, and to liberate those still in bondage is almost overwhelming. And yet the path is unclear. It seems a perfect time to regroup, to keep an eye on world events, to help a neighbor close by and imagine the future. And this book revisits the quest for freedom using unique rhetorical tools that include the languages of cosmology, Africana thought, philosophies of liberation, and the impetus toward moral fulfillment.[17]

My quoting Holmes is in order to suggest that in thinkers even such as she, who is in tune with black experience as manifolds of manifestations and powers of presentations, it is difficult to resist the seduction of grasping our cultural resources as tools of criticism without also endowing them with a binding moral and spiritual force in articulations of a black scholarly aesthetics.

Black feminist critic Barbara Christian identifies this irony. She argues that as Black Arts theorists critiqued the dominant literature and representations of black experience, which were defined by assimilation, decadence, and pathology, and that theorized black culture forms by reversal, they "re-theorized" black experience by a new radical, militant, and Africanized black consciousness. Within these cultural moves, race discourse recoiled. It turned on itself, replicating and reinscribing forms of black identity stylized into race-defining cultural images. The result was strategic essentialism. With strategic essentialism, black expressive culture registers signs and symbols of a near "monolithism" and cultural monotheism, says Christian:

> It is true that the Black Arts Movement resulted in a necessary and important critique both of previous Afro-American literature and of the white-established literary world. But in attempting to take over power, it, as Ishmael Reed satirizes so well in *Mumbo Jumbo*, became much like its opponent, monolithic and downright repressive. Inevitably, monolithism becomes a metasystem, in which

> there is a controlling ideal, especially in relation to pleasure. Language as one form of pleasure is immediately restricted, and becomes heavy, abstract, prescriptive, monotonous.[18]

On Christian's reading, the black scholarly aesthetics not only displayed a tendency toward "monolithism"; it also produced a repressive "monotheism," which produced an iconography of "blackness."

When that happened, black culture signified expressive elements that connect cultural moves and forms with black identity. Said is helpful here:

> First of all it means all those practices, like the arts of description, communication, and representation, that have relative autonomy from the economic, social, political realms and that often exist in aesthetic forms, one of whose principal aims is pleasure. Included, of course, are both the popular stock of lore about distant parts of the world and specialized knowledge available in such learned disciplines as ethnography, historiography, philology, sociology, and literary history.[19]

Said interrogates culture in relation to empire, but he also critiques counter-imperial cultural criticism for its tendencies toward maintaining "otherness" at all cost of "the other." In this case, Said appeals to culture to "become the method colonized people use to assert their own identity and the existence of their own history."[20]

In the black scholarly aesthetics, appeals to culture produce possibilities not only for the critique of hegemonic discursive formations of power, but such appeals also re-coil in a doubling loop in black studies and religious thought. Said illuminates the ironic effects, which I see so threatening in our contemporary grasping of black experience in the appeals of my students, who evoke strategic essentialism in their efforts to come to terms with the meaning of blackness in contemporary black popular culture. Said describes culture as "a refining and elevating element, each society's reservoir of the best that has been known and thought."[21] Within the black scholarly aesthetics, we work toward social transcendence from the everyday brutalities of a social life world and social practices through which hegemonic power, what I call analogous nature, contains black experience against manifolds of manifestations and powers of presentations. Strategic essentialism, also analogous nature, stands in to unite black agency into a counter-discourse of white supremacy and debilitating social market forces that then define black experience as self-transcendence from these death-dealing forces of white supremacy within analogous nature.

Black culture constructs a grand metanarrative of itself as blackness-coming-into-being, signifying a singular identity. Said describes this phenomenon thus:

> [C]ulture comes to be associated, often aggressively, with the nation or the state; this differentiates "us" from "them." . . . Culture in this sense is a source of identity, and a rather combative one at that, as we see in recent "returns" to culture and tradition. These "returns" accompany rigorous codes of intellectual and moral behavior that are opposed to the permissiveness associated with such relatively liberal philosophies as multiculturalism and hybridity. In the formally colonized world, these "returns" have produced varieties of religious and nationalist fundamentalism.[22]

Culture operates duplicitously, signifying both a tendency to form distinctiveness or singularity, which marks an identity, while within its circuitry, the manifolds of manifestations and powers of presentations in the private and social practices of black people that signify black experience are morally integrated into this singularity of "us" or "we" as expressed in speech as "we or us as a people." The product of this circuitry is a black cultural canon, or as Murray terms it, an African American Form. When this cultural circuitry canonizes black experience, forming as it were a strategic essentialism as countercultural discourse to white hegemony, the effect is not only the singular "us" distinguished from "them" but black cultural "henotheism." Culture is a religious idea operating in the black scholarly aesthetics and represents an iconography of an African American Form, canonized black experience.

As I introduced the religious critic into the black scholarly aesthetics elsewhere, religious criticism analyzes and promotes representations of black experience that contribute to the furtherance of our needs for social, moral, spiritual, economic, political, and cultural fulfillment.[23] The religious critic is not content with describing only the dark sides of our cultural forms, articulated and critiqued in black studies and religion. Religious criticism also affirms, in a self-reflexive manner, the creative possibilities of our cultural productions for the fulfillment of our political, social, and spiritual strivings. The self-reflexive criticism that the scholarly aesthetics of the religious critic performs on black experience as manifolds of manifestations and powers of presentations is displayed most eloquently in Toni Morrison's scholarly aesthetics. Morrison says:

> Writing and reading are not all that distinct for a writer. Both exercises require being alert and ready for unaccountable beauty, for intricateness or simple elegance of the writer's imagination, for the world that imagination evokes. Both require being mindful of the places where imagination sabotages itself, locks its own gates, pollutes its vision. Writing and reading mean being aware of the writer's notions of risk and safety, the serene achievement of, or sweaty fight for, meaning and response-ability.[24]

Morrison is not so much interested in the creation of an African American Form, the canonization of black experience by black cultural moves as in Du Bois's "genius," Murray's "style," or Gates's "canon." Within what I have called analogous nature, she maintains a "racial realism" in which race is an inevitable category of writing and reading in black expressive culture.[25] It will not be ignored. So in very telling remarks, Morrison comes to terms with black experience and its cultural forms, saying: "My project is an effort to avert the critical gaze from the racial object to the racial subject; from the described and imagined to the describers and imaginers; from the serving to the served."[26] "The kind of work I have always wanted to do," Morrison says, "requires me to learn how to maneuver ways to free up the language from its sometimes sinister, frequently lazy, almost always predictable employment of racially informed and determined chains."[27]

For the religious critic, the scholarly aesthetics is imagined and performed as a rigorous iconoclasm. This scholarly aesthetics requires attention to writing and reading from a self-reflexive position that critiques discursive formations of discourse that bind the black scholarly aesthetics between subject and object, white and black, innocence and guilt, victim and victimizers, virtuous and perverse, and all iconographies of blackness in canon, form, style, and genius. The religious critic is the cultural iconoclast. Our work is driven by a view of black experience that highlights identity within manifolds of manifestations and powers of presentations.

When I talk about black experience as manifolds of manifestations and powers of presentations, which space prevents me here from developing fully, I have something like this in mind. When I see a cube, borrowing from Robert Sokolowski's phenomenological illustration, I do not consciously grasp merely a thing before my eyes. Immediately, I recognize this thing as a cube. I know it from its defining aspects cognitively. In this case, I know that this is a cube and has six squares combined and welded together, whose profile presents four sides, a top, and a bottom. While interesting enough, my cognitive recognition has little meaning or significance for me. Although I cannot see all of its sides at the same time, I nevertheless have confidence from my angle of vision that what is presented to me is a cube. Its identity is that of a cube. But I do not only experience the cube by its aspects and profiles. I experience myself consciously taking up the cube with interest: perhaps as a thing of puzzlement as in a puzzle, or a thing of play as in hiding in a box, or perhaps in one moment I attend to it with inquisitiveness as in wondering what's in this box, a gift or a hat? It occurs to me perhaps as a thing of art, or in another moment, perhaps as a makeshift shelter as in a home. In each of these ways of taking into my conscious life the cube—the cube as cube—its identity has not changed; it looks like a cube and behaves like a cube, with all of its proper aspects and profiles, its identity is its reality, namely, a cube. What has happened in all these instances, I have only grasped its identity (cube) within manifolds of manifestations and presentations as a puzzle, a hiding place, gift box, a hatbox, a work of art, and a shelter. I have come to difference within identity beyond essence or essentialism.

In each manifestation and presentation, identity in difference is irreducible to a single meaning or significance. The cube presents itself to me as "such and such." Its powers of presentations are within manifolds of manifestations. My curiosity is not divorced from the aesthetic dimension of my conscious life. The manner in which I understand the possible meanings of the cube is by way of its powers of presentations in manifold. My understanding the identity of the cube this time as a puzzle, at another time a gift box, and still another moment as a shelter, is given through its powers of presentations, the manner in which it is present to me through manifolds of manifestations, which simultaneously evoke my appreciation and relation to this particular identity. "Each manifold is different, each is proper to its identity, and the identities are different in kind."[28]

We have now come to what I have called black experience as manifolds of manifestations and powers of presentations, what Sokolowski calls "manifolds of appearances" and "identities."[29] Our cube is not a self-contained closed world. Its reality, that is, its identity, is related meaningfully with many other identities constituted by our lived experienced of things and events. Likewise, black culture is not the totality of black experience, which is open to manifolds of manifestations and powers of presentations. Culture is representational. It presents in possible manifolds of manifestations distinct ways of being, living, and experiencing life in the world: expressively, intellectually, morally, spiritually, politically, playfully, and in still yet unimagined manifolds and powers. "Manifolds of appearances" and "identity" are analogous terms.[30]

> The identity of an art object is different from the identity of a political event, and yet, both are identities, and both have their proper ways of being given. By spelling out the diverse manifolds and identities, phenomenology helps us to preserve the reality and distinctiveness of each. It helps us avoid reductionism by bringing out what is proper to each kind of being, not only in its independent existence, but also in its power of presentation.[31]

With this understanding of difference in identity, the scholarly aesthetics of the religious critic performs not only the deconstructive work of criticism turned on totalizing form, style, canon, or genius, or as Morrison does in the quote above, learning "how to maneuver ways to free up the language from its sometimes sinister, frequently lazy, almost always predictable employment of racially informed and determined chains."[32] As a religious critic, I have no particular replacement vision to fill in the void vacated by carrying out such modes and aims of reflexive criticism proposed by Morrison. Rather, the scholarly aesthetics of the religious critic is more like the watchman standing at the city gates, looking for, keeping watch over, alerting, and serving to keep our discourses on black experience, black culture, and black religion open and porous.

In the operations of this scholarly aesthetics, the cultural critic as religious critic values most the exercise of the freedom of thought, of will, and of expression in the productions of counter-hegemonic discourses of black experience as manifolds of manifestations and powers of presentations. With the performance of this scholarly aesthetics, the puzzlement, inquisitiveness, and sometimes bewilderment expressed by my seminar students over the cultural meaning of "blackness" in black experience, when they ask "Mama: is Victor black too?" is for me a scholarly achievement.

## Notes

1. Nancy Cunard, *Negro: An Anthology* (1933; reprint, New York: Continuum 1966), xxxi.
2. Ibid.
3. W. E. B. Du Bois, *Souls of Black Folk* (1905; reprint, New York: NAL Penguin, 1969).
4. Victor Anderson, *Beyond Ontological Blackness: An Essay on African American Religious and Cultural Criticism* (1994; reprint, New York: Continuum, 1998).
5. Henry Louis Gates Jr., *Loose Canons: Notes on the Culture Wars* (New York: Oxford University Press, 1992), 26.
6. Ibid.

7. Ibid., 29.

8. Amiri Baraka and Larry Neal, *Black Fire: An Anthology of Afro-American Writing* (1968; reprint, Baltimore: Black Classics, 2007).

9. Gates, 30.

10. Gates, 31.

11. Albert Murray, *The Omni-Americans: Black Experience and American Culture* (New York: Da Capo, 1970), 54–55.

12. Ibid., 55.

13. Ibid., 56.

14. Ibid.

15. James H. Cone, *A Black Theology of Liberation* (1970; reprint, Maryknoll, NY: Orbis, 1991), 27.

16. Edward Said, *Culture and Imperialism* (New York: Alfred A. Knopf, 1993), xiiff.

17. Barbara A. Holmes, *Liberation and the Cosmos: Conversations with the Elders* (Minneapolis: Fortress Press, 2008), x.

18. Barbara Christian, "The Race for Theory," in *The Black Feminist Reader*, ed. Joy James and T. Denean Sharpley-Whiting (Malden, MA: Blackwell, 2000), 18–19.

19. Said, xii.

20. Ibid.

21. Ibid., xiii.

22. Ibid.

23. Anderson.

24. Toni Morrison, *Playing in the Dark: Whiteness and the Literary Imagination* (New York: Vintage, 1992), xi.

25. Ibid., 11.

26. Ibid., 90.

27. Ibid., xi.

28. Robert Sokolowski, *Introduction to Phenomenology* (New York: Cambridge University Press, 2000), 31.

29. Ibid.

30. Ibid.

31. Ibid.

32. Morrison, xi.

14

# Embodying Womanism

## *Notes toward a Holistic and Liberating Pedagogy*

**Arisika Razak**

Drawing from twenty-three years of work in the field of women's healthcare and over a decade of academic teaching in a small, private, graduate institution in the San Francisco Bay area, I offer a framework for constructing an embodied, holistic spiritual and liberating pedagogy that can be successfully employed in the pluralistic humanities[1]classroom of twenty-first-century United States of America, by using Alice Walker's womanist definition.[2]

As a womanist teacher, my pedagogy is informed by the scholarly fields of feminism, women-of-color feminisms, critical thinking, postcolonial discourse, and ethnic and religious studies. It utilizes diversity theory and antiracist praxis, experiential exercises and therapeutic movement, personal sharing and written narratives, and art, journaling, and music. I also use Buddhist meditation practices, rituals from "African Derived Traditions,"[3] and yoga or chi gung in order to provide a supportive space for liberatory transformation for the students.

While I do not claim that the womanist epistemology and pedagogy I propose is appropriate for all socially marginalized groups, I believe that it supports the educational empowerment and liberatory transformation of black women and other women of color who claim diverse religious traditions and class backgrounds, and who embody an assortment of national, gender, sexual, ethnic, or racial identities, etc.[4] In my experience, a womanist pedagogy has been a successful teaching vehicle for supporting the empowerment of other marginalized members of the dominant society—e.g., Euro-American women, lesbians, and older women.

## Standpoint

I embrace Alice Walker's definition because Walker's affirmation of the self, the body, and the sacredness of nature echo my own personal beliefs. While I am not a Christian like many of the other scholars in womanist religious thought, I regularly invoke the memory of my enslaved African ancestors who transformed the Christianity of their owners into a soulful refuge and a spiritual home. The Christianity they created was a vehicle for self-love, liberation, profound faith, and moral and ethical behavior. But I also prize the religions that enslaved Africans brought from Africa—religions in which God was female (at least some of the time), women were priestesses, and sexuality was a sacred act that could be talked about in polite company. If I choose to venerate African deities—which I sometimes do—I believe that I celebrate my foremothers' gods.

Walker's definition of womanism asks that we pay attention to the dynamic tension between the personal and the political. The womanist she describes is not only fiercely committed to the struggle for liberation, but has *personally* resisted the ubiquitous racist, classist, homophobic, patriarchal, fat-phobic, and heteronormative oppression of American society. She has successfully affirmed her right to love herself, her body, her people, her culture, and the natural world, "*[r]egardless*."[5] Writing about Walker's affirmation of self-love, Cheryl Townsend Gilkes notes:

> I read the last reference to love, ". . . (loves) herself. Regardless," to be a critical admonition for those seeking to emancipate and empower women, especially and most critically black women. . . . The failure to love self makes it impossible to love others, and our hateful acts toward others are often a measure of our feelings about self. Some of the greatest threats to human development among the poor and the non-poor, among the black and the non-black are rooted in low self-esteem.[6]

As a midwife and women's healthcare worker, my sense of the sacred is inextricably linked to the physical realities of the female body. For twenty-three years of my life, I worked as an inner-city midwife serving the needs of indigent women and their families from over seventy countries. Standing as witness, companion, and helper to women in labor was a life-changing event for me, as was my own experience of birth at home. Nothing I had ever experienced before had prepared me for the holiness of the moment in which a laboring woman turns away from her preoccupation with the world to focus on the world making within her body—a moment that for me, revealed the face of God/dess making the world again.

However, my work with women also demonstrated the immense constrictions under which women live. As a midwife working in a county hospital, I learned all the good, bad, and ugly ways that women became pregnant. I witnessed firsthand the ways that faith has been used to compromise women's beliefs in themselves, their cultures, or their right to life. I also witnessed women's strengths—and the loud or quiet courage accompanying their efforts to make a better life for themselves and their children. It is my work with women and birth that grounded my belief in the worth, capability, and intelligence of women, especially women of color.

I identify with that part of Walker's definition that declares that a "womanist is a black feminist or feminist of color,"[7] and I resonate with *both* parts of this statement. I appreciate womanism's origin in black women's experience, for my life has been shaped by the experience of living as a black woman in the USA during the last half of the twentieth century. However, my life has also been deeply affected by forty years of work with multicultural groups of women. As an abused child, I was also "other-mothered" by white, Jewish, and Japanese activists and their families.[8]They exposed me to other traditions, struggles, and ways of being. Living in diverse households and working with multiethnic groups of women for social change and personal and spiritual development helps me resonate with Vanessa Sheared's statement that "[w]e are more than black women. We are black women connected to all brothers and sisters engaged in the struggle against oppression based on race, gender and class."[9]

## Educational Setting for the Pedagogical Use of Womanism

I currently direct a Women's Spirituality Program at the California Institute of Integral Studies (CIIS), a small graduate institution in the San Francisco Bay Area. At CIIS, Women's Spirituality is a broadly defined inter- and transdisciplinary field that draws from the intersection of Women's Studies, Ethnic Studies, Philosophy, and Religion. One of our school's ideals is feminism, and our Women's Spirituality program defines itself as "feminist" or "womanist-feminist."

While most of my program's students identify as women, some identify as gender-fluid or transgender individuals. Since the program is more than 95 percent women, students have been heavily impacted by issues of violence against women. Many are survivors of sexual abuse or domestic violence. Others have experienced abuse based on sexist, patriarchal, or heterosexist norms within their original religious traditions, and they want a program based in "spirituality" rather than religion.

I don't think it's surprising that our students represent a plurality of world religions: some follow animist, "pagan," or African Derived Traditions; others embrace Muslim, Jewish, or Christian beliefs; others practice Buddhism, Hinduism, Druze, or other faiths. Our black students are spiritually diverse too—they are Wiccans, Buddhists, Jews, and Christians or practitioners of African Derived spiritualities and New Thought religions. In our setting, a pedagogy based on a Christian understanding of womanism—e.g., steeped in Christian logic, language, metaphor, and ethics—would not be appropriate for many of our students.

However, it is precisely because Walker's definition does not apply solely to the practice of Christianity—or to any one faith tradition practiced by (black) women—that I find it inclusive enough to serve as a framework for a liberatory pedagogy for students of diverse faiths and sociocultural locations. I believe that attention to a diversity of spiritual perspectives and sociocultural locations is necessary for the integration of spirituality and feminism, as well as for promoting twenty-first-century pedagogy.

Vanessa Sheared speaks to the importance of an education that addresses diverse constituents in her article "Giving Voice: An Inclusive Model of Instruction—A Womanist Perspective." She states:

> Educators in general and adult educators in particular are becoming increasingly concerned by the question, How are we to deliver course content in such a way that classroom discourse acknowledges all voices—the multiple ways in which people interpret and reflect their understanding of the world?[10]

## Feminist Pedagogies

Many black scholars have argued about whether womanism and black feminism are separate, equal, opposed, or related. In her 1996 essay "What's in a Name? Womanism, Black Feminism, and Beyond," Patricia Hill Collins wrote, "Current debates about whether black women's standpoint should be named 'womanism' or 'black feminism' reflect [the] basic challenge of accommodating diversity among black women . . . many African American women see little difference between the two since both support a common agenda of black women's self-definition and self-determination."[11] As a third wave womanist, I acknowledge that the pedagogy I call "womanist" may well be called "feminist" or "black feminist" by others. I use these terms interchangeably—at least for the purposes of this article. A number of scholars do so, including Walker in her original definition. Self-identified black feminist bell hooks has written about liberatory pedagogies for almost two decades.[12] She offers the following description of her pedagogy:

> My pedagogical practices have emerged from the mutually illuminating interplay of anticolonial, critical, and feminist pedagogies. This complex and unique blending of multiple perspectives has been an engaging and powerful standpoint from which to work. Expanding beyond boundaries, it has made it possible for me to imagine and enact pedagogical practices that engage directly both the concern for interrogating biases in curricula that reinscribe systems of domination (such as racism and sexism) while simultaneously providing new ways to reach diverse groups of students.[13]

For several decades, Euro-American feminists have documented their attempts to bring women's issues into the academy. In *Women's Ways of Knowing*, Belenky et al. suggest that a successful pedagogy for women 1) acknowledges the student as a source of knowledge; 2) encourages articulation of the student's knowledge; 3) supports expansion and development of the student's knowledge base; 4) encourages application of the student's knowledge to the world outside of the classroom; 5) creates a *connected community* of teacher-learners; 6) tolerates ambiguity and uncertainty; 7) welcomes diversity of opinion; 8) focuses on the student as *subject;* and 9) has women's development as its overarching educational goal.[14]

I call my pedagogy *womanist* because: 1) it acknowledges body, mind, heart, and spirit as human dimensions of being that must be brought into the classroom; 2) it privileges the development of a liberatory consciousness; 3) it takes an oppositional stance against racist, sexist, and homophobic oppression in theory and practice; 4) it encourages human review of our place within a sacred *earthly* world; 5) it is based on acceptance and tolerance for *all* members of the human family; and 6) it underscores our need for rest and replenishment—a conceptual combination that, for me, was initially presented by Walker's womanist definition.

## Womanist Pedagogy

The pedagogy that I wish to outline is also based in Layli Phillips's womanist perspective, which emerges from an activist consideration of the entirety of Walker's original definition:

> Womanism is a social change perspective rooted in Black women's and other women of color's everyday experiences and everyday methods of problem solving in everyday spaces extended to the problem of ending all forms of oppression for all people, restoring the balance between people and the environment/nature, and reconciling human life with the spiritual dimension.[15]

What kind of pedagogy emerges if womanism is at the center, or if a womanist perspective serves as a foundation? First of all, if a womanist perspective is at the center, it demands an inclusive liberatory pedagogy that integrates a variety of theories, canons, methodologies, and perspectives. It would "walk its talk": its process would embody its theories and its theories would promote social change. It would promote personal *and* planetary transformation, and honor activism, rest, healing, and contemplation. It would speak to all aspects of human life and seek to liberate our minds and consciousness from the misrepresentations and falsehoods that are the result of historic inequities, social-cultural oppression, and injustice. It would also promote respect and tolerance among a variety of worldviews, abilities, and learning styles. In her affirmation of womanism as a pedagogical foundation, Vanessa Sheared suggests that:

> The womanist perspective seeks to expose the differences and similarities that human beings experience in the classroom as a result of skin color, language, economic status, and personal experiences. . . . I believe that the womanist perspective is . . . inclusive and that it challenges us to think critically about such issues as racism, sexism, language, religious orientation, and sexual orientation. More important, its aim is to reinterpret the word—the ways in which we read, hear and ultimately speak to one another.[16]

## Notes from an Embodied Womanist Pedagogy

I'd like to bring in a few examples of how I utilize a womanist pedagogy. Each of these notes relates to a real-world example that arose in my classroom. I have changed the names of all the students.

## Note I: Bringing Body, Mind, Heart, and Spirit into the Classroom

The class is titled "Women's Embodiment, Healing, and Sexuality." It provides a "personal, multicultural and womanist exploration of the spiritual gifts inherent in physical existence in the female body." Readings are drawn from the diverse fields of women's spirituality, earth-based spiritual traditions, science and medicine, psychology, feminism, and the writings and literature of women of color. These readings are augmented by the student's own experience to provide a journey though basic themes of female embodiment: women and nature; female growth and maturation; the effects on women of disability and illness; women's spiritual, cultural, ethnic, and sexual identity; sexuality, menarche, childbirth, and menopause; and women's experience/s of sexual abuse, healing, and recovery. I explicitly state that art, ritual, writing, sound, and movement will be used to create a safe container to hold our stories of descent, healing, and transformation.

At the beginning of class we sit in a circle. Some of the texts we use are embodied narratives that bring the heart, mind, body, and spirit of a woman into the classroom. Each narrative outlines resistance to sexual, physical, and emotional abuse or presents real-life descriptions of conscious or unconscious opposition to social and cultural norms that deny women's agency, intellect, and power.[17] Each woman's story is emotionally compelling—and can provoke anger, tears, or memories of abuse. I talk with the class about the effect of reading these narratives and remind them of the power of "breaking the silence."[18] I inform them that the history of the oppression of women, lesbians, people of color, and other targeted populations has often been denied and hidden—and I tell them that while we are most familiar with our own oppression, it is crucial that we know about and understand the oppressions of others.

I solicit responses from the students. Then I guide them through an exercise designed to place boundaries between emotionally charged material and its effect on the body. I begin with conscious breathing. Then I ask the students to remember or visualize a (mildly) charged issue. I ask each student to breathe into her/his own body and to notice where the tension emerges. Is the stomach clenched? Is the throat tight? Do they feel numb or absent? I ask the students to breathe into their hearts and to send love and healing to the parts of the body or the self that feel affected. I ask them to send love and healing to their former or present body. I ask them to scan their bodies in present time, establishing a real-world connection to the "here and now" of their presence in the room, and to image themselves surrounded by a loving community, which may—or may not—include the presence of spirit.

When we ask our students to engage with a liberatory curriculum, we must also make room for the *feelings* evoked by histories of oppression, resistance, war, or other traumas. In a multicultural classroom populated by women, a liberatory curriculum that engages with diverse feminisms will call up *embodied* responses from students. The oppression we read about often reflects our own; the struggles we learn about have hidden costs that our bodies remember. If we ask our students to bring their bodies into the classroom, we must create safe spaces to hold the diverse experiences and emotions that the body contains. Mind-body-spirit-based ways of knowing, and energy-clearing methodologies, are essential parts of a womanist scholar's toolkit.

### Note II: Development of Liberatory Consciousness

The class is beginning. Lucy, a young Euro-American student, raises her hand. She indicates that the readings she has done on women's health issues contain words like "breast," "uterus," and "vagina." She discloses that she is a sexual abuse survivor and that these words are causing her to dissociate. She is "all in her head." Most of us are momentarily startled—and there is a half-moment of unexpected silence. I ask the students to take a breath with me so that we may hear this truth with our hearts. I acknowledge Lucy's courage in speaking, and thank her for her reminder that many of us are survivors. I thank her for demonstrating that we don't need to be defined by our abuse—that we can grow and change, take our lives back, and move on.

I ask if other people share Lucy's experience. There are several nods. I go around the room to give everyone a chance to say what they're feeling, and to see what stories have been evoked in the room. Can we move on or is everyone "stuck"? I ask the students how their bodies are doing. Sarah, a young white woman, states that she was never abused—she's not "triggered" by the readings, but she appreciates the sharing. A young Euro-American man states that he feels that men should hear these stories. Then Vanessa, one of the black women, speaks out. She apologizes in advance for a comment that may be racist. Looking directly at Sarah, she states that Sarah's claim of "innocence" makes her "white" and "pure" and "clean," while her own experience of abuse makes her feel "black" and "soiled" and "dirty."

We breathe together again to take in this statement. The room is charged. I thank Vanessa for acknowledging her truth. I explain to the class that Sarah's statement isn't racist—it's a statement based in the everyday racism of the

English language. English links concepts of purity, innocence, and goodness with "whiteness; it links concepts of evil, dirt, and ugliness with "blackness." I tell Sarah, the white student, that she didn't invent this system—but that she does benefit from it. I tell Vanessa, the black student, that I *always* see her beauty and her inner light. I acknowledge that her gut response points us toward a powerful truth about the effect of racism in language.

When working with women in a womanist classroom, we must explicitly reject patriarchal dichotomies of good girls, bad girls, virgins and whores, recognizing instead the many struggles that women go through as they attempt to claim their sexuality or take back their lives in the aftermath of rape, incest, violence, and sexual abuse. We must let our students know that we see them as strong, intelligent, empowered, and sacred.

Our liberatory consciousness arises as we examine, confront, resist, and ultimately reject the forces of oppression that pervade our lives. The moments for liberatory engagement emerge from multiple sites in a womanist classroom—and while the teacher, the curriculum, and the pedagogy must support the goal of liberatory transformation, they are not the only sites that initiate shifts in consciousness. As teachers, we must not only pay attention to the moments that signal critical engagement and learning that arises from the students, we must welcome, foster, and encourage these moments, integrating them into the flow of our lesson plans.

## Note III: Taking a Stance against Racist, Sexist, and Homophobic Oppression

We are discussing women's body issues and discussing Naomi Wolf's *The Beauty Myth.*[19] Marilyn, one of the African American students, has an insight. She tells the class that the problem with the fashion industry is that it's run by gay men. I know immediately that I have to intervene, since this statement scapegoats another oppressed minority. I begin by thanking Marilyn for opening the dialogue about a really important issue, and I tell the class that as a young woman, I, too, heard this rationale. I explain that dominant systems of oppression often pit socially marginalized and targeted groups against each other. I remind the class about Wolf's statistics on the beauty industry's corporate profits and ask the students if they believe gay people own these corporations—or are major shareholders. We talk about the process of scapegoating, and how it functions today.

I watch Marilyn's face fall. I can't figure out how to support her in the moment. Her face haunts me. Next week, I tell the class that I want to revisit the discussion. I ask Marilyn how it felt to have her comment be a major point of discussion. She's a little hesitant, but she realizes that I want to know—and that she won't be penalized. She tells me she hated it—she felt diminished and ashamed. I apologize for my clumsiness. I tell the class that I really want them to express their opinions—and that sometimes I will disagree. I might not do this often, but it will occur. I remind them that our contract is to learn together—to respect each other—and to have different opinions. I tell them that I want the class to feel safe, but that discussions of our relative privilege are incredibly difficult. I state that none of us grew up in a culture where we received loving criticism—and I praise them for wanting to learn and grow.

If liberation is a pedagogical goal, the curriculum must draw from a canon that includes a diversity of teachings that speak to multiple sites of oppression. This curriculum must support and encourage acts of social change and resistance and provide us with tools for unlearning racism, sexism, and homophobia. It must promote alliance building. As a teacher who is guided by womanist pedagogy, I cannot privilege any position that is grounded in oppression. I may experience times of uncertainty and off-centeredness because of this, but the rewards of this commitment outweigh the difficulties.

## Other Thoughts

While I cannot review all the characteristics of the womanist pedagogy that I use, I would like to share a few more thoughts about it. Rest and replenishment are necessary components of our bodies' health. This is the least-discussed and perhaps least-appreciated part of Walker's definition. We need time apart—time alone with the self and with nature—to encourage understanding of our place in the natural world. We also desperately need the healing and balance that we only find in nature. As teachers, we must take time out for our own renewal, and we must support our students' need to do the same. I *know* this is not easy—and that it means transforming our sites (or styles) of work and activism so that we may live sustainable lives.

Awareness of the natural world and acknowledgment of the need for healing and rest must also come through our teaching. The classroom must be a site that incorporates our connection to the natural world and the many species with whom we interdependently cohabit the earth. In an urban classroom environment, my guided visualizations often reference the elements, the seasons, or the plants and trees. I often remind students that everything we touch, breathe, feel, or perceive is created of elements native to this planet.

An embodied womanist pedagogy demands that we bring the truths of our bodies—multicolored, differently-abled, queerly gendered, young or old—into the classroom with us. It means bringing our cultures and the hard-won insights that emerge from our experience. Of course it also means incorporating the scholarly issues and theories that have emerged over the last half-century of feminist, womanist, and postcolonial writings.[20] But it also means that we must recognize our bodies as living texts.[21]

### Conclusion

As I have indicated earlier, I find refuge, identity, and meaning in Walker's four-part womanist definition.[22] For me, liberation struggles for racial justice, women's rights, social and economic empowerment for *all* members of society, sexual and reproductive freedoms and choice—including the right to freely choose who and how I love, sexually and nonsexually—are all part of a dynamic tapestry that includes my freedom to worship the Sacred as I know and name it, along with my commitment to love and honor my body's need for rest, renewal, and healing, and my recognition of and engagement with the sacredness of the natural world of which I am part. For me, this holistic tapestry of liberation is best named by the term "womanist."

This tapestry of liberation helps provide the spiritual and intellectual frame for my classroom teaching. It is augmented by a variety of artistic and transformational methodologies that offer physical grounding and spiritual and emotional support for students journeying through my classes. Together with my co-learners and co-teachers I hope to create an environment that helps my students rebirth themselves as activists, scholars, healers, teachers, and people of faith and vision who will change the world.

## Notes

1. While womanism as a methodological framework may have applicability beyond the humanities, my experience is only in a humanities classroom. See also bell hooks, *Teaching Community: The Politics of Hope* (New York: Routledge, 2003), 2–6.

2. All references to Alice Walker's womanist definition are found in Alice Walker, *In Search of Our Mothers' Gardens: Womanist Prose* (San Francisco: Harcourt Brace Jovanovich, 1983), xi–xii.

3. I am grateful to Shani Settles for this term. See Shani Settles, "The Sweet Fire of Honey: Womanist Visions of Osun as a Methodology of Emancipation," in *Deeper Shades of Purple:*

*Womanism in Religion and Society*, ed. Stacey M. Floyd-Thomas (New York: New York University Press, 2006), 191–206.

4. The embodied pedagogies I describe that sometimes emphasize physical movement may not be ideal for differently-abled individuals even though I modify them. Third-gender/gender-fluid individuals may find the term *woman* offensive since it can be perceived as reifying the binary nature of gender.

5. Walker, xi.

6. Cheryl Townsend Gilkes, *If It Wasn't for the Women . . . Black Women's Experience and Womanist*

7. Walker, xi.

8. During my adolescence, I lived with Japanese American activist Yuri Kochiyama, who at that time was extremely active in black liberation movements; I also lived with and/or was mentored by Jewish activist Janet Carlson and Euro-American Bunty Barus, all of whom offered me refuge during periods when my mother would not allow me to live with her.

9. Vanessa Sheared, "Giving Voice: An Inclusive Model of Instruction—A Womanist Perspective," *The Womanist Reader*, ed. Layli Phillips (New York: Routledge, 2006), 272.

10. Sheared, 269.

11. Patricia Hill Collins, "What's in a Name? Womanism, Black Feminism, and Beyond," in *The Womanist Reader*, ed. Layli Phillips (New York: Routledge, 2006), 58.

12. See the following works by bell hooks: *Teaching to Transgress: Education as the Practice of Freedom* (New York: Routledge, 1994), *Teaching Community: A Pedagogy of Hope* (New York: Routledge, 2003), and *Teaching Critical Thinking: Practical Wisdom* (New York: Routledge, 2010).

13. hooks, *Teaching to Transgress*, 10.

14. Mary Field Belenky, Blythe McVicker Clinchy, Nancy Rule Goldberger, and Jill Mattuck Tarule, *Women's Ways of Knowing: The Development of Self, Voice, and Mind* (New York: Basic, 1986), 214–29.

15. Phillips, xx.

16. Sheared, 270–71.

17. For example: "Claiming One's Life" pairs El Saadawi's *A Daughter of Isis* with bell hooks's *Wounds of Passion*; "Erotic Outlaws" compares Roy's *The God of Small Things* to Feinberg's *Stone Butch Blues*, and "Double and Triple Jeopardies" contrasts Allison's *Bastard Out of Carolina* with hooks's *Bone Black*.

18. In the 1970s and 80s this term was often applied to women who broke the silence about childhood molestation, incest, and other instances of familial sexual abuse.

19. Naomi Wolf, *The Beauty Myth* (New York: Morrow, 1991).

20. While it is beyond the scope of this article to fully enumerate the texts I draw from, the canon I utilize draws from diverse feminist traditions (e.g., feminism, black feminism, womanism, Chicana/*xicanista* and Latino feminism, Muslim/Islamic feminism, mestiza theory, tribalism and postcolonial feminism, feminist/woman's spirituality, etc.). A partial list of writings of women-of-color theorists and scholars includes: self-identified black feminists Patricia Hill Collins, Audre Lorde, Beverly Guy-Sheftall, and bell hooks; avowed womanists like Alice Walker, Stephanie Mitchem, and Cheryl Townsend Gilkes; Latina, Chicano, and mestiza theorists like Gloria Anzaldua, Ana Castillo, and Aurora Levins Morales; Asian feminists like Sonia Shah, Iris Chang, Lora Jo Foo, and Janice Mirikatani; Native American authors Paula Gunn Allen, Leslie Marmon Silko, Barbara Mann, and Ella Deloria; Islamic feminists Amina Wadud, Nawal El Sadaawi, and Muslim womanist philosopher Debra Mubashshir Majeed; and Ifa priestess and chief Luisah Teish. Contemporary analysis of global postcolonial populations require that we be knowledgeable about the work of more recent postcolonial theoreticians and feminist critics like Haunani Kay Trask, Vandana Shiva, and Andrea Smith. Scholars that might be of particular importance to religious studies include postcolonial, womanist, mujerista, mestiza, and borderlands writings edited by Kwok Pui-Lan/Laura Donaldson, Anzaldua/Analouise Keating, Maria Pilar Aquino/Daisy L. Machado; works by Gloria Mercy Oduyoye, Ada Maria Isasi-Diaz, Chung Hyun Kyung,

Arundati Roy, and Luisah Teish; and the works of African gender theorists Oyeronke Oyewumi and Ifi Amadiume.

21. Stephanie Y. Mitchem, *Introducing Womanist Theology* (Maryknoll, NY: Orbis, 2002), 47.

22. Arisika Razak, "Response to 'Must I Be Womanist?'" *Journal of Feminist Studies in Religion* 22, no. 1 (Spring 2006): 99–107.